Contents

1 Introduction

The APPLE II and the APPLE II e are very popular computers. And most of the users have a lot of experience in programming. In most cases the programming language BASIC is used. The aim of this book is to show how to use machine code and the exciting language FORTH. Therefore this book is divided into three sections, BASIC, Machine Language and FORTH.

Some words for a newcomer in programming:

A program is the realization of a problem in a language which is understood by a computer. There are many problems, such as data base management, mathematical computations, the control of machines or robots etc.

For the solution of these problems with a computer, an algorithm must be found. This is a recipe how to translate the problem into a language a computer understands. To find such an algorithm is often not very easy. Let us make an example.

We have a list of names, and we search for a name in this list. How is it done without a computer? If it is a short list, one starts at the beginning and compares name by name until the desired name is found. This method can not be used if it is a long list of names like in a phone book. Then a sorted list must be used. Here we start the search in the middle and check if the wanted name is in the upper or in the lower half of the list. If it is in the upper part of the list, the search commences in the middle of this part. This method is repeated until the name is found. This search is much faster than the other, but we must have a sorted list. There are several algorithms used to sort a list. Some are very slow as the BUBBLE or RIPPLE. Some are much faster as the SHELL, HEAP or QUICK sort.

Another feature of a computer must be mentioned here. If we search the name MULLARSKY in the list, but we have misspelled it as MULARSKI, a human being will find this name; a computer won't. A computer is not intelligent. It is only as intelligent as its programmer. If an error occurs in a program, not the computer has made this error, but the programmer.

If an algorithm is found to solve a problem, it has to be coded in a programming language. If there is no need for quick computing , code it in BASIC. This very easy. If the program must run fast, machine code is used. This coding is a little bit harder. If one wants easy programming and fast programs, then FORTH is the language. One may ask why we didn't mention PASCAL here. This is an excellent language for learning how to program and to solve some special problems. But it is an epic language. Writing a FORTH program or a PASCAL program is the same as writing a short story or a book like WAR and PEACE.

Let us summarize what programming means:
First, finding an algorithm which solves the problem.

Second, coding this algorithm in a language which the computer understands.

2 Basic-Section

The programs found in the BASIC-section contain some programming techniques, which are different from those commonly found in other BASIC programs. The program CASH-REGISTER, for example, doesn't use the menu like

QTY: 5 <RETURN>

DESCRIPTION: SCREWDRIVER <RETURN>

SALES PRICE: 1.95 <RETURN>

Instead, the input is done as

5 SCREWDRIVERS 1.95

The three words are divided by one space character. The program divides this string into three strings and converts the strings 5 and 1.95 into numbers.

The program NOTE-BOOK uses linked lists to sort the keywords. This makes it easy to turn over the sheets of the note book and step through the entries.

The next program KEYWORD FILE uses binary trees for sorting the keywords. Binary trees are widely used in DBMS programs. The advantage of binary trees is a very fast access to a keyword.

All these programs are models. One may change them to one's own convenience.

The next programs deal with statistics. Two programs show how to represent statistical data. They also show how to mix numbers and lines in high resolution graphics. Another program analyzes statistical data.

Graphics are very useful. A picture is always more evident than thousands of numbers. Therefore the programs LINEAR and 3-D PLOT are used to draw linear or three dimensional functions.

The program FOURIER ANALYSES is used to analyze a periodic function. The results are shown as numbers and as graphics.

The last programs of the BASIC section are for fun and recreation. There are some computer graphics and a game, RUNNING THROUGH A MAZE. The program LUNAR PHASE shows you the shape of the moon for a given day when one can't go to the front door and actually view the moon.

The printout of these programs was made with the PRETTY-PRINT program, described in the machine language section.
Now let us look at some programming techniques used in the following programs.

2.11 Dividing Strings

The program cash-register uses the input form

5 SCREWDRIVER 1.95

The program STRDIV in Figure 2-1 shows how to divide the inputted string into single strings.

I$ is the input string. There are two spaces added to this string. In line 1020 the first space character is searched. After it is found, the left part of I$ is moved to W$(0) and is removed from I$. The length L is changed to the length of the remaining string.

Now the next space character is searched in the same way. The new left hand part is stored in W$(1). After this the last part of the string is stored in W$(2).

```
1000  ONERR  GOTO 9000
1002  HOME : VTAB 2
1005  INPUT " ?";I$:V$ = I$:
      I$ = I$ + "  "
1010  K = 0:L =  LEN (I$):
      I = 1
1020  IF  MID$ (I$,I,1) <  > " " THEN I
      = I + 1: GOTO 1020
1030  W$(K) =  LEFT$ (I$,I - 1):
      I$ =  RIGHT$ (I$,L - I):
      K = K + 1:L = L - I:
      I = 1
1040  IF K = 3 THEN  GOTO 1100
1050  GOTO 1020
1100  N =  VAL (W$(0)):P =  VAL (W$(2))
1110  PRINT N: PRINT W$(1):
      PRINT P
1120 END
9000  VTAB 23: PRINT V$;" ?":
      GET A$
9010  GOTO 1002
```

Figure 2-1: Program STRDIV

The subroutine starting in line 9000 is executed if the system detects an error. The input of

5SCREWDRIVER 1.95

will cause the subroutine to display

5SCREWDRIVER 1.95 ?

This shows the erroneous input. After pressing any key the program jumps back to line 1000 and waits for another input.

In line 1100 the strings W$(0) and W$(2) are converted to numbers via the VAL function and are printed on the screen.

A similar technique can be used for menus. The program MENU in Figure 2-2 shows an example. Our menu has four words:

INPUT
WRITE DISK
WRITE LIST
END

The words INPUT, WRITE and END are stored in the string array K$. The menu is displayed in lines 500-540. The input is expected in line 1020. Line 1060 searches for a space character. If no space is found, the input is a single word. This word is searched in the string array K$. If it is found, the program jumps to the specified line number in the ON ... GOTO statement. If it is not found, the input is displayed via the error routine at line 9000.

If in line 1060 a space character is found, the input is divided into the two strings V$ and U$. V$ is now searched in the dictionary K$. If it is found, the program jumps to the given line number. Here the second part U$ is used to branch the program.

```
 100  K$(1) = "INPUT"
 110  K$(2) = "WRITE"
 120  K$(3) = "END"
 130  GOTO 1000
 500  HOME : VTAB 5: HTAB 10:
      PRINT "INPUT"
 510  HTAB 10: PRINT "WRITE DISK"
 520  HTAB 10: PRINT "WRITE LIST"
 530  HTAB 10: PRINT "END"
 540  RETURN
1000  GOSUB 500
1020  VTAB 17: HTAB 1: PRINT "?";:
      INPUT " ";I$
```

```
1030  VTAB 17: HTAB 1: PRINT L$;
1040  L =  LEN (I$)
1050  FOR I = 1 TO L
1060    IF  MID$ (I$,I,1) = " " THEN  GOTO 1100
1070  NEXT I
1080  V$ = I$: GOTO 1110
1100  V$ =  LEFT$ (I$,I - 1):
      U$ =  RIGHT$ (I$,L - I)
1110  FOR I = 1 TO 3
1120    IF V$ = K$(I) THEN  GOTO 1200
1130  NEXT I
1140  GOTO 9000
1200  ON I GOTO 2000,3000,4000
2000  REM  INPUT
2010  VTAB 17: HTAB 1: PRINT "START OF AN
      INPUT ROUTINE"
2020  GET A$: GOTO 1000
3000  REM  WRITE
3005  VTAB 17: HTAB 1
3010  IF U$ = "DISK" THEN  PRINT "I WRITE
      TO DISK": GOTO 2020
3020  IF U$ = "LIST" THEN  PRINT "I MAKE
      A LIST": GOTO 2020
3030  GOTO 9000
4000  REM  END
4010 END
9000  H = 0:V = 17: GOSUB 900:
      PRINT V$;" ?";
9005  GET I$:H = 0:V = 17:
      GOSUB 900: PRINT L$;:
      GOTO 1020
```

Figure 2-2: Program MENU

One may ask why use this menu technique. One has to type more letters than otherwise. I found that many people who are unfamiliar with computers but very familiar with typewriters like it more. To type a word rather than choose a letter from a menu.

2.12 Linked Lists

If one takes a closer look at mailing lists, inventory managements or other data base management programs, he will find that all records are separate units. They have no relation to the predecessor or the successor. Sorting such files, even if one uses index sequential files, means moving a lot of bytes around in the memory.

Let us look at an example:

You have a index sequential file with 400 existing records. The next record has to be entered as the 150 th record. Every index takes four bytes. In order to make place for one index number you have to move 4*250 = 1000 bytes. This shows Figure 2-3.

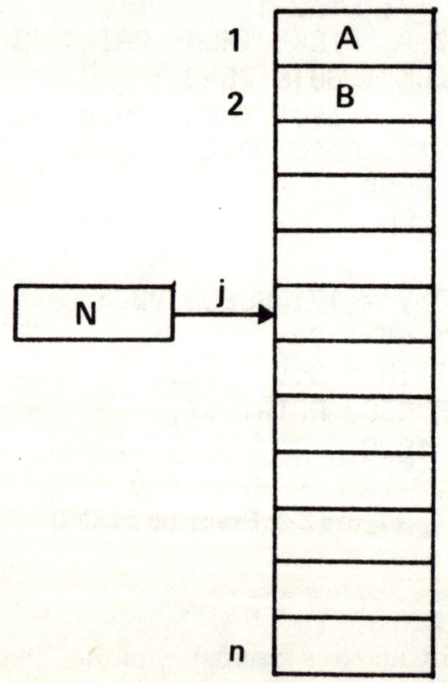

Figure 2-3: Inserting an Index Number

The execution time of sorting procedures is determined by the number of bytes which have to be moved. This moving can be avoided by using linked lists.

A. Linear Lists

Beside the information stored in the record, a linked list contains a pointer. This pointer is the address of the next record. Pointers are data types used in PASCAL or in the language C. Figure 2-4 shows a linear linked list.

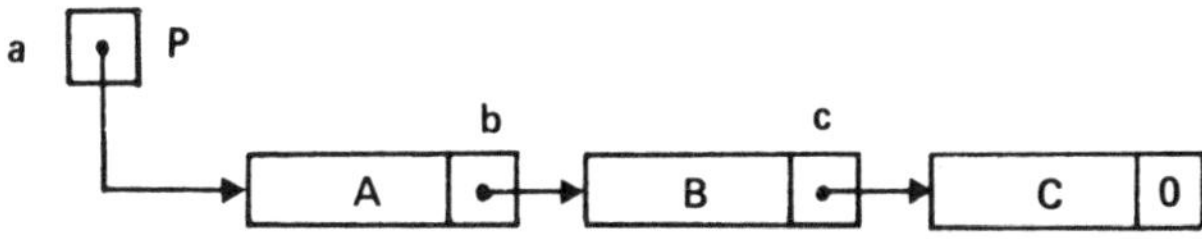

Figure 2-4: Linear Linked List

The variable P in Figure 2-4 is a pointer variable. It contains the address of the first record. This is the Address a of the Record A. The pointer of A is the Address b of Record B. The pointer of the last record is zero. This marks the end of the list.

Inserting a new record is shown in Figure 2-5. The Record J should be inserted between Record A and Record B.

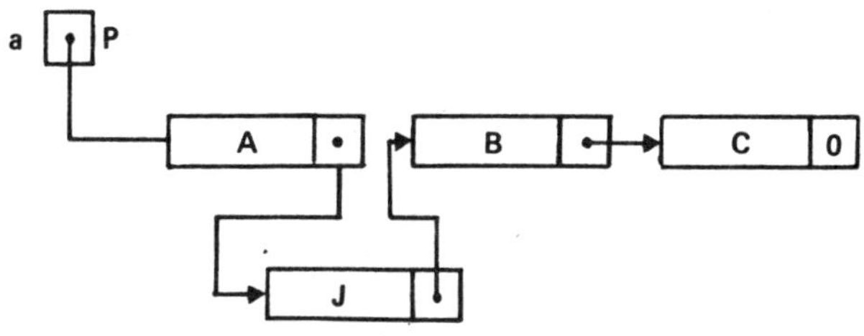

Figure 2-5: Inserting a New Record

The Record J is stored somewhere in the memory at Address j.

This address is written into the pointer of A. The former pointer of A (b) is written into the pointer of J. The Record J now fits logically into the linked list though it was stored somewhere in memory.

The program LILI in Figure 2-6 is a demonstration program for linear linked lists. Line 100 dimensions two arrays N$ and Z. The length of both arrays is set to 10. In the Array N$ the data (names, security numbers, articles etc..) is stored. The Array Z contains the pointers. The program expects the input of data in line 500 through 540. If the input is finished the program links the entries. This is done in line number 200 to 299.

The pointer variable P is zero at the beginning. This shows an empty list. The linking starts with P = 1 and Z(1) = 0. In line 250 it is determined if the new record has to be placed before the first record. Line 270 places the new record between two existing records, while line 280 places it at the end of the list.

```
100  N = 10: DIM N$(N),Z(N)
110  GOSUB 500
120  GOSUB 200
140  GOSUB 1000
150  PRINT : PRINT
160  GOSUB 1020
170  STOP
200  REM  LINK LIST
210  P = 0
220  IF P = 0 THEN Z(1) = 0:
     P = 1
230  FOR J = 2 TO N
240    I = P
250    IF N$(J) < N$(P) THEN Z(J) = P:
       P = J: GOTO 295
260    K = I:I = Z(I)
270    IF N$(J) < N$(I) THEN Z(K) = J:
       Z(J) = I: GOTO 295
280    IF I = 0 THEN Z(K) = J:
       Z(J) = 0: GOTO 295
290    GOTO 260
295  NEXT J
299  RETURN
```

```
500  REM  INPUT
510  FOR J = 1 TO N
520    INPUT ":";N$(J)
530  NEXT J: RETURN
1000 FOR I = 1 TO N: PRINT N$(I):
     NEXT
1010 RETURN
1020 I = P
1030 IF I = 0 THEN  RETURN
1040 PRINT N$(I)
1050 I = Z(I): GOTO 1030
```

Figure 2-6: Linear Linked Lists

Lines 1000 - 1010 print the list in the entered order; lines 1020 - 1050 print the sorted linked list. An example is illustrated in Figure 2-7.

```
                       P=4
1  MILLER PAUL      6  ARCHER DAVID
2  WAYNE JOHN       8  DUCK DONALD
3  STEVENS DAN      5  GOLWEEN SAM
4  ARCHER DAVID     9  MILLER PAUL
5  UNCLE SAM        2  ROBERTS ANDREW
6  ROBERTS ANDREW   3  STEVENS DAN
7  ZARSKY ED        0  UNCLE SAM
8  WOZNIAC STEVE    7  WAYNE JOHN
9  DUCK DONALD      10 WOZNIAC STEVE
10 GOLWEEN SAM      1  ZARSKY ED
```

Figure 2-7: Example Linked List

In Figure 2-7 on the left hand side, the names are listed as they were entered. The Pointer P points to the fourth name ARCHER DAVID. Its pointer points to name # 9. A sorted list is printed on the right hand side. The last name, ZARSKY ED has the pointer 0. This is the end of the list.

Erasing a record is also very simple. Figure 2-8 shows this. The Record B should be removed from the list. The pointer of B (c) is written into the pointer of A.

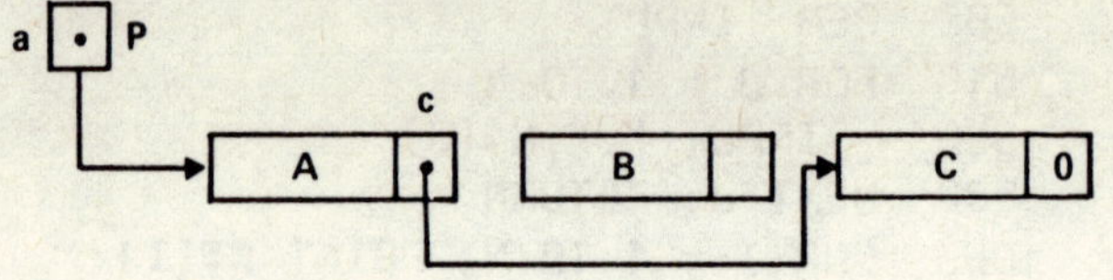

Figure 2-8: Erasing a Record

B. Double Linked List

Figure 2-9 shows a double linked list. Every record has two pointers. One pointer points to the predecessor, the other pointer to the successor. A double linked list can be passed in both directions. The left pointer of the first record and the right pointer of the last record are zero.The program NOTE-BOOK uses such a double linked list.

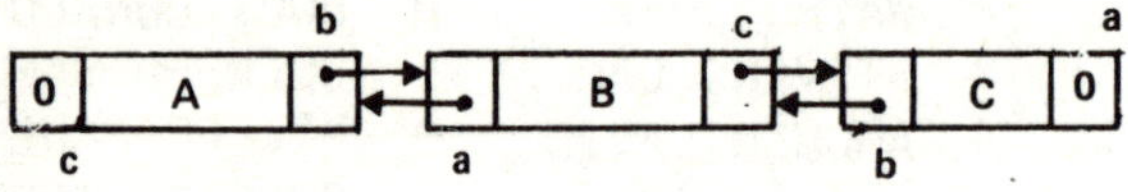

Figure 2-9: Double Linked List

2.13 Hashing

One of the main problems in database management is to find in a very short time one record in a very large file. But this demand for a short access time in a large database seems unrealistic. Instead of sorting and searching, hashing can be used.

The method of hashing is shown in an example. We have a sequential list of names as in Figure 2-10. The length of the names may vary; however the length of a record is constant. The records are not sorted.

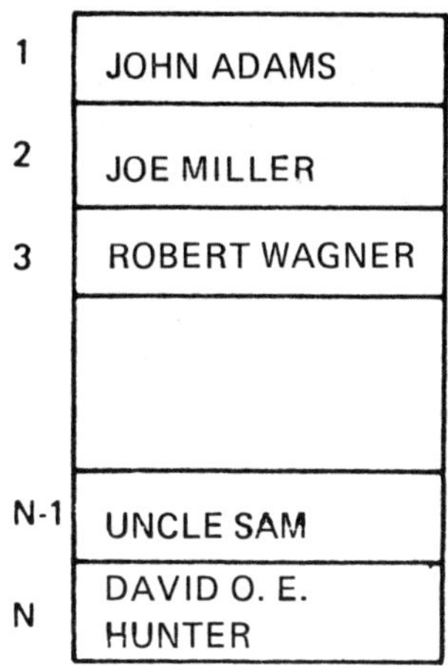

Figure 2-10: List of Names

Besides this list a second list is used. This list contains pointers to the records. These pointers can be found in various ways. One way is, for example, to give numbers to the characters. "A" equals 1, and "Z" equals 26. The smallest number in our example is 1. The name consists of only of the letter A. The largest number is 520 (20*Z). The sum of the letters of the first name JOHN ADAMS is 85. The sum of the second name JOE MILLER is 99. This can be calculated with the program in Figure 2-11.

```
 10  INPUT "NAME: ";A$
 20  GOSUB 100
 30  PRINT S
 40 END
100  L =  LEN (A$)
110  S =  ASC ( LEFT$ (A$,1)) - 64
120  FOR I = 2 TO L - 1
130    N =  ASC ( MID$ (A$,I,1))
140    IF N < 64 GOTO 170
150    IF N > 90 GOTO 170
160    S = S + N - 64
170  NEXT I
180  S = S +  ASC ( RIGHT$ (A$,1)) - 64
190  RETURN
```

Figure 2-11: Calculating the HASH-Number by the Sum of the Letters.

Figure 2-12 shows the relation between the list of names and the second list. At the beginning, all fields of the pointer list are zero. The HASH-number of the first name was 85. Therefore a 1 is written in 85th field of the pointer list. The 99 th field gets the number 2.

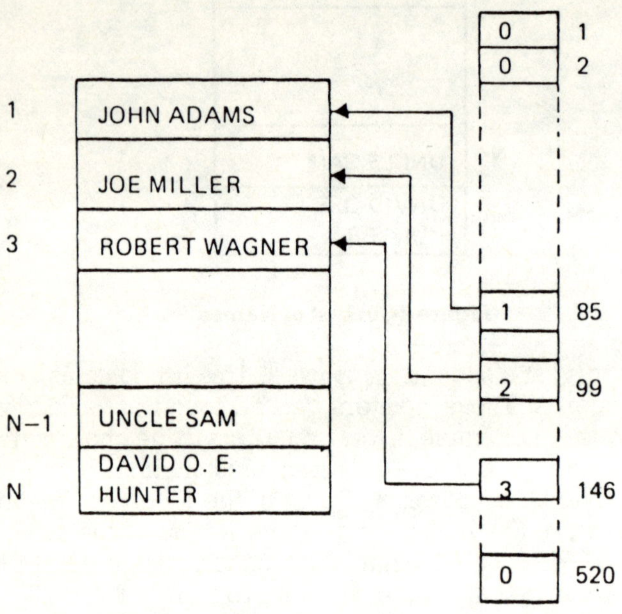

Figure 2-12: List of Names and the Pointer-List.

It is now very easy to find a name. If one wants to find JOE MILLER, he has to calculate the HASH-value. This number gives the number of the field where the pointer to the name is stored. This is very easy and a provides fast access to the record. Let us now look at two other names, ROBERT WAGNER and DAVID O.E. HUNTER. Both have the HASH-number 146, if we use our method to calculate this value. This means a collision. Now you have the problem to find a method for calculating the HASH-value with less collisions surfaces. Other methods are:

-number of the first letter plus number of the last letter times the length of the name.

-number of the first letter plus number of the second letter to the power two plus number of the third letter to the power three.

-use another distribution of numbers.

-add only consonants.

But in all cases you will get collisions. There are several methods to work with collisions. One is mentioned here. To our list of names and the pointer list a third list is added. This is a two dimensional list. This is shown in Figure 2-13.

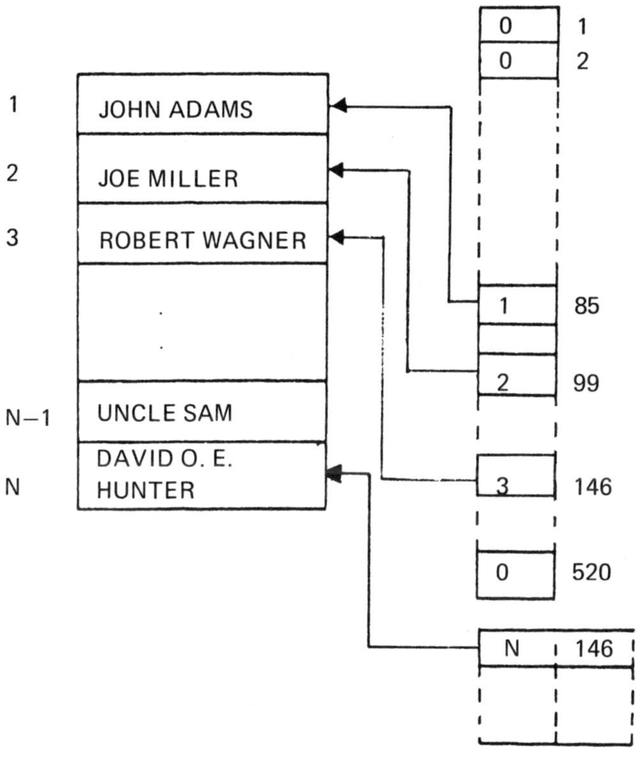

Figure 2-13: Working with Collisions

If a collision is detected, the number of the entry and the HASH-number are stored in the third list. For finding a name one has to take two steps. The first step is to get the name via the pointer list. If it is not the desired name, the correct name is searched in

the third list.
For some methods the HASH-numbers are very large. Then one should use the MODULO-division to get a number within an upper limit. For a list of 300 names a HASH-number between 0 and 300 is expected. This is done by the MODULO-division

```
Q=INT(S/300)
R=(S/300-Q)*300
```

Q is the quotient and R the remainder of the division. R is always equal or greater than zero and less than 300.

There is no program in the BASIC section which uses HASHING. Make your own program and test it on various data types.

2.2 Cash Register

The program in Figure 2-16 simulates a cash register. It uses the input and menu technique described in the previous chapter.

Figure 2-14 shows the printout of the screen. It is divided into three parts. The upper part shows the date and the total amount of all inputs. The lower part shows all words which can be entered at this moment.
The date is entered by typing

DATE MM/DD/JJ

For example:

DATE 06/17/83

The date is used as a filename when writing on disk.

The word INPUT opens the cash register. The input is entered in the following form:

QTY DESCRIPTION SALES PRICE DEPARTMENT

For example:

5 T-SHIRTS 9.95 3

There is no space character allowed in the description. After hitting return the total sales price is calculated and added to the amount of the department and the total amount. The totals of the departments (0 - 9) are displayed on the right hand side of the middle part of the screen. The input for one receipt is limited to 15 items. The input mode is left with CTRL-A RETURN.

```
                 CASH-REGISTER
DATE:08/04/83                TOTAL:    56.50
--------------------------------------------



                                      2.85/1

                                     49.75/3

                                      3.90/5

 ? DATE 08/04/83
 ? INPUT
 ? 5 T-SHIRTS 9.95 3
 ? 1 MOUNTAIN-CHABLIS 2.85 1
 ? 2 CORN-CHIPS 1.95 5
 ?
--------------------------------------------
QTY  ITEM SALES PRICE DEPT.
FOR EXAMPLE 5 T-SHIRTS 9.95 3
CTRL-A EXITS INPUT MODE
```

Figure 2-14: Screenprint Cash Register

The words WRITE DISK save the total and the totals of the departments on disk. They can be read from disk with READ <DATE>. For example:

READ 06/17/83

Be sure that you type the correct date.

The words WRITE RECEIPT write a receipt as it is shown in Figure 2-15. First the tax is entered. Type 0 for no tax. The receipt is written.

```
CHAOT ENTERPRISES                                   08/04/83
JOHN D. MILLER
SCHAEFFER AVE 8
CHINO CA 92123
                                  RECIEPT

     5      T-SHIRTS                         9.95      49.75
     1      MOUNTAIN-CHABLIS                 2.85       2.85
     2      CORN-CHIPS                       1.95       3.90

                             NET AMOUNT                56.50
                             TAX    6.5%                3.67
                             TOTAL                     60.17

                             CASH                      65.00
                             RETURN                     4.83
```

Figure 2-15: Printout Receipt

It is assumed that the printer interface is in slot # 1. Otherwise lines 7035 and 7325 must b changed. At the end of the printout the program asks for the cash received. The return cash is shown on the screen and both amounts are printed.

The word END ends the program. Be sure that the data is saved on disk before.

Some remarks to the program.

The main input routine starts at line 1000. Line 2000 starts the input of the date. Lines 3000 - 3130 read the file of a date from disk and display the results on the screen. Lines 4000 - 4180 write the file of a date to disk. If the date has been entered as 06/17/83, the file is saved as D06/17/83. The D is automatically added in reading or writing to disk.

Lines 5000-5010 end the program. Maybe a note to save on disk can be entered here prior to jumping back into BASIC. The input for one receipt is entered in lines 6000 - 6340. All items (up to 15) are stored in the string array S$. The subroutine starting at 6300 divides the input of one item in the four parts. If an error is detected there by the system, the program jumps to an error routine at 6200.

The subroutine starting at line 1600 is used to format the numbers for printing. The number is transferred to the subroutine via the variable P. This number is converted to a string P$. Then the routine searches for a decimal point. If there is no decimal point, the string ".00" is added to P$. If a decimal point is found but is followed by only one character, a "0" is added.

The printout of a receipt starts at line 7000. The address of the company is stored in N$(0) to N$(4). The date and the word receipt are printed. Then the contents of S$ are printed and the totals calculated and added. At the end of the receipt the net amount, the tax and the total amount is printed - at least the cash received and the cash return.

For formatting the printout two subroutines are used.The subroutine starting at 7400 prints a string left justified at the vertical TAB position VT. At the beginning of a line the variable VP is zero. Then it contains the actual print position of the print head. The length of a string should not exceed 20 characters, and the string is transferred to the subroutine via the variable A$.

The subroutine starting at line 7600 prints a string right justified in field with the length VF. The vertical TAB position of the beginning of the field is determined by the variable VT.

```
 105  D$ =  CHR$ (13) +  CHR$ (4)
 110  DIM K$(6),S$(15),GP(10)
 115  DIM N$(4): GOSUB 7500
 120  K$(1) = "DATE":K$(2) = "READ":
      K$(3) = "WRITE":K$(4) = "END":
      K$(5) = "INPUT"
 130  L$ = "                    ":
      REM   20 SPACES
 199  GOTO 1000
 900  POKE 37,V: POKE 36,H:
      CALL  - 990: RETURN
1000  HOME : HTAB 10: PRINT "CASH-REGISTER"
1010  VTAB 2: PRINT "DATE:
      ";: HTAB 25: PRINT "TOTAL:
      "
1012  VTAB 3:
      FOR I = 0 TO 39: PRINT "-";:
      NEXT
1014  VTAB 19:
      FOR I = 0 TO 39: PRINT "-";:
      NEXT
1015  GOSUB 1500
1020  V = 17:H = 1: GOSUB 900:
      PRINT "?";: INPUT " ";I$
1030  V = 17:H = 1: GOSUB 900:
      PRINT L$;
1040  L =  LEN (I$)
1050  FOR I = 1 TO L
1060    IF  MID$ (I$,I,1) = " " THEN  GOTO 1100
1070  NEXT I
1080  V$ = I$: GOTO 1110
1100  V$ =  LEFT$ (I$,I - 1):
      U$ =  RIGHT$ (I$,L - I)
1110  FOR I = 1 TO 5
1120    IF V$ = K$(I) THEN  GOTO 1200
1130  NEXT I
1140  GOTO 9000
1200  ON I GOTO 2000,3000,4000,5000,6000
1500  POKE 34,19: CALL  - 958:
      H = 0:V = 19: GOSUB 900
1502  CALL  - 958
1504  PRINT "DATE MM/DD/JJ, INPUT, END,"
1505  PRINT "READ <DATE>, WRITE DISK,"
```

```
1507  PRINT "WRITE RECIEPT"
1510  POKE 33,30: POKE 34,3:
      POKE 35,18
1520  RETURN
1600  P$ =  STR$ (P):L =  LEN (P$)
1610  FOR I = 1 TO L
1620    IF  MID$ (P$,I,1) = "." THEN  GOTO 1640
1630  NEXT I:P$ = P$ + ".00"
1640  IF I = L - 1 THEN P$ = P$ + "0"
1650  RETURN
2000  REM  INPUT DATE
2010  DA$ = U$: VTAB 2: HTAB 6:
      PRINT U$: GOTO 1020
3000  REM  READ DISK
3005  VTAB 2: HTAB 6: PRINT U$:
      PRINT
3010  U$ = "D" + U$
3020  PRINT D$;"OPEN";U$
3030  PRINT D$;"READ";U$
3040  INPUT T
3050  FOR I = 0 TO 9: INPUT GP(I):
      NEXT
3060  PRINT D$;"CLOSE";U$
3065  POKE 33,40
3070  H = 0:V = 4: GOSUB 900:
      HOME
3072  P = T: GOSUB 1600
3075  V = 1:L =  LEN (P$):
      H = 38 - L: GOSUB 900
3077  PRINT P$
3080  FOR J = 0 TO 9
3090    P = GP(J): GOSUB 1600
3100    V = J + 5:L =  LEN (P$):
        H = 38 - L: GOSUB 900
3110    PRINT P$;"/";J
3120  NEXT J
3130  POKE 33,30: GOTO 1020
4000  REM  WRITE
4010  IF U$ = "DISK" THEN  GOTO 4100
4020  IF U$ = "RECIEPT" THEN  GOTO 7000
4030  GOTO 1020
4100  U$ = "D" + DA$: PRINT
```

```
4110  PRINT D$;"OPEN";U$
4120  PRINT D$;"DELETE";U$
4130  PRINT D$;"OPEN";U$
4140  PRINT D$;"WRITE";U$
4150  PRINT T
4160  FOR I = 0 TO 9: PRINT GP(I):
      NEXT
4170  PRINT D$;"CLOSE";U$
4180  GOTO 1020
5000  POKE 33,40: POKE 34,0:
      POKE 35,24
5010  HOME : STOP
6000  REM  INPUT
6010  POKE 35,24: POKE 34,19:
      H = 0:V = 19: GOSUB 900
6012  CALL  - 958
6020  PRINT "QTY  ITEM SALES PRICE DEPT."
6030  PRINT "FOR EXAMPLE 5 T-SHIRTS 9.95
      3"
6040  PRINT "CTRL-A EXITS INPUT MODE"
6045  J = 0
6050  I$ = "": POKE 34,3:
      POKE 35,18
6055  V = 17:H = 1: GOSUB 900
6060  PRINT "?";: INPUT " ";I$:
      I$ = I$ + "  "
6065  S$(J) = I$:J = J + 1:
      IF J > 14 THEN 9000
6070  IF  ASC (I$) = 1 THEN  POKE 35,24:
      GOTO 1014
6080  GOSUB 6300
6120  N =  VAL (W$(U)):P =  VAL (W$(2)):
      G =  VAL (W$(3))
6130  P = P * N:PO = P:P = P + GP(G):
      GP(G) = P: GOSUB 1600
6135  POKE 33,40
6140  V = G + 5:L =  LEN (P$):
      H = 38 - L: GOSUB 900:
      PRINT P$;"/";G
6150  P = T + PO:T = P: GOSUB 1600
6160  V = 1:L =  LEN (P$):
      H = 38 - L: GOSUB 900:
      PRINT P$;
```

```
6170  POKE 33,30: GOTO 6050
6200  H = 0:V = 17: GOSUB 900
6210  J = J - 1: PRINT S$(J);" ?":
      GET A$
6220  GOTO 6055
6300  K = 0:L =  LEN (I$):
      I = 1
6310  IF  MID$ (I$,I,1) <  > " " THEN I
      = I + 1: GOTO 6310
6320  W$(K) =  LEFT$ (I$,I - 1):
      I$ =  RIGHT$ (I$,L - I):
      K = K + 1:L = L - I:
      I = 1
6330  IF K = 4 THEN  RETURN
6340  GOTO 6310
7000  REM  WRITE RECIEPT
7010  H = 0:V = 4: GOSUB 900:
      HOME
7020  H = 1:V = 17: GOSUB 900
7030  INPUT " TAX:";T$
7035  PRINT D$;"PR#1"
7040  VP = 0
7042  VT = 0:A$ = N$(0):
      GOSUB 7400
7044  VT = 54:A$ = DA$: GOSUB 7400
7046  PRINT :VP = 0
7050  VT = 0:A$ = N$(1):
      GOSUB 7400
7055  PRINT :VP = 0
7060  VT = 0:A$ = N$(2):
      GOSUB 7400
7065  PRINT :VP = 0
7070  VT = 0:A$ = N$(3):
      GOSUB 7400
7075  PRINT :VP = 0
7080  VT = 30:A$ = "RECIEPT":
      GOSUB 7400
7085  PRINT :VP = 0
7090  T = 0
7100  FOR Z = 0 TO J - 2
7110    I$ = S$(Z): GOSUB 6300
7120    PRINT :VP = 0
7130    VT = 0:VF = 5:A$ = W$(0):
        GOSUB 7600
```

```
7140      VT = 10:A$ = W$(1):
          GOSUB 7400
7150      VT = 30:VF = 10:
          A$ = W$(2): GOSUB 7600
7160      N =  VAL (W$(0)):
          P =  VAL (W$(2)):P = N * P:
          T = T + P
7170      GOSUB 1600
7180      VT = 40:VF = 10:
          A$ = P$: GOSUB 7600
7190   NEXT Z
7200   PRINT : PRINT :VP = 0
7210   VT = 25:A$ = "NET AMOUNT":
       GOSUB 7400
7220   P = T: GOSUB 1600:
       VT = 40:VF = 10:A$ = P$:
       GOSUB 7600
7230   PRINT :VP = 0
7240   VT = 25:A$ = "TAX":
       GOSUB 7400:VT = 31:
       A$ = T$ + "%": GOSUB 7400
7245   TA =  VAL (T$):P =  INT (T * TA + .5)
       / 100
7250   GOSUB 7390
7252   PRINT :VP = 0
7254   VT = 25:A$ = "TOTAL":
       GOSUB 7400
7255   P = P + T: GOSUB 7390
7260   PRINT D$;"PR#0"
7270   H = 1:V = 17: GOSUB 900
7280   INPUT "CASH: ";A$
7290   P1 =  VAL (A$): IF P1 < P THEN  GOTO 7270
7300   H = 1:V = 17: GOSUB 900
7310   P2 = P1 - P:P = P2:
       GOSUB 1600
7320   PRINT "RETURN: ";P$
7325   PRINT D$;"PR#1"
7328   PRINT :VP = 0
7330   VT = 25:A$ = "CASH":
       GOSUB 7400
7340   P = P1: GOSUB 7390
7345   PRINT :VP = 0
7350   VT = 25:A$ = "RETURN":
       GOSUB 7400
```

```
7360  P = P2: GOSUB 7390
7365  PRINT D$;"PR#0"
7370  GOTO 1020
7390  GOSUB 1600:VT = 40:
      VF = 10:A$ = P$: GOTO 7600
7400  L =  LEN (A$)
7410  IF VT = VP THEN  PRINT A$;:
      VP = L: GOTO 7499
7430  IF VT - VP > 20 THEN  PRINT L$;:
      VP = VP + 20: GOTO 7410
7440  A$ =  LEFT$ (L$,VT - VP) + A$:
      PRINT A$;:VP = VT + L
7499  RETURN
7500  REM  SALES ADDRESS
7510  N$(0) = "CHAOT ENTERPRISES"
7520  N$(1) = "JOHN D. MILLER"
7530  N$(2) = "SCHAEFFER AVE 8"
7540  N$(3) = "CHINO CA 92123"
7550  RETURN
7600  L =  LEN (A$): IF L > VF THEN VT = VT
      - (L - VF)
7610  IF VP > VT + VF THEN  PRINT A$;:
      VP = VP + L: GOTO 7699
7620  IF VT - VP > 20 THEN  PRINT L$;:
      VP = VP + 20: GOTO 7620
7630  IF VT - VP <  > 0 THEN  PRINT  LEFT$ (L$,
      VT - VP);:VP = VT
7640  A$ =  LEFT$ (L$,VF - L) + A$:
      PRINT A$;:VP = VP + VF
7699  RETURN
9000  G
9005  H = 0:V = 17: GOSUB 900:
      PRINT L$;: GOTO 1020
```

Figure 2-16: Program: Cash Register

2.3 Notebook

The program NOTEBOOK in Figure 2-18 uses double linked lists. There are two arrays used for the pointers R(i) and L(i). The Pointer R(i) points to the next keyword which is greater, and L(i) points to the keyword which is smaller. One entry is logically right from the actual entry, the other is left from the entry. In the memory they are stored in different places.

In linking a double linked list there are five possibilities:

1. The list is empty. Then P = 0.

2. There is only one entry. Then P = 1, R(1) = 0 and L(1) = 0.

3. The next entry j is bigger than all entries in the list. Then R(j) = 0, L(j) = k, R(k) = j. K is the number of the former last entry.

4. The next entry j is smaller than all entries. Then R(j) = p, L(j) = 0, L(p) = j and P = j.

5. The next entry has to be placed between entry k and i. Then R(k) = j,R(j) = i,L(j) = k and L(i) = j.

This linking is programmed in lines 200 - 299 .

Figure 2-17 shows the structure of the notebook.

Keyword 15 Characters

Text 50 Characters

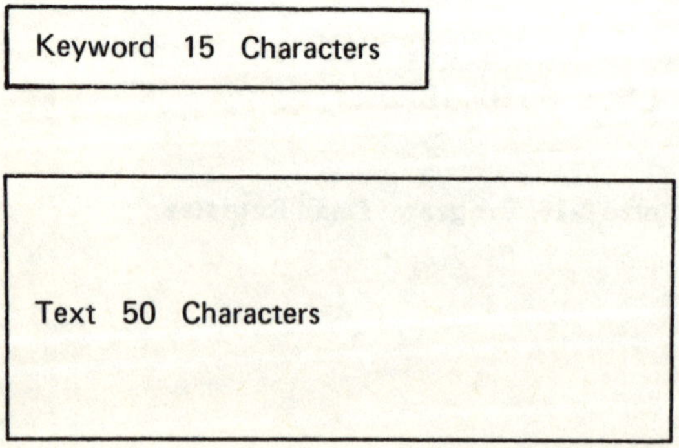

Figure 2-17: Structure of the Notebook

The length of the keyword is up to 15 characters and the length of one entry may have up to 50 characters. The input mode is entered by the word ENTRY. As an example we will use cities as keywords and make some remarks regarding these cities in our note-book.

E.G. KEYWORD: LAS VEGAS

TEXT: DON'T MISS THE SHOW AT CESARS

In the lower part of the screen appears the sign --> ?. Hitting the right arrow key lets one make another entry. Any other key causes the program to jump back to the menu.

To find an entry in the note-book one has to enter

SEARCH <KEYWORD>

For example:

SEARCH LAS VEGAS

The keyword and the text is displayed on the screen. Now you see the signs <-- --> ? in the lower part of the screen. The left arrow key is used to step to the next smaller keyword or the right arrow key to the next bigger keyword in the notebook. The message END OF LIST is printed if one of either ends of the list is reached. Hitting any other key than the cursor keys cancels the stepping through the notebook and leads back to the menu.

The word PRINT prints all keywords sorted on the screen.

With WRITE <FILENAME> the notebook can be saved on disk. With READ <FILENAME> the note-book goes back into memory. The word END terminates the program.

```
100  N = 40:Z = 0:C = 0
105  DIM N$(N),R(N),L(N)
110  DIM K$(6),E$(N)
120  K$(1) = "ENTRY":K$(2) = "SEARCH"
130  K$(3) = "END"
140  K$(4) = "WRITE":K$(5) = "READ":
     K$(6) = "PRINT"
150  L$ = "                    ":
     REM  20 SPACES
160  D$ =  CHR$ (4)
199  GOTO 1000
200  REM  MAKE DOUBLE LINKED LISTS
210  R(1) = 0:L(1) = 0:
     P = 1
220  FOR J = 2 TO Z
230    I = P
250    IF N$(J) < N$(P) THEN R(J) = P:
       L(J) = 0:L(P) = J:P = J:
       GOTO 295
260    K = I:I = R(I)
265    IF I = 0 THEN R(K) = J:
       R(J) = 0:L(J) = K: GOTO 295
270    IF N$(J) < N$(I) THEN R(K) = J:
       R(J) = I:L(J) = K:L(I) = J:
       GOTO 295
290    GOTO 260
295  NEXT J
298  C = 1: RETURN
1000 HOME : VTAB 3: HTAB 5:
     PRINT "ENTRY"
1005 HTAB 5: PRINT "SEARCH <KEYWORD>"
1008 HTAB 5: PRINT "READ   <FILENAME>
1010 HTAB 5: PRINT "WRITE  <FILENAME>
1014 HTAB 5: PRINT "PRINT  (KEYWORDS)
1018 HTAB 5: PRINT "END"
1020 VTAB 20: INPUT " ? ";I$
1030 VTAB 20: PRINT L$
1040 L =  LEN (I$)
1050 FOR I = 1 TO L
1060   IF  MID$ (I$,I,1) = " " THEN  GOTO 1100
1070 NEXT I
1080 V$ = I$: GOTO 1110
```

```
1100  V$ =  LEFT$ (I$,I - 1):
      U$ =  RIGHT$ (I$,L - I)
1110  FOR I = 1 TO 6
1120    IF V$ = K$(I) THEN  GOTO 1200
1130  NEXT I
1140  GOTO 9000
1200  ON I GOTO 2000,3000,4000,5000,6000,
      7000
2000  REM  MAKE ENTRY
2005  HOME
2010  Z = Z + 1
2020  INPUT "KEYWORD: ";N$(Z)
2030  INPUT "TEXT:";E$(Z)
2040  VTAB 20: PRINT "—>"
2045  C = 0
2050  GET I$: IF  ASC (I$) = 21 THEN  GOTO 2005
2060  GOTO 1000
3000  REM  SEARCH
3010  HOME : IF C = 0 THEN  PRINT "I'M LINKING":
      GOSUB 200
3020  I = P
3030  IF I = 0 THEN  GOTO 3080
3040  IF N$(I) = U$ THEN  HOME :
      VTAB 2: PRINT N$(I):
      VTAB 4: PRINT E$(I):
      VTAB 20: PRINT "<— —>":
      GOTO 3100
3050  I = R(I): GOTO 3030
3080  VTAB 20: PRINT I$;" ? ":
      GOTO 9005
3100  GET I$:
3110  IF  ASC (I$) = 21 THEN K = I:
      I = R(I): GOTO 3200
3120  IF  ASC (I$) = 08 THEN K = I:
      I = L(I): GOTO 3200
3130  GOTO 1000
3200  HOME : IF I = 0 THEN  GOTO 3240
3210  VTAB 2: PRINT N$(I):
      VTAB 4: PRINT E$(I):
      VTAB 20: PRINT "<— —>":
      GOTO 3100
3240  PRINT "END OF FILE"
3250  I = K: GET I$: GOTO 3210
```

```
4000  VTAB 20: PRINT "WRITE TO DISK (Y/N)"
4010  GET I$: IF I$ = "Y" THEN  GOTO 1000
4020 END
5000  REM  WRITE TO DISK
5003  HOME
5010  PRINT D$;"OPEN";U$
5020  PRINT D$;"DELETE";U$
5030  PRINT D$;"OPEN";U$
5040  PRINT D$;"WRITE";U$
5050  PRINT Z
5060  FOR I = 1 TO Z
5070    PRINT N$(I):
      NEXT I
5080  FOR I = 1 TO Z
5090    PRINT E$(I):
      NEXT I
5100  PRINT D$;"CLOSE";U$
5110  GOTO 1000
6000  REM  READ FROM DISK
6010  ONERR  GOTO 9000
6020  PRINT D$;"OPEN";U$
6030  PRINT D$;"READ";U$
6040  INPUT Z
6050  FOR I = 1 TO Z
6060    INPUT N$(I):
      NEXT I
6070  FOR I = 1 TO Z
6080    INPUT E$(I):
      NEXT I
6090  PRINT D$;"CLOSE";U$
6095  PRINT "MUST LINK":
      GOSUB 200
6100  GOTO 1000
7000  REM  PRINT KEYWORDS
7005  IF C = 0 THEN  HOME :
      PRINT "I'M LINKING":
      GOSUB 200
7010  HOME :I = P:K = 0
7020  PRINT N$(I):I = R(I)
7030  IF I = 0 THEN  GOTO 7100
7040  IF K < 18 THEN K = K + 1:
      GOTO 7020
7045  VTAB 20: PRINT "-->"
```

```
7050  GET I$: IF  ASC I$ = 21 THEN  HOME :
      GOTO 7020
7060  GOTO 1000
7100  PRINT "END OF KEYWORDS":
      GET A$: GOTO 1000
9000  VTAB 20: PRINT V$;" ?"
9005  GET I$: GOTO 1000
```

Figure 2-18: Program Notebook

2.4 Keyword-File

One of the most important applications for computers is to store data. The problem is, as it was mentioned earlier, to have a fast access to the data and find the information in a very short time.

To store data in numeric or alphabetical order is possible only in RAM, not on disk. On disk, if a new entry is made or an existing entry is erased, then too many records would have to be moved. A new entry should cause only the change of few bytes. The program NOTEBOOK uses therefore linked lists. The program KEYWORD-FILE in Figure 2-23 uses another method: BINARY TREES. Figure 2-21 shows the representation of a binary tree. As in linked lists every record has pointers.

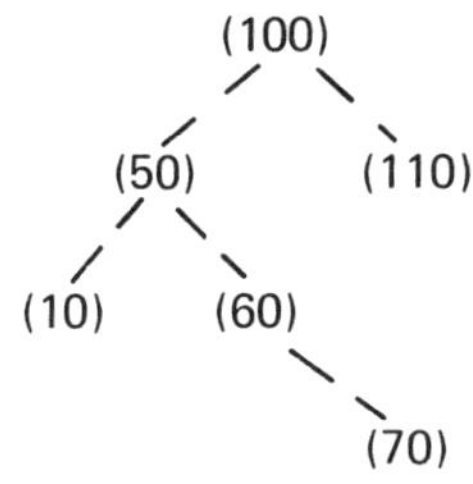

Figure 2-21: Representation of a Binary Tree.

The binary tree uses three pointers. One points to the predecessor, one to the successor which is less and the third to the successor which is greater then the actual record (less or greater refer to the lexical order).

The search of a record starts at the root and steps to the right if the record is greater, or to the left if the record is smaller than the root. This is continued until the wanted record is found.

Making a new entry starts in the same manner as searching the entry. If it is found, in fact an error message appears. Otherwise the tree is stepped through until the end of a branch is reached. There is no successor, and the pointer value is therefore zero. As example we search the place for 40 in the binary tree in Figure 2-21. The result is shown in Figure 2-22.

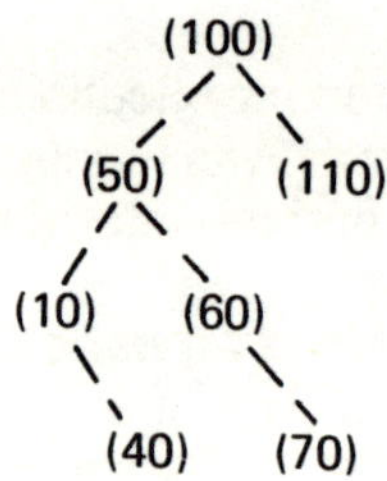

Figure 2-22: Insertion of 40 into the Binary Tree.

40 is smaller than 100, so we have to go to the left. It is also smaller than 50 and we proceed on the left branch. The next element is 10 and we have to step to the right. There is no successor and we have found the place for 40. The pointer for the right branch of 10 contains the address of 40.

A little bit more work has to be done for erasing an entry. We must consider three possible cases:

a) The record has no successor. The only thing we have to do for erasing the record is to set the pointer of the predecessor to zero.

b) The record has only one successor. Then the pointer of the predecessor is changed to the successor and vise versa. This is the same procedure as deleting an entry in a double linked list.

c) The record has two successors. The first step is to find the next smaller entry. This is done by stepping first to the left and then as far as possible to the right. If it is found, it replaces the record which has to be erased. To erase the 50 in Figure 2-22, for example, the 40 is removed from the end of the branch by changing the pointers in such a manner that it is now on the place of the 50.

To save disk capacity the empty place of the erased record can be overwritten by the last entry of the file. The file length pointer is reduced by one.

NOTES TO THE PROGRAM:

The length of one record is 64 bytes. There are 47 bytes for the keyword and text. The remaining rest is used for three pointers (12 bytes) and five bytes for dividing the entries within one record.
A program written in machine language is added, which allows the input of colons, question marks and commas into the text. If more characters for text are wanted line 3800 and line 1020 must be changed.

One application of this program is storing comments to the contents of special periodicals. The time to find one specific entry out of 650 takes about six seconds.

```
 10  REM
 20  REM  KEYWORD-FILE
 30  REM
 35  REM W.BAUER 1983
 40  REM
 90  D$ =  CHR$ (4): PRINT D$"BLOADINPUT1"
100  TEXT : HOME : PRINT "  KEYWORD-FILE
      :": PRINT "----------------------------
                  -----------":
     POKE 34,3
110  INPUT "FILENAME:";F$:
     FL = 1: ONERR  GOTO 1900
112  GOSUB 3800: PRINT D$"READ"F$",R0":
     INPUT FL
```

```
115  POKE 216,0: PRINT D$"CLOSE"
120  VTAB 1: HTAB 25: PRINT "MENU
        ": HOME : PRINT  TAB( 5)"1:
     INPUT   ": PRINT : PRINT  TAB( 5)"2:
     SEARCH ": PRINT : PRINT  TAB( 5)"3:
     OUTPUT IN ALPHABETICAL ORDER":
     PRINT : PRINT  TAB( 5)"4:
     ERASE"
130  VTAB 18: INPUT "WHICH  FUNCTION:
     ";A$
140  A =  VAL (A$): IF A < 1 OR A > 4 THEN 130
150  ON A GOTO 1000,2000,3000,4000
1000 VTAB 1: HTAB 25: PRINT "INPUT  ":
     HOME
1010 PRINT : PRINT "KEYWORD:
     ": CALL 768,KW$: IF KW$ = "" THEN 120
1020 PRINT : PRINT "DATA :
     ": CALL 768,DA$: IF  LEN (DA$ + KW$)
     > 47 THEN  PRINT "TOO LONG!!":
     GOTO 1010
1030 IF DA$ = "" THEN 1010
1100 GOSUB 3800: IF FL = 1 THEN  PRINT D$"WRITE"F$"
     R1": PRINT KW$: PRINT DA$:
     GOTO 1800
1120 GOSUB 3900: IF KW$ = KO$ THEN  PRINT "KEYWORD
     IS PRESENT!!": GOTO 1820
1130 IF KW$ < KO$ THEN 1160
1140 IF R <  > 0 THEN T = R:
     GOTO 1120
1150 PRINT D$"WRITE"F$",R"T:
     PRINT KO$: PRINT DO$:
     PRINT B","L","FL: PRINT D$"WRITE"F$",
     R"FL: PRINT KW$: PRINT DA$:
     GOTO 1800
1160 IF L <  > 0 THEN T = L:
     GOTO 1120
1170 PRINT D$"WRITE"F$",R"T:
     PRINT KO$: PRINT DO$:
     PRINT B","FL","R: PRINT D$"WRITE"F$",
     R"FL: PRINT KW$: PRINT DA$:
     GOTO 1800
1800 PRINT T",0,0":FL = FL + 1:
     PRINT D$"WRITE"F$",R0":
     PRINT FL
```

```
1820  PRINT D$"CLOSE": GOTO 1010
1900  POKE 216,0: IF  PEEK (222) = 5 THEN 115
1910  PRINT : PRINT "ERROR:
      " PEEK (222): GET A$:
      GOTO 120
2000  VTAB 1: HTAB 25: PRINT "SEARCH":
      HOME : PRINT "WILDCARD CHARACTER:
       '@'": PRINT : PRINT "EXAMPLE :
       'COM@' SEARCHES ALL WORDS WHICH START
      WITH 'COM'"
2010  PRINT  CHR$ (4)"CLOSE":
      PRINT : PRINT "KEYWORD:
      ": CALL 768,KW$: IF KW$ = "" THEN 120
2015  IF  RIGHT$ (KW$,1) = "@" THEN KW$
      =  LEFT$ (KW$, LEN (KW$) - 1):
      DA$ = KW$ +  CHR$ (127):
      GOSUB 3040: GOTO 2010
2020  GOSUB 3800
2040  GOSUB 3900: IF KW$ = KO$ THEN  PRINT ">>>"DO$:
      GOTO 2010
2050  IF KW$ > KO$ THEN 2080
2060  IF L <  > 0 THEN T = L:
      GOTO 2040
2070  PRINT "NOT IN FILE !!":
      GOTO 2010
2080  IF R = 0 THEN 2070
2090  T = R: GOTO 2040
3000  VTAB 1: HTAB 25: PRINT "ALPHA OUT":
      HOME
3010  PRINT : PRINT "FROM KEYWORD:
      ": CALL 768,KW$: IF KW$ = "" THEN 120
3020  PRINT : PRINT "TO  KEYWORD:
      ": CALL 768,DA$
3030  IF KW$ > DA$ THEN A$ = KW$:
      KW$ = DA$:DA$ = A$
3040  GOSUB 3800
3100  GOSUB 3900: IF KW$ = KO$ THEN 3420
3110  IF KW$ < KO$ THEN 3140
3120  IF R <  > 0 THEN T = R:
      GOTO 3100
3130  GOTO 3430
3140  IF L <  > 0 THEN T = L:
      GOTO 3100
```

```
3150  GOTO 3420
3400  GOSUB 3900
3410  IF L < > 0 THEN T = L:
      GOTO 3400
3415  IF KO$ > DA$ THEN 3460
3420  PRINT KO$ TAB( 20)DO$
3430  IF R < > 0 THEN T = R:
      GOTO 3400
3440  A = T:T = B: GOSUB 3900:
      IF A = L THEN 3415
3450  IF A < > 1 THEN 3440
3460  PRINT D$"CLOSE": IF RIGHT$ (DA$,1)
      = CHR$ (127) THEN RETURN
3470  GOTO 3010
3800  PRINT D$"OPEN"F$",L64":
      T = 1: RETURN
3900  PRINT D$"READ"F$",R"T:
      CALL 768,KO$: CALL 768,DO$:
      INPUT B,L,R: RETURN
4000  VTAB 1: HTAB 25: FLASH :
      PRINT "ERASE   ": NORMAL :
      HOME
4010  PRINT : PRINT "KEYWORD:
      ": CALL 768,KW$: IF KW$ = "" THEN 120
4020  GOSUB 3800
4030  GOSUB 3900: IF KW$ = KO$ THEN 4100
4040  IF KW$ > KO$ THEN 4070
4050  IF L < > 0 THEN T = L:
      GOTO 4030
4060  PRINT "NOT IN FILE    ":
      GOTO 4290
4070  IF R < > 0 THEN T = R:
      GOTO 4030
4080  GOTO 4060
4100  T2 = T: IF L < > 0 THEN 4310
4110  IF R < > 0 THEN T = R:
      GOTO 4300
4120  T = B:TX = 0: IF T2 = 1 THEN PRINT "MEMORY
      TOTALLY ERASED !!": PRINT D$"DELETE"F$:
      GET A$: GOTO 100
4130  GOSUB 3900: IF T2 = L THEN L = TX:
      GOTO 4150
4140  R = TX
```

```
4150  PRINT D$"WRITE"F$",R"T:
      PRINT KO$: PRINT DO$:
      PRINT B","L","R
4160  T = FL - 1: IF T2 = T THEN 4280
4165  GOSUB 3900: PRINT D$"WRITE"F$",R"T2:
      PRINT KO$: PRINT DO$:
      PRINT B","L","R
4170  LL = L:RL = R:T = B:
      GOSUB 3900: IF L = FL - 1 THEN L = T2:
      GOTO 4190
4180  R = T2
4190  PRINT D$"WRITE"F$",R"T:
      PRINT KO$: PRINT DO$:
      PRINT B","L","R
4200  IF RL <  > 0 THEN T = RL:
      GOSUB 3900: PRINT D$"WRITE"F$",R"T:
      PRINT KO$: PRINT DO$:
      PRINT T2","L","R
4210  IF LL <  > 0 THEN T = LL:
      GOSUB 3900: PRINT D$"WRITE"F$",R"T:
      PRINT KO$: PRINT DO$:
      PRINT T2","L","R
4280  FL = FL - 1: PRINT D$"WRITE"F$",R0":
      PRINT FL
4290  PRINT D$"CLOSE": GOTO 4010
4300  IF T2 = 1 THEN 4400
4305  BL = B: GOSUB 3900:
      PRINT D$"WRITE"F$",R"T:
      PRINT KO$: PRINT DO$:
      PRINT BL","L","R:TX = T:
      T = BL: GOTO 4130
4310  IF R = 0 THEN T = L:
      GOTO 4300
4320  T = L:LL = L:RL = R:
      BL = B
4330  GOSUB 3900: IF R <  > 0 THEN T = R:
      GOTO 4330
4340  PRINT D$"WRITE"F$",R"T2:
      PRINT KO$: PRINT DO$:
      PRINT BL","LL","RL:
      GOTO 4100
```

```
4400  GOSUB 3900: PRINT D$"WRITE"F$",R1":
      PRINT K0$: PRINT D0$:
      PRINT "1,"L","R:T2 = T
4410  LL = L: IF R <  > 0 THEN T = R:
      GOSUB 3900: PRINT D$"WRITE"F$",R"T:
      PRINT K0$: PRINT D0$:
      PRINT "1,"L","R
4420  IF LL <  > 0 THEN T = LL:
      GOSUB 3900: PRINT D$"WRITE"F$",R"T:
      PRINT K0$: PRINT D0$:
      PRINT "1,"L","R
4430  GOTO 4160
```

```
0300-   20 BE DE    JSR   $DEBE
0303-   A9 2C       LDA   #$2C
0305-   8D FF 01    STA   $01FF
0308-   20 2C D5    JSR   $D52C
030B-   AD 00 02    LDA   $0200
030E-   C9 03       CMP   #$03
0310-   D0 03       BNE   $0315
0312-   4C 63 D8    JMP   $D863
0315-   85 75       STA   $75
0317-   86 7F       STX   $7F
0319-   84 80       STY   $80
031B-   20 E3 DF    JSR   $DFE3
031E-   85 85       STA   $85
0320-   84 86       STY   $86
0322-   A5 B8       LDA   $B8
0324-   A4 B9       LDY   $B9
0326-   85 87       STA   $87
0328-   84 88       STY   $88
032A-   A6 7F       LDX   $7F
032C-   A4 80       LDY   $80
032E-   86 B8       STX   $B8
0330-   84 B9       STY   $B9
0332-   20 B1 00    JSR   $00B1
0335-   A5 B8       LDA   $B8
0337-   A4 B9       LDY   $B9
0339-   20 58 03    JSR   $0358
033C-   20 3D E7    JSR   $E73D
033F-   20 7B DA    JSR   $DA7B
0342-   20 B7 00    JSR   $00B7
```

```
0345-   A5 B8       LDA   $B8
0347-   A4 B9       LDY   $B9
0349-   85 7F       STA   $7F
034B-   84 80       STY   $80
034D-   A5 87       LDA   $87
034F-   A4 88       LDY   $88
0351-   85 B8       STA   $B8
0353-   84 B9       STY   $B9
0355-   60          RTS
0356-   A9 00       LDA   #$00
0358-   85 0E       STA   $0E
035A-   85 0D       STA   $0D
035C-   4C ED E3    JMP   $E3ED
```

Figure 2-23: Program Keyword File

2.5 Presentation of Statistical Data

There are many possibilities to present statistical data. We will show here two examples, the histogram or bar graph and the pie chart.

2.51 The Bar Graph

Figure 2-24 shows the presentation of statistical data as a bar graph.

The program is shown in Figure 2-25. The input of data starts in line 1000. The program can draw a bar graph up to 14 different data. After entering the number of data, the data itself is entered. The program asks if the sum of all data or the maximum has to be set to 100%. Then the bar graph is drawn in high resolution graphics. The program can draw numbers into the high resolution graphic. The shapes of

- . / 0 1 2 3 4 5 6 7 8 9

are stored as data statements in the lines 40 to 100. The statement

DRAW 4 AT 140,90

draws a 0 in the middle of the screen. The parameters HCOLOR=, SCALE= and ROT= must be properly set.

The subroutine starting at line 600 draws the left hand scale. The plot of the bar graph starts at line 1300.

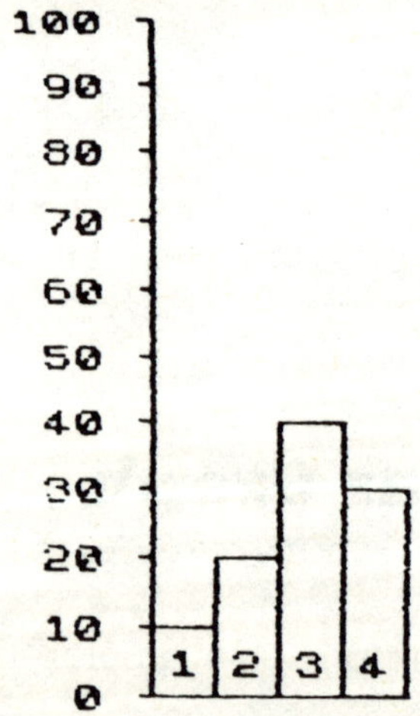

Figure 2-24: The Bar Graph

```
10  GOTO 1000
30  HIMEM: 38144: LOMEM: 16384
40  DATA  13,0,28,0,34,0,36,0,43,0,57,
    0,64,0,75,0,86,0,96,0,107,0,121,0,129,
    0
```

```
  50  DATA  141,0,192,56,13,45,4,0,4,0,216,
      12,12,12,12,4,0,101,36,36,28,63,23,54,
      54
  60  DATA  14,4,96,12,4,0,107,39,36,36,
      188,6,0,9,63,63,100,12,101,228,63,23
  70  DATA  6,0,216,14,45,12,228,103,12,
      60,63,55,0,33,44,28,36,188,23,23,46,
      45
  80  DATA  0,216,14,45,12,36,28,63,39,44,
      45,53,0,2,101,228,63,150,28,36,100
  90  DATA  12,45,6,155,0,35,36,97,12,60,
      63,55,0,101,228,103,33,28,63,23,174,
      23
 100  DATA  118,5,0,216,42,101,12,36,36,
      59,63,50,14,45,5,0
 110  FOR I = 0 TO 153
 120    READ A: POKE 38144 + I,A
 130  NEXT I
 140  RESTORE
 370  POKE 232,0: POKE 233,149
 600  HGR : HCOLOR= 3: SCALE= 1:
      ROT= 0
 610  HPLOT 30,155 TO 30,5
 620  FOR I = 0 TO 10
 625    U = 155 - I * 15
 630    HPLOT 28,U TO 32,U
 640  NEXT I
 650  FOR I = 0 TO 10
 660    DRAW 4 AT 20,158 - I * 15
 670  NEXT I
 680  FOR I = 1 TO 10:A = I:
        IF I = 10 THEN A = 0
 690    DRAW A + 4 AT 12,158 - I * 15
 700  NEXT I
 710  DRAW 5 AT 5,8
 720  RETURN
1000  REM  DATA INPUT
1005  IF  PEEK (233) <  > 149 THEN  GOSUB 30
1010  TEXT : HOME : INPUT "QTY:
      ";N
1020  DIM E(N)
1030  FOR I = 1 TO N
```

```
1040    PRINT "D";I;"=";:
        INPUT "";E(I)
1050  NEXT I
1060  FOR I = 1 TO 500:
      NEXT I
1070  HOME : VTAB 2: HTAB 2:
      PRINT "100%=S)UM"
1080  VTAB 3: HTAB 7: PRINT "M)AXIMUM"
1090  GET A$: IF A$ = "S" THEN  GOTO 1100
1095  IF A$ = "M" THEN  GOTO 1200
1099  GOTO 1090
1100  REM  SUM
1110  E = 0
1120  FOR I = 1 TO N:E = E + E(I):
      NEXT I
1130  FOR I = 1 TO N:E(I) = 155 - E(I) / E
        * 150:
      NEXT I
1140  GOTO 1300
1200  REM  MAXIMUM
1210  E = E(1)
1220  FOR I = 2 TO N
1230    IF E(I) > E THEN E = E(I)
1240  NEXT I
1250  GOTO 1130
1300  REM  PLOT DATA
1310  GOSUB 600
1315  HPLOT 30,155 TO 30 + 15 * N,155
1320  FOR I = 1 TO N
1325    U = 15 + 15 * I:
        V = 15 + U
1330    HPLOT U,155 TO U,E(I) TO V,E(I)
        TO V,155
1335  NEXT I
1340  FOR I = 1 TO N:A = I
1345    IF I > 9 THEN A = A - 9
1350    DRAW A + 3 AT 22 + 15 * I,150
1360  NEXT I
1370  VTAB 24: PRINT ;
```

Figure 2-25: Program Bar Graph

2.52 Pie Chart

The program in Figure 2-27 draws a pie chart as shown in Figure 2-26. For the input of data the program uses the same routines like the program bar graph. The subroutine starting in line 600 draws the circle at 140, 80 and the radius of 70 pixels. In a pie chart only the sum can be set to 100%. The drawing of the pieces of the pie starts at line 1300.

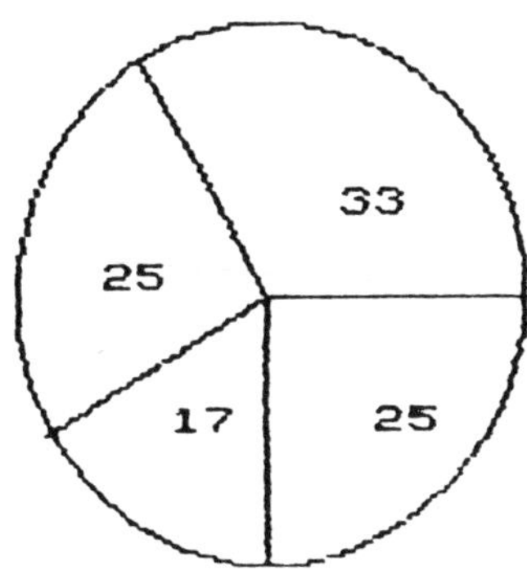

Figure 2-26: Pie Chart

The same subroutine as in the previous program is used to mix lines and numbers.

```
10  GOTO 1000
30  HIMEM: 38144: LOMEM: 16384
40  DATA  13,0,28,0,34,0,36,0,43,0,57,
    0,64,0,75,0,86,0,96,0,107,0,121,0,129,
    0
50  DATA  141,0,192,56,13,45,4,0,4,0,216,
    12,12,12,12,4,0,101,36,36,28,63,23,54,
    54
60  DATA  14,4,96,12,4,0,107,39,36,36,
    188,6,0,9,63,63,100,12,101,228,63,23
70  DATA  6,0,216,14,45,12,228,103,12,
    60,63,55,0,33,44,28,36,188,23,23,46,
    45
```

```
 80  DATA  0,216,14,45,12,36,28,63,39,44,
     45,53,0,2,101,228,63,150,28,36,100
 90  DATA  12,45,6,155,0,35,36,97,12,60,
     63,55,0,101,228,103,33,28,63,23,174,
     23
 100 DATA  118,5,0,216,42,101,12,36,36,
     59,63,50,14,45,5,0
 110 FOR I = 0 TO 153
 120   READ A: POKE 38144 + I,A
 130 NEXT I
 140 RESTORE
 370 POKE 232,0: POKE 233,149
 375 RETURN
 600 HGR : HCOLOR= 3: SCALE= 1:
     ROT= 0
 610 PI = 3.151596235
 620 U0 = 140:V0 = 80:R = 70
 630 HPLOT U0 + R,V0
 640 FOR I = 0 TO 360 STEP 5
 650   W = I * PI / 180
 660   X = R *  COS (W):
       Y = R *  SIN (W)
 670   XP = X + U0:YP = V0 - Y
 675   HPLOT  TO XP,YP
 680 NEXT I
 690 RETURN
1000 REM  DATA INPUT
1005 IF  PEEK (233) <  > 149 THEN  GOSUB 30
1010 TEXT : HOME : INPUT "QTY:
     ";N
1020 DIM E(N),F(N)
1030 FOR I = 1 TO N
1040   PRINT "D";I;"=";:
       INPUT "";E(I)
1050 NEXT I
1060 FOR I = 1 TO 500:
     NEXT I
1100 REM  SUM
1110 E = 0
1120 FOR I = 1 TO N:E = E + E(I):
     NEXT I
1130 FOR I = 1 TO N:E(I) = E(I) / E * 360:
     NEXT I
```

```
1140  E = 0
1150  FOR I = 1 TO N
1160    LET E = E(I) + E:
        F(I) = E
1170  NEXT I
1300  REM  PLOT DATA
1310  GOSUB 600
1320  HPLOT U0,V0 TO U0 + R,V0
1325  FOR I = 1 TO N
1330    X = R *  COS (PI * F(I) / 180)
1340    Y = R *  SIN (PI * F(I) / 180)
1350    XP = U0 + X:YP = V0 - Y
1360    HPLOT XP,YP TO U0,V0
1370  NEXT I
1380  FOR I = 1 TO N
1390    W = PI * (F(I) - E(I) / 2) / 180
1395    X = 2 * R / 3 *  COS (W):
        Y = R / 2 *  SIN (W)
1400    XP = X + U0:YP = V0 - Y
1410    N =  INT (E(I) / 3.6 + 0.5):
        NN =  INT (N / 10)
1420    DRAW NN + 4 AT XP,YP
1430    NN = N - 10 * NN
1440    DRAW NN + 4 AT XP + 7,YP
1450  NEXT I
1460  VTAB 24: PRINT
```

Figure 2-27: Program Pie Chart

2.6 Plotting Functions

2.61 Linear Functions

The program in Figure 2-31 plots linear functions of the form y=f(x). First there must be defined a system of coordinates for the function. Figure 2-30 shows an example.

We want to plot the function y=sin(x)/x in the range -10>x>10.

The first input u0,v0 is the center of the coordinates. This center should be in the middle of the screen. We choose u0=140 and v0=80. Next we have to determine the length of the axes. The X-axis should be 200 pixels long and the Y-axis 100 pixels. The x-values range from xa=-10 to xe=10. For the y-range we have to make estimations. Good values are ya=-1 and ye=1. The last input concerns the partition of the axes. The X-axis is divided into 10 parts (xt=10) and the Y-axis into four parts (yt=4).

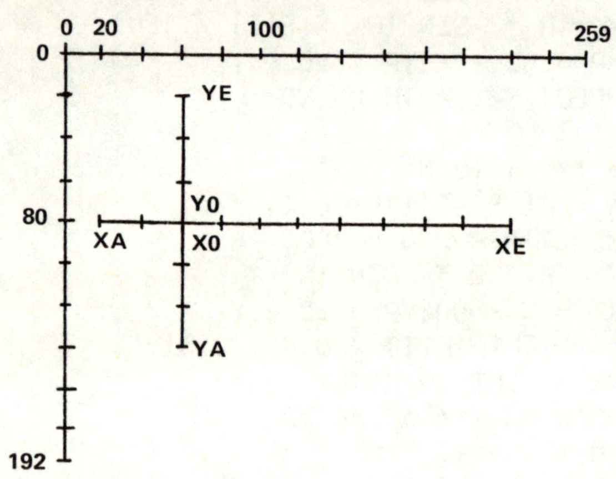

Figure 2-30: Definition of a system of coordinates.

```
 100  GOSUB 3000
1000  REM  FUNCTION
1005  VTAB 20: PRINT
1010  INPUT "STEP RATE S:
      ";S
1020  FOR X = XA TO XE STEP S
1030    IF X <  > 0 THEN Y =  SIN (X) / X
1040    GOSUB 2200
1050  NEXT X
1999  STOP
2000  REM  SYSTEM OF COORDINATES
2005  HOME
2010  PRINT " DATA FOR THE SYSTEM OF COORDINATES":
      PRINT
2015  INPUT "CENTER OF COORDINATES X0,Y0:
      ";X0,Y0
```

```
2020  INPUT "LENGTH OF THE AXES XL,YL:
      ";XL,YL
2030  INPUT "RANGE FOR X; XA,XE:
      ";XA,XE
2040  INPUT "RANGE FOR Y; YA,YE:
      ";YA,YE
2045  INPUT "DIVISION OF THE AXES XT,YT:
      ";XT,YT
2050  XG =  ABS (XA) +  ABS (XE):
      YG =  ABS (YA) +  ABS (YE)
2060  X1 = XL / XG * XA:
      X2 = XL / XG * XE
2065  X1 = X1 + X0:X2 = X2 + X0
2068  YL =  - YL
2070  Y1 = YL / YG * YA:
      Y2 = YL / YG * YE
2075  Y1 = Y1 + Y0:Y2 = Y2 + Y0
2080  MX = XL / XG:MY = YL / YG
2085  XT = XL / XT:YT = YL / YT
2100  HGR : HCOLOR= 3
2110  HPLOT X1,Y0 TO X2,Y0
2120  HPLOT X0,Y1 TO X0,Y2
2130  FOR X = X1 TO X2 STEP XT
2132    HPLOT X,Y0 - 2 TO X,Y0 + 2:
      NEXT X
2134  FOR Y = Y1 TO Y2 STEP YT
2136    HPLOT X0 - 2,Y TO X0 + 2,Y:
      NEXT Y
2140  RETURN
2200  XP = X * MX + X0:YP = Y * MY + Y0
2205  HCOLOR= 3
2210  IF XP < 0 OR XP > 279 THEN  GOTO 2230
2220  IF YP < 0 OR YP > 159 THEN  GOTO 2230
2225  HPLOT XP,YP
2230  RETURN
3000  READ X0,Y0,XL,YL,XA,XE,YA,YE,XT,YT
3010  GOSUB 2050: RETURN
3020 END
3100  DATA    140,80,200, 100,-10,10,-0.5,
      1,10,3
```

Figure 2-31: Program Function

After the input for the system of coordinates is finished, the program calculates the scale factors. The function itself is programmed in lines 1000 - 1050. The variables x and y are the parameters transferred to the plot-routine starting at line 2200. Figure 2-32 shows the result.

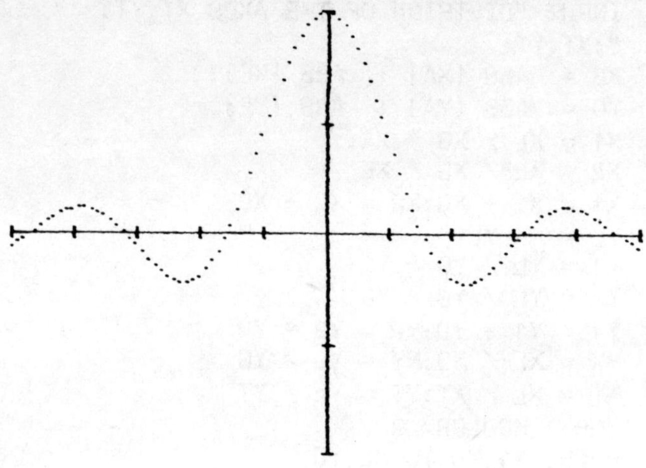

Figure 2-32: Example 1: y=sin(x)/x

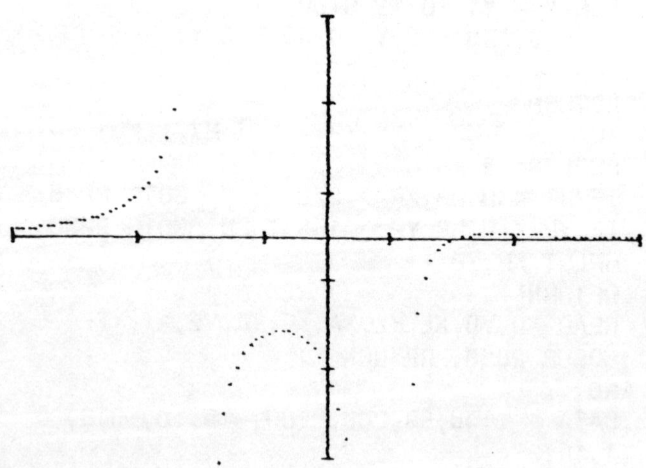

Figure 2-33: Example Broken Rational Function

The data for the system of coordinates can be stored in data statements in lines 3100 - 3120. If line 100 is changed to GOSUB 3000 the input at lines 2000 - 2070 is ignored. Another example shows Figure 2-33. This is the plot of the function

$$y=(3x-6)/((x-1)*(x-1)*(x+2))$$

The x-range is -5>x>5. The division by zero at the poles must be avoided. Line 130 then reads:

```
1030     IF X < > 1 OR X < > - 2 THEN Y
         = (3 * X - 6) / ((X - 1) * (X
         - 1) * (X + 2))
```

2.62 Three-Dimensional Functions

The program in Figure 2-31 is now expanded to plot three dimensional functions. The program in Figure 2-35 is used to plot three dimensional functions in a two dimensional plane. The transition from the three dimensional coordinates x,y,z to the two dimensional coordinates u,v is shown in Figure 2-34.

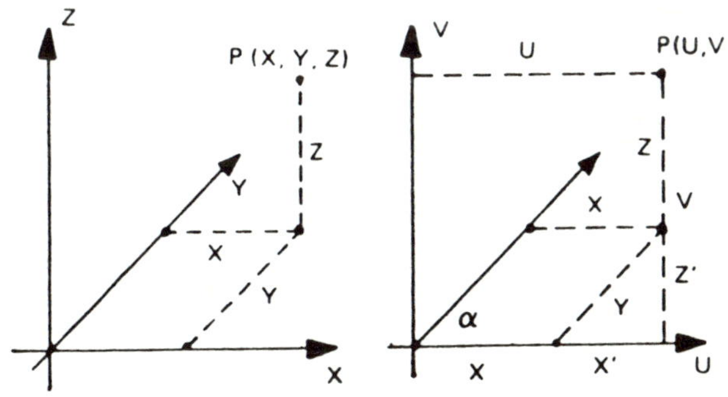

Figure 2-34: Transition from 3D to 2D Coordinates.

Alpha is the angle between the X-axis and the Y-axis in the two-dimensional presentation. The new coordinates U,V are:

$$U = X + X' \; ; \; V = Z + Z' \; ,$$

with X' = Y*cos(A) and Z' = Y*sin(A).

The input of data is similar as in the previous program. The system of coordinates is entered in lines 2000 - 2045. The function is programmed in lines 1000 - 1999. The sine and cosine values are calculated only once to increase computing speed.

```
 100  PI = 3.141592653
 110  GOSUB 3000
1000  REM  FUNCTION
1005  Z = 0:R = 0.75:S = 0.03
1010  FOR A = 0 TO 2 * PI STEP S
1020    X = R *  COS (A):
        Y = R *  SIN (A)
1030    GOSUB 2400:
      NEXT A
1040  Y = 0
1050  FOR A = 0 TO 2 * PI STEP S
1060    X = R *  COS (A):
        Z = R *  SIN (A)
1070    GOSUB 2400:
      NEXT A
1080  X = 0
1090  FOR A = 0 TO 2 * PI STEP S
1100    Y = R *  COS (A):
        Z = R *  SIN (A)
1110    GOSUB 2400:
      NEXT A
1999  STOP
2000  REM  SYSTEM OF COORDINATES
2005  HOME
2010  PRINT " DATA FOR THE SYSTEM OF COORDINATES":
      PRINT
2015  INPUT "CENTER OF COORDINATES U0,V0:
      ";U0,V0
2020  INPUT "LENGTH OF THE AXES XL,YL,ZL:
      ";XL,YL,ZL
```

```
2025  INPUT "RANGE FOR X; XA,XE:
      ";XA,XE
2030  INPUT "RANGE FOR Y; YA,YE:
      ";YA,YE
2035  INPUT "RANGE FOR Z; ZA,ZE:
      ";ZA,ZE
2040  INPUT "DIVISION OF THE AXES XT,YT,
      ZT:";XT,YT,ZT
2045  INPUT "ANGLE ALPHA:
      ";WI
2050  XG =  ABS (XA) +  ABS (XE):
      YG =  ABS (YA) +  ABS (YE):
      ZG =  ABS (ZA) +  ABS (ZE)
2060  X0 = U0:Z0 = V0:Y0 = 0
2070  X1 = XL / XG * XA + X0:
      X2 = XL / XG * XE + X0
2080  Y1 = YL / YG * YA + Y0:
      Y2 = YL / YG * YE + Y0
2090  Z1 = ZL / ZG * ZA + Z0:
      Z2 = ZL / ZG * ZE + Z0
2100  MX = XL / XG:MY = YL / YG:
      MZ = ZL / ZG
2110  XT = XL / XT:YT = YL / YT:
      ZT = ZL / ZT
2120  CO =  COS (PI * WI / 180):
      SI =  SIN (PI * WI / 180)
2200  REM  DRAW SYSTEM OF COORDINATES
2210  HGR : HCOLOR= 3
2220  HPLOT X1,Z0 TO X2,Z0
2230  HPLOT X0,Z1 TO X0,Z2
2240  FOR X = X1 TO X2 STEP XT
2250    HPLOT X,Z0 - 2 TO X,Z0 + 2:
      NEXT X
2260  FOR Z = Z1 TO Z2 STEP ZT
2270    HPLOT X0 - 2,Z TO X0 + 2,Z:
      NEXT Z
2280  UA = U0 + CO * Y1:
      VA = V0 - SI * Y1
2290  UE = U0 + CO * Y2:
      VE = V0 - SI * Y2
2300  HPLOT UA,VA TO UE,VE
2310  FOR Y = Y1 TO Y2 STEP YT
```

```
2320      U = U0 - CO * Y:
          V = V0 + SI * Y
2340      HPLOT U,V - 2 TO U,V + 2:
        NEXT Y
2350    RETURN
2400    REM  PLOT FUNCTION
2410    XP = X * MX:YP = Y * MX:
        ZP = Z * MZ
2420    U = XP + CO * YP + U0:
        V =   - ZP - SI * YP + V0
2430    IF U < 0 OR U > 279 THEN  GOTO 2460
2440    IF V < 0 OR V > 159 THEN  GOTO 2460
2450    HPLOT U,V
2460    RETURN
3000    READ U0,V0,XL,YL,ZL,XA,XE,YA,YE,ZA,
        ZE,XT,YT,ZT,WI
3010    GOTO 2050
3100    DATA    140,80,140,140,140,-1,1,-1,
        1,-1,1,4,4 ,4,45
```

Figure 2-35: Program Plot-3D

To enter the values for the system of coordinates, change line 110 in GOSUB 2000. Use GOSUB 3000 if they are stored in DATA statements.

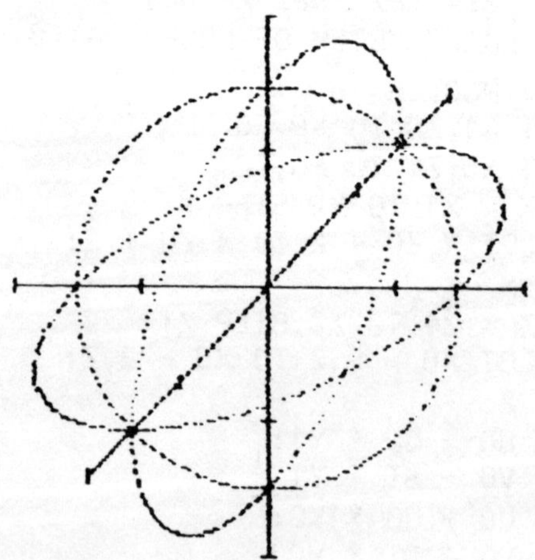

Figure 2-36: Three Circles in Different planes.

In the first example we plot three circles in three different planes. The center of the coordinates is at u0=140, v0=80. The length of the axes is 140, the range for the coordinates is -1 to 1. The axes are divided into four parts and the angle is 45 degrees.

Our second example draws a sphere. The following lines have to be inserted:

```
1002  FOR B =  - PI / 2 TO PI / 2
1005    R = 0.75:S = 0.06
1020    X = R *  COS (A) *  COS (B):
        Y = R *  SIN (A) *  SIN (B):
        Z =  SIN (B)
1035  NEXT B
```

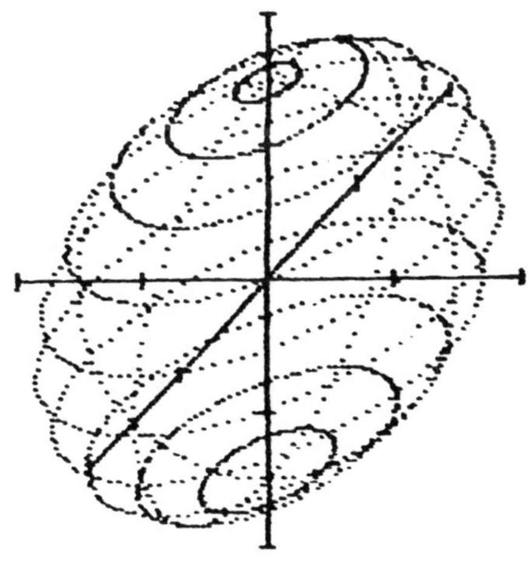

Figure 2-37: Sphere.

2.7 Fourier Analysis

The Fourier analysis determines the DC-component, the fundamental and the harmonics of a periodic signal. Using a mathematical method the coefficients c(0), s(n) and c(n) of the formula

$$f(t) = c(o) + \sum_{n=1}^{N} (s(n) \sin n\omega t + c(n) \cos n\omega t)$$

are computed.

The mathematical method isn't discussed here. It can be found in [1]. It is a recursive method. The used trigonometric terms are computed only once. This speeds up the execution time.

For the analysis of a periodic signal we must have samples with constant intervals in time within one period. The number of samples NP must be greater than 2*NH + 1. NH is the number of harmonics to be calculated. Figure 2-38 shows the sampling of a square wave. This is Example 3 in our program.

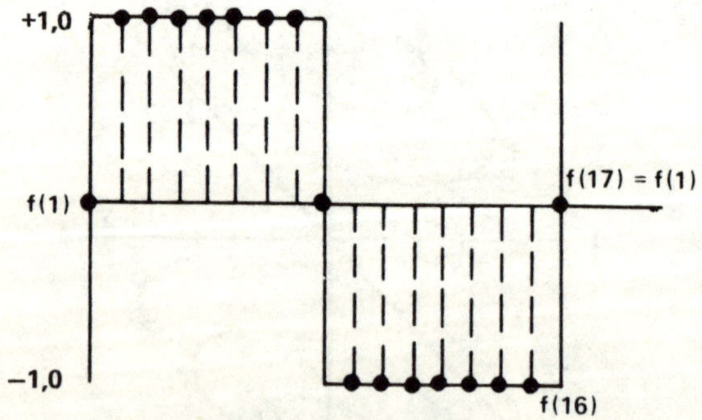

Figure 2-38: Square wave

If there is a jump in the function, the arithmetic mean of upper and lower limits is taken as sample. The following results are obtained with NP=16 and NH=7. The numeric results are shown in Figure 2-39.

N	COS	SIN
0	0	0
1	0	1.2685
2	0	0
3	0	.4103
4	0	0
5	0	.2309
6	0	0
7	0	.148

Figure 2-39: Fourier Coefficients

The results show that all cosine and all even sine terms are zero. The spectrum is shown in Figure 2-40.

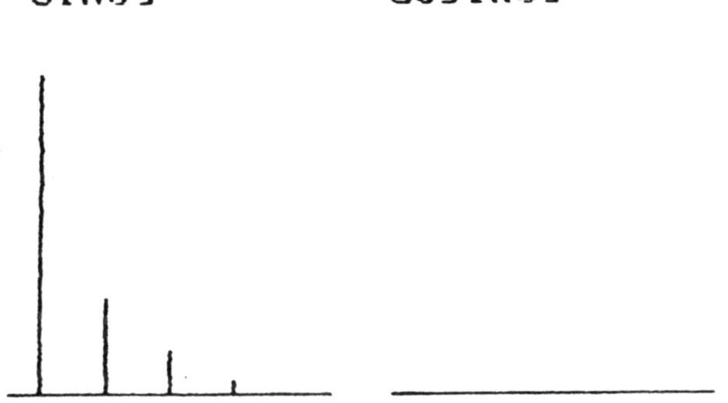

Figure 2-40: Spectrum of a Square Wave

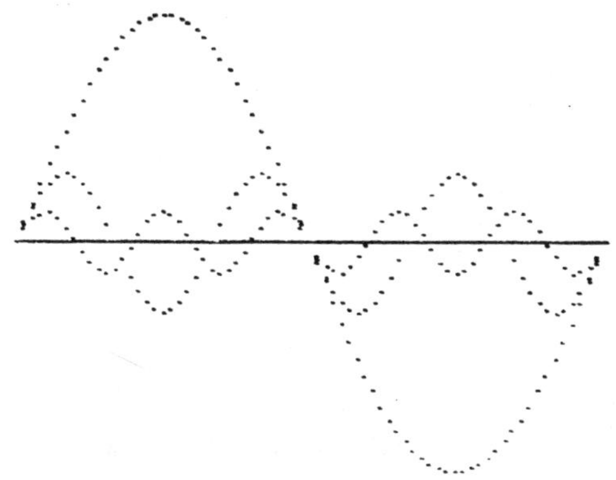

Figure 2-41: Fundamental and Harmonics

The fundamental and the harmonics are shown in Figure 2-41.

The next Figure 2-42 is a Fourier synthesis. The fundamental and the harmonics are added and compared with the samples.

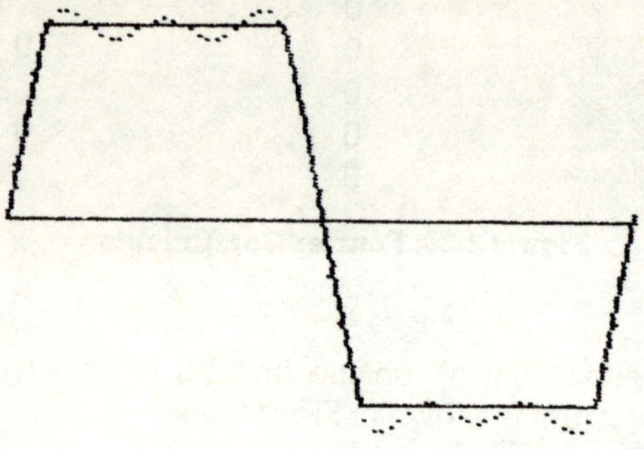

Figure 2-42: Fourier Synthesis.

The Figure 2-43 and 2-44 show two different sawtooth functions. They are used in Examples 1 and 2 in the program.

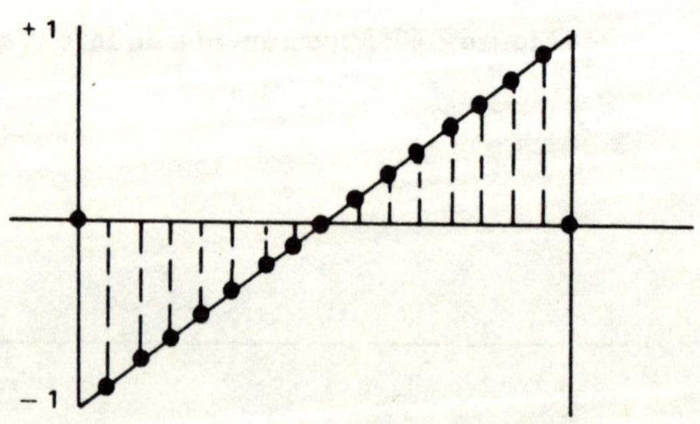

Figure 2-43: Example 1: Sawtooth 1

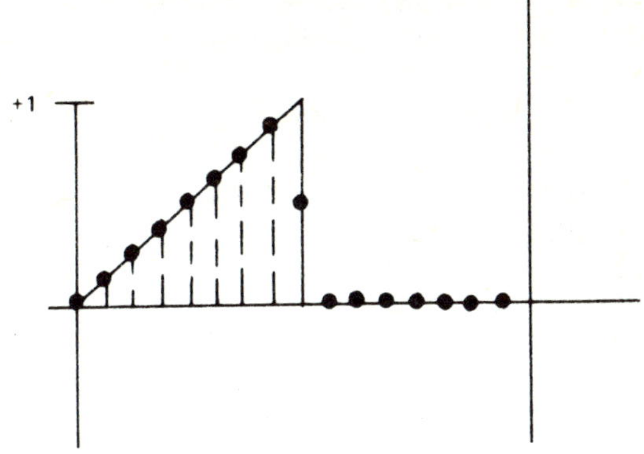

Figure 2-44: Example 2: Sawtooth 2

The program is shown in Figure 2-45. The menu and the input of NP and NH start in line 20. The examples are programmed in lines 100, 200 and 300. The Fourier analysis starts in line 500. The pictures are drawn at line 1000, 1200 and 1400. The program restarts and is terminated by entering a five.

```
10  TEXT : HOME : PRINT "FOURIER ANALYSIS":
    PRINT : PRINT "WHICH EXAMPLE ?":
    PRINT
15  PRINT " A SAWTOOTH 1"
20  PRINT " B SAWTOOTH 2"
25  PRINT " C SQUARE WAVE"
28  PRINT : INPUT "(A/B/C)";A$
30  IF A$ = "A" THEN  GOSUB 100:
    GOTO 40
32  IF A$ = "B" THEN  GOSUB 200:
    GOTO 40
34  IF A$ = "C" THEN  GOSUB 300:
    GOTO 40
36  PRINT "": GOTO 20
40  PRINT : PRINT "END OF PROGRAM"
42 END
44  GOTO 20
45  PRINT "INPUT OF THE QUANTITY OF HARMONICS
    AND
46  PRINT "THE NUMBER OF SAMPLE POINTS
    NP"
```

```
 47  PRINT "IT MUST BE NP > 2*NH+1"
 50  INPUT "QTY OF HARMONICS NH:
     ";NH
 60  INPUT "QTY OF SAMPLE POINTS:
     ";NP
 70  IF NP < 2 * NH + 1 THEN  GOTO 50
 80  RETURN
100  REM  EXAMPLE SAWTOOTH 1
105  GOSUB 45
110  DIM F(NP),S(NP),C(NP)
115  F(0) =  - 1:DY = 2 / NP
120  FOR I = 1 TO NP - 1
125    F(I) = F(I - 1) + DY:
     NEXT I
128  F(0) = 0
130  GOSUB 500
140  RETURN
200  REM  SAWTOOTH 2
205  GOSUB 45
210  DIM F(NP)
215  F(0) = 0:DY = 2 / NP
220  FOR I = 1 TO NP / 2 - 1
225    F(I) = F(I - 1) + DY:
     NEXT I
230  F(NP / 2) = 0.5
240  FOR I = NP / 2 + 1 TO NP - 1
245    F(I) = 0:
     NEXT I
250  GOSUB 500
260  RETURN
300  REM  SQUARE WAVE
302  GOSUB 45
305  DIM F(NP)
310  F(0) = 0:F(NP / 2) = 0
315  FOR I = 1 TO NP / 2 - 1:
       F(I) = 1:
     NEXT I
320  FOR I = NP / 2 + 1 TO NP - 1:
       F(I) =  - 1:
     NEXT I
330  GOSUB 500
340  RETURN
500  PI = 3.141592653
```

```
 502  HOME : PRINT
 503  PRINT "N"; TAB( 15);"COS"; TAB( 31);"SIN";:
      PRINT : PRINT
 505  PRINT
 510  Z = 2 / NP
 520  C1 =  COS (Z * PI):
      S1 =  SIN (Z * PI)
 530  C = 1:S = 0:P = 0
 540  U1 = 0:U2 = 0
 550  KLN = NP - 1
 560  U0 = F(KLN) + 2 * C * U1 - U2
 570  U2 = U1:U1 = U0:KLN = KLN - 1
 580  IF KLN = 0 GOTO 600
 590  GOTO 560
 600  A = Z * (F(0) + C * U1 - U2)
 605  B = Z * S * U1
 610  EPS = 1E - 6
 620  IF  ABS (A) < EPS THEN A = 0
 630  IF  ABS (B) < EPS THEN B = 0
 632  J% = 10000
 634  A =  INT (J% * A) / J%:
      C(P) = A
 636  B =  INT (J% * B) / J%:
      S(P) = B
 638  IF P = 0 THEN A = A / 2:
      C(P) = A
 640  PRINT P,A,B
 650  IF P = NH GOTO 999
 660  Q = C1 * C - S1 * S
 670  S = C1 * S + S1 * C
 680  C = Q:P = P + 1: GOTO 540
 999  GOSUB 1500
1000  REM  SPECTRAL LINES
1005  HOME :MY = 60
1010  HGR : HCOLOR= 3
1020  VTAB 22: HTAB 2: PRINT "COSINE";:
      HTAB 22: PRINT "SINE";
1030  VTAB 24: HTAB 9: PRINT "FOURIER-COEFFICIENTS"
1040  HPLOT 10,150 TO 110,150:
      HPLOT 150,150 TO 250,150
1050  FOR I = 0 TO NH
1060    HPLOT 10 * I + 10,150 TO 10 * I
        + 10,150 - 100 *  ABS (C(I))
```

```
1070  NEXT I
1080  FOR I = 0 TO NH
1090    HPLOT 10 * I + 150,150 TO 10 * I
        + 150,150 - 100 *  ABS (S(I))
1095  NEXT I
1099  GOSUB 1500
1100  REM  HARMONICS
1110  HOME : VTAB 24: HTAB 9:
      PRINT "SINGLE FREQUENCIES"
1120  HGR : HCOLOR= 3: HPLOT 20,80 TO 200,
      80
1130  FOR P = 0 TO NH
1140    IF S(P) = 0 THEN  GOTO 1200
1150    FOR I = 0 TO 360 STEP 5
1160      Y = S(P) *  SIN ((P) * 2 * PI
          * I / 360):
          Y = 80 - Y * MY
1170      X = I / 2 + 20
1180      HPLOT X,Y
1190    NEXT I
1200    IF C(P) = 0 THEN  GOTO 1260
1210    FOR I = 0 TO 360 STEP 5
1220      Y = C(P) *  COS ((P) * 2 * PI
          * I / 360):
          Y = 80 - Y * MY
1230      X = I / 2 + 20
1240      HPLOT X,Y
1250    NEXT I
1260  NEXT P
1295  GOSUB 1500
1300  REM  FOURIER-SYTHESIS
1310  HOME : HGR : HCOLOR= 3
1320  VTAB 24: HTAB 9: PRINT "FOURIER-SYNTHESIS"
1330  HPLOT 20,80 TO 200,80
1340  FOR I = 0 TO 360 STEP 5
1350    Y = 0
1360    FOR P = 0 TO NH
1370      W = P * 2 * PI * I / 360
1380      Y = Y + S(P) *  SIN (W) + C(P)
          *  COS (W)
1390    NEXT P
1400    Y = 80 - Y * MY:
        X = I / 2 + 20
```

```
1410      HPLOT X,Y
1420    NEXT I
1430    X = 180 / NP:Y = 80 - 70 * F(0):
        XP = 20
1440    HPLOT XP,Y
1450    FOR I = 1 TO NP
1460      Y = 80 - MY * F(I):
          XP = X * I + 20
1470      HPLOT  TO XP,Y
1480    NEXT I
1495    GOTO 1500
1500    VTAB 24: PRINT "FOR MORE PRESS ANY
        KEY";: GET A$: RETURN
```

Figure 2-45: Program Fourier Analysis

2.8 Computer-Graphics

The following three programs use high resolution graphics. The first draws shapes, the second is a little game and the third draws the shape of the moon.

2.81 Graphics 1

The program draws a regular polygon around the center of the screen. This polygon is turned around the center and around one corner. To increase the speed of plotting the sine and cosine values are stored in a table. Line 200 sets the high resolution mode and HCOLOR to white. In line 350 the coordinates of the center of the screen are determined. Line 530 draws a line from the last point to the point X1 and Y1. After finishing the picture the program beeps and is waiting for a keypress. Figure 2-46 shows an example.

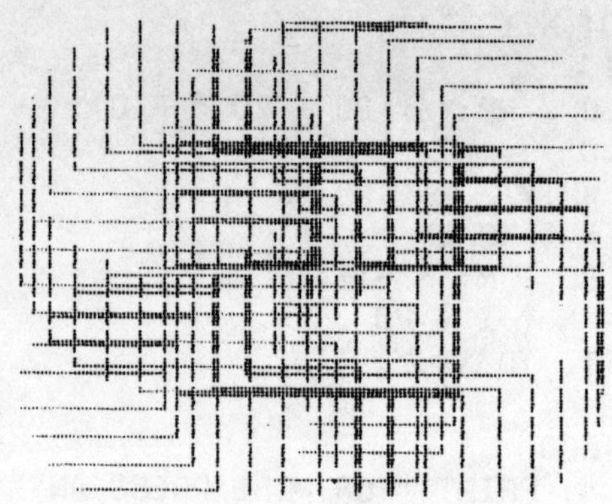

Figure 2-46: Example Graphics 1

```
 10  DIM C(100),S(100):
     P = 3.14159265
 20  HOME : PRINT "COMPUTER-GRAPHICS":
     PRINT : PRINT "PLEASE WAIT FOR A MOMENT"
100  FOR I = 0 TO 2 * P STEP P / 50:
       S(X) =  SIN (I):C(X) =  COS (I):
       X = X + 1:
     NEXT
120  PRINT
125  INPUT " TURN 1:";D1
130  INPUT " TURN 2:";D2
140  INPUT " SIZE 1:";G1
150  INPUT " SIZE 2:";G2
160  INPUT " # OF CORNERS:
     ";E:D3 = 100 / E
170  INPUT " # OF DRAWN CORNERS:
     ";E
200  HGR2 : HCOLOR= 3
300  R1 = 0:R2 = 0
350  X = 140:Y = 95: GOTO 410
400  X = 140:Y = 95
405  IF R1 < .1 OR R1 > 99.9 THEN  IF R2
     < .1 OR R2 > 99.9 THEN  PRINT
     CHR$ (7): GET A$:
     TEXT : GOTO 120
410  R1 = R1 + D1: IF R1 > 100 THEN R1
     = R1 - 100
```

```
420  X1 = X + C(R1) * G1:
     Y1 = Y + S(R1) * G1
430  HPLOT X1 + .5,Y1 + .5
500  FOR I = 1 TO E
```

Figure 2-47: Program Graphics 1

The input for this picture was:

```
TURN 1= 44
TURN 2= 25
SIZE 1= 36
SIZE 2= 35
# OF CORNERS= 4
# OF CORNERS DRAWN= 2
```

The input values have the following meanings:

TURN 1: Rotation after each sequence around the center of the screen. This is a number between 0 and 100. 100 is a turn of 360 degrees.
TURN 2: Rotation of the polygon around one corner.
SIZE 1: Radius of the polygon.
SIZE 2: Size of the polygon.
of the corners and # of the corners drawn.

The following examples are recommended:

T1	T1	S1	S1	Cn	Cnd
44	25	36	35	4	2
2	99.5	45	45	1	1
2	99	40	40	3	3
46	12.5	10	35	8	4
12.5	42	50	20	4	4
40	42	50	20	5	5
98	3.2	50	30	1	1

2.82 Maze

There are only a few people who have been inside a maze. The program MAZE allows one to walk through a maze and try to find the exit. Additionally one may view the maze from abuve to see one ' s location

The size in x-direction is limited to 38, the size in y-direction to 22

GOOD LUCK

```
10  TEXT : NORMAL : HOME :
    PRINT  TAB( 11)"***   MAZE    ***"
20  PRINT : PRINT : PRINT "YOU HAVE TO
    FIND THE EXIT OF A MAZE IN "
30  PRINT : PRINT "WHICH YOU ARE WALKING
    AROUND !"
50  PRINT : PRINT "IF YOU PRESS THE 'RETURN'
    KEY, YOU"
60  PRINT : PRINT "MOVE ONE SEGMENT FOREWARD.":
    PRINT
70  PRINT "IF YOU PRESS THE KEYS '<-'
    OR '->' "
80  PRINT : PRINT "YOU MAKE A TURN OF
    90 DEGREES TO THE"
81  PRINT : PRINT "LEFT OR TO THE RIGHT."
82  PRINT : PRINT "THE EXIT IS MARKED
    WITH A CROSS."
84  PRINT : PRINT "PLEASE PRESS THE KEY
    ->";: GET A$
85  HOME : PRINT "IF YOU PRESS 'X' THE
    MAZE IS SHOWN   ": PRINT :
    PRINT "FROM ABOVE."
92  PRINT : PRINT : PRINT "INPUT:
    ": PRINT
100 INPUT "SIZE IN X-DIRECTION  :
    ";WX: PRINT : IF WX < 4 OR WX > 38 THEN
    PRINT "BETWEEN  4 AND 38 PLEASE!!":
    PRINT : GOTO 100
```

```
105  INPUT "SIZE IN Y-DIRECTION  :
     ";WY: PRINT : IF WY < 4 OR WY > 22 THEN
     PRINT "BETWEEN  4 AND 22 PLEASE!!":
     PRINT : GOTO 105
106  IF  INT (WX / 2) <  > WX / 2 THEN WX
     = WX + 1
107  IF  INT (WY / 2) <  > WY / 2 THEN WY
     = WY + 1
110  PRINT : INPUT "LEVEL OF SKILL (1-4):
     ";S: IF S < 1 OR S > 4 THEN 110
210  DIM A(WX,WY)
220  PRINT : PRINT "PLEASE WAIT ":
     X =  INT (WX / 2):Y =  INT (WY / 2):
     A(X,Y) = 1
230  IF  RND (1) > .51 THEN XS =  SGN (
     RND (1) - .5):
     YS = 0: GOTO 250
240  XS = 0:YS =  SGN ( RND (1) - .5)
250  FOR I = 0 TO 1:X = X + XS:
       Y = Y + YS:A(X,Y) = 1
255    IF F THEN  IF X = 1 OR X = WX - 1
       OR Y = 1 OR Y = WY - 1 THEN 280
260    IF X = 0 OR X = WX OR Y = 0 OR Y
       = WY THEN 280
270  NEXT : GOTO 230
280  F = F + 1: IF F < S THEN 220
2000 HOME : HCOLOR= 3
2010 X =  INT (WX / 2):
     Y =  INT (WY) / 2:X1 = X:
     Y1 = Y:R = 0
2020 X(0) = 1:Y(0) = 0:
     X(1) = 0:Y(1) =  - 1:
     X(2) =  - 1:Y(2) = 0:
     X(3) = 0:Y(3) = 1
2030 RR = R + 1: IF RR > 3 THEN RR = 0
2035 XR = X(RR):YR = Y(RR)
2040 X1 = X:Y1 = Y:I = 1.5:
     HGR2 : GOSUB 3000
2050 I = I + .5:X1 = X1 + X(R):
     Y1 = Y1 + Y(R)
2051 IF X1 < 0 OR X1 > WX OR Y1 < 0 OR Y1
     > WY THEN  GOSUB 3300:
     GOTO 2065
```

```
2052  IF A(X1,Y1) = 0 THEN 2065
2055  GOSUB 3000
2060  GOTO 2050
2065  GOSUB 4000
2070  GET A$: IF A$ =  CHR$ (21) THEN R
      = R + 1: GOTO 2200
2080  IF A$ =  CHR$ (8) THEN R = R - 1:
      GOTO 2200
2085  IF A$ = "X" THEN  GOSUB 5000:
      GOTO 2040
2090  IF A$ < > CHR$ (13) THEN 2070
2100  X1 = X + X(R):Y1 = Y + Y(R):
      IF X1 < 0 OR X1 > WX OR Y1 < 0 OR Y1
      > WY THEN 6000
2110  IF A(X1,Y1) = 0 THEN 2070
2115  X = X1:Y = Y1: GOTO 2030
2200  IF R < 0 THEN R = 3:
      GOTO 2030
2210  IF R > 3 THEN R = 0
2220  GOTO 2030
3000  A1 = 140 + 139 / I:
      B1 = 95 + 94 / I:B2 = 191 - B1:
      A3 = 279 - A1:B3 = B1:
      B4 = B2
3010  C1 = 140 + 139 / (I - .5):
      D1 = 95 + 94 / (I - .5):
      D2 = 191 - D1:C3 = 279 - C1:
      D3 = D1:D4 = D2
3015  XT = X1 + XR:YT = Y1 + YR:
      IF XT < 0 OR XT > WX OR YT < 0 OR YT
      > WY THEN 3040
3020  IF A(XT,YT) = 1 THEN 3040
3030  HPLOT C1,D1 TO A1,B1:
      HPLOT C1,D2 TO A1,B2:
      GOTO 3050
3040  HPLOT C1,B1 TO A1,B1:
      HPLOT C1,B2 TO A1,B2
3050  HPLOT A1,B1 TO A1,B2
3090  XT = X1 - XR:YT = Y1 - YR:
      IF XT < 0 OR XT > WX OR YT < 0 OR YT
      > WY THEN 3140
3100  IF A(XT,YT) = 1 THEN 3140
```

```
3130  HPLOT C3,D3 TO A3,B3:
      HPLOT C3,D4 TO A3,B4:
      GOTO 3150
3140  HPLOT C3,B3 TO A3,B3:
      HPLOT C3,B4 TO A3,B4
3150  HPLOT A3,B3 TO A3,B4
3200  RETURN
3300  HPLOT A1,95 TO A3,95:
      HPLOT 140,B2 TO 140,B1:
      RETURN
4000  HPLOT A1,B1 TO A3,B1:
      HPLOT A1,B2 TO A3,B2:
      RETURN
5000  TEXT : HOME :
      FOR Z = 0 TO WY:
        FOR Q = WX TO 0 STEP  - 1
5010      IF A(Q,Z) = 0 THEN 5040
5015      INVERSE : IF Z = 0 OR Z = WY OR Q
          = 0 OR Q = WX THEN  FLASH :
          PRINT "A";: GOTO 5050
5020      IF Q = X THEN  IF Z = Y THEN
          FLASH : PRINT "*";:
          GOTO 5050
5040      PRINT " ";: NORMAL
5050      NORMAL :
        NEXT : PRINT :
      NEXT : PRINT "PRESS KEY '->'";:
      GET A$: RETURN
6000  TEXT : HOME : FLASH :
      PRINT  TAB( 6)"YOU GOT IT !!!"
6010  PRINT : NORMAL : PRINT "CONGRATULATIONS"
6020  PRINT : PRINT : PRINT "S=SAME MAZE
      ONCE MORE"
6030  PRINT "E=END OF PROGRAM"
6040  PRINT "N=NEW MAZE"
6050  GET A$: IF A$ = "N" THEN  CLEAR :
      HOME : GOTO 100
6060  IF A$ = "E" THEN END
6070  IF A$ <  > "S" THEN 6000
6080  GOTO 2000
```

Figure 2-48: Program Maze

2.83 The Lunar Phase

The program in Figure 2-49 draws the lunar shape. The date and the time is entered, and you can see the moon on the TV screen.

```
10  HOME :
    FOR I = 1 TO 6: PRINT  CHR$ (7):
    NEXT
15  FOR I = 1293 TO 1305:
      POKE I,32: POKE I + 512,32:
    NEXT
20  FOR I = 1421 TO 1679 STEP 128:
      POKE I,32: POKE I + 12,32:
    NEXT
25  POKE 1551,141: POKE 1553,143:
    POKE 1555,144: POKE 1557,136:
    POKE 1559,129
30  VTAB 10: PRINT "PROGRAM TO CALCULATE
    THE LUNAR PHASE": PRINT
35  PRINT "FOR A GIVEN DAY":
    PRINT
45  VTAB (17): PRINT  TAB( 8)"COPYRIGHT
     OKTOBER 1980
50  PRINT  TAB( 9)"BY  WOLFGANG F. HAHN
100 VTAB 23: INPUT "DO YOU WANT INSTRUCTIONS?
    (Y/N)";A$
105 IF A$ = "N" GOTO 500
110 IF A$ < > "Y" GOTO 100
115 HOME
120 PRINT "FOR CALCULATING YOU CAN USE
    THE DATE"
125 PRINT "OF THE LAST NEW MOON OR A DATE
    WITHIN"
130 PRINT "THE PROGRAM"
140 PRINT "ENTER THE DATE AS FOLLOWS:
    ": PRINT
145 PRINT "  1. MONTH (1 - 12)":
    PRINT
150 PRINT "  2. DAY ( 1 - 31 )":
    PRINT
```

```
 155  PRINT "  3. YEAR (FOUR DIGITS)":
      PRINT
 160  PRINT "  4. TIME (1 - 12 AM/PM)":
      PRINT : PRINT
 165  PRINT "E.G. MAY 3 1981,9 PM  :
      5,3,1981,9,PM"
 170  PRINT : PRINT
 185  PRINT "THE PROGRAM CAN SHOW YOU A
      DOTTED"
 190  PRINT "CIRCLE WHICH REPRESENTS THE
      FULL MOON."
 200  VTAB 23: PRINT " (PRESS ANY KEY FOR
      MORE).."
 205  VTAB (23): HTAB (40)
 210  GET A$
 500  HOME
 505  RESTORE : DIM WN$(6)
 510  READ X0,Y0,RADIUS,SM
 515  READ P1,P2
 520  FOR W = 0 TO 6
 525    READ WN$(W):
      NEXT
 530  DATA  140,80,75
 535  DATA  29.53
 540  DATA  6.283185307,4.712388981
 545  DATA  SUNDAY,MONDAY,THUESDAY,WEDNESDAY,
      THURSDAY,FRIDAY,SATURDAY
 550  RR = RADIUS ^ 2
1000  PRINT "DO YOU WANT TO ENTER THE DATE
      OF ": PRINT
1005  PRINT "A NEW MOON (=1) OR USE THE
      DATE ": PRINT
1010  INPUT "WITHIN THE PROGRAM (=2) ";A
1015  PRINT : IF A = 1 GOTO 1030
1020  IF A <  > 2 GOTO 1000
1025  DN = 723111.16: GOTO 1055
1030  PRINT "DATE OF THE NEW MOON"
1032  INPUT "(M,D,Y,T) ";M,T,J,S,N$
1034  IF  LEFT$ (N$,1) = "P" THEN S = S
      + 12
1035  GOSUB 3005
1040  GOSUB 3040: IF FL = 0 GOTO 1030
1045  DN=DAYS
```

```
1050  HOME : PRINT : PRINT
1055  PRINT : PRINT "FOR WHAT DATE DO YOU
      WANT THE LUNAR ": PRINT
1060  INPUT "PHASE? (M,D,Y,T) ";M,T,J,S,
      N$
1062  IF  LEFT$ (N$,1) = "P" THEN S = S
      + 12
1065  J1 = J: GOSUB 3005
1070  GOSUB 3040: IF FL = 0 GOTO 1055
1075  D = DAYS - DN
1500  MA = D * P1 / SM
1505  F =  COS (MA)
1510  IF  SIN (MA) < 0 GOTO 1530
1515  REM  FIRST AND SECOND QUARTER
1520  VX = 1: GOTO 2005
1525  REM  THIRD AND LAST QUARTER
1530  VX =  - 1
2000  REM  FULL MOON REFERENCE
2005  PRINT : PRINT "DO YOU WANT THE REFERENCE
      ": PRINT
2010  INPUT "OF THE FULL MOON (Y/N) ";A$
2015  IF A$ = "N" GOTO 2200
2020  IF A$ <  > "Y" GOTO 2005
2025  HGR
2030  FOR I = 0 TO P1 STEP P2 / 18
2035    X = X0 + RADIUS *  COS (I):
        Y = Y0 + RADIUS *  SIN (I)
2040    HPLOT X,Y
2045  NEXT
2050  GOTO 2205
2200  HGR
2205  VTAB (21)
2210  FOR I =  - 75 TO 75
2215    Y =  ABS (I):YP = I + 80
2220    X = VX *  SQR (RR - Y ^ 2)
2225    XK = X0 + X:XE = X0 + F * X
2230    HPLOT XK,YP TO XE,YP
2235  NEXT
2240  VTAB (21)
2242  N$ = "AM": IF S > 12 THEN S = S - 12:
      N$ = "PM"
2245  PRINT "LUNAR PHASE AT ";WN$(W)", THE
      ";M;"/";T;"/";J1;"
```

```
2250  PRINT "AT ";S;" ";N$
2255  INPUT "ONCE MORE AGAIN (Y/N)";A$
2260  IF A$ = "Y" GOTO 1055
2265  IF A$ <  > "N" GOTO 2255
2270  HGR : TEXT : HOME
2275 END
3000  REM  SUBROUTINE DATE
3005  DAYS = 0
3010  DAYS = (T - 1) + 31 * (M - 1) + 365
      * (J - 1)
3015  IF M > 2 GOTO 3025
3020  J = J - 1
3025  DAYS = DAYS -  INT (.4 * M + 2.3)
      +  INT (J / 4) + S / 24
3030  W =  INT (DAYS -  INT (DAYS / 7) * 7)
3035  RETURN
3040  IF DAYS < 693699 OR DAYS > 766715
      GOTO 3050
3045  FL = 1: RETURN
3050  PRINT : PRINT : PRINT  CHR$ (7)
3055  PRINT " DATE NOT CORRECT":
      PRINT
3060  FL = 0: RETURN
```

Figure 2-49: The Lunar Phase

NOTES

3 Machine Language Section

Many books have been written for the 6502 CPU. Here we will make a short introduction in programming in machine language and then we will look at some specific problems. Two main programs are included in this section. The PRETTY-PRINT prints our BASIC programs in a more readable form, and the RT-CLOCK is used to measure the time. The latter program uses interrupts, and we will explain how to use this technique. In short programs we will discuss how to use the & statement from BASIC, how to make sound, and how to use some graphic routines. Let us start with a look to the programming model of the 6502 CPU.

3.1 The Programming Model

Figure 3-1 shows the programming model of the 6502. We have four eight-bit registers: the accumulator, the X- and Y-registers and the status register. The program counter is 16 bit wide to address the range from 0 to 65535 (0 to $FFFF).

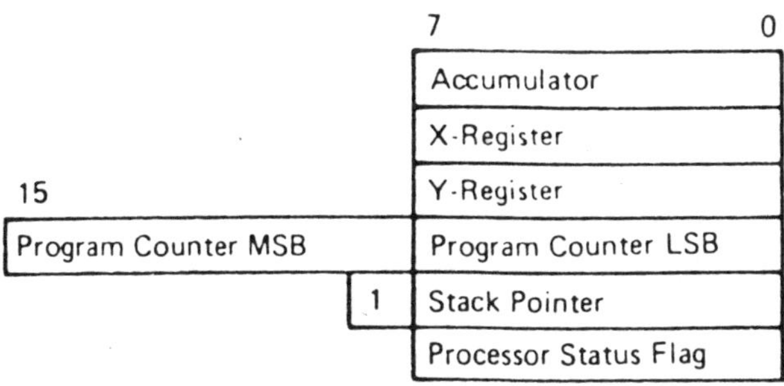

Figure 3-1: The Programming Model of the 6502 CPU.

The stack pointer is a nine bit register, but the ninth bit is always one. The stack pointer contains an address which points to a memory location between $100 and $1FF. The use of stacks is shown in the third section of this book (FORTH).

What are the registers used for ?

The accumulator is the main register of the processor. All arithmetic and most of the transfer commands are executed via this register. The X- and Y-registers are called index registers. They are used for counting and for modifying addresses.

The status register contains the status of the processor. Figure 3-1 shows the significance of the single bits.

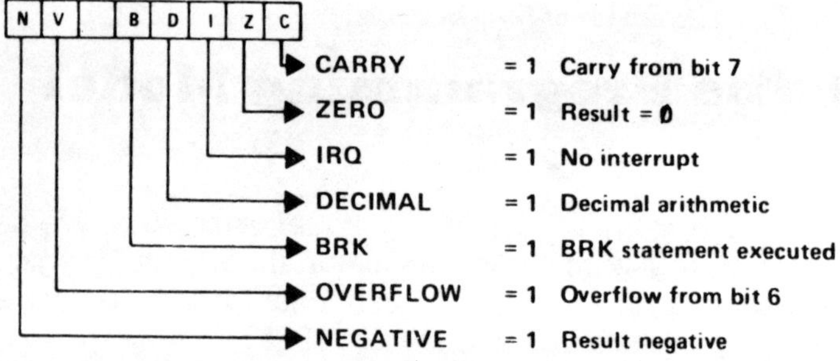

Figure 3-2: The Status Register.

For example the zero flag is set if the result of an operation is zero. The rightmost column in Table A-1 in the appendix shows which bits are affected by the single commands.

The flow of data between the registers and the memory is shown by Figure 3-3. The LOAD-instructions fetch the contents of a memory location and store them in the register. The STORE-instructions take the contents of a register and store it in memory. The TRANSFER-instructions take the contents of a register and place them in another register.

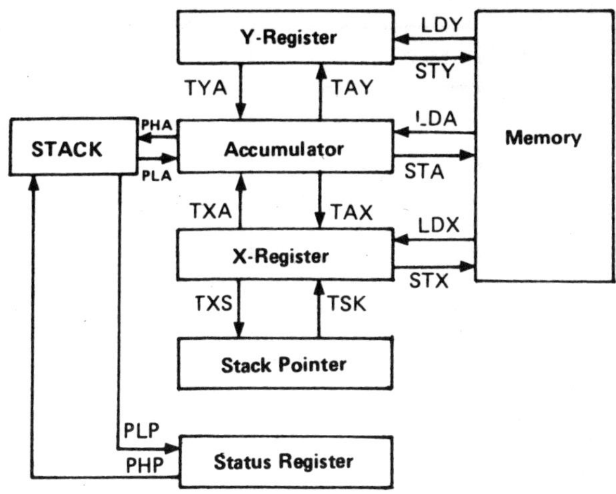

Figure 3-3: Transfer of Data between Registers and Memory.

There is no direct exchange of data between the X- and Y-registers. This has to be done via the accumulator. The contents of the stack pointer can only be stored or loaded via the X-register. To get the contents of the status register into the accumulator one has to push them onto the stack and pull them into the accumulator.

Figure 3-4 shows the memory configuration of the APPLE II computer.

On the right side, the addresses are given in hexadecimal; on the left side, in decimal. As we will see later, integer numbers greater than $7FFF represent negative integers.

With a 6502 CPU the zero page and the stack have fixed addresses.We will see the use of both later on. At $200 the input buffer for BASIC starts. If one types a line in BASIC, a subroutine from the monitor places the input there. The RAM area from $300 to $3FF is used for vectors and jump tables. The memory for the screen starts at $400. If BASIC or HI-RES graphics are not used the free RAM starts at $800 and goes until $9600.Here the disk operation system starts. The addresses from $2000 to $5FFF are reserved for high resolution graphics. The RAM area starting at $C000 is used for input and output. We will take a closer look at this later.

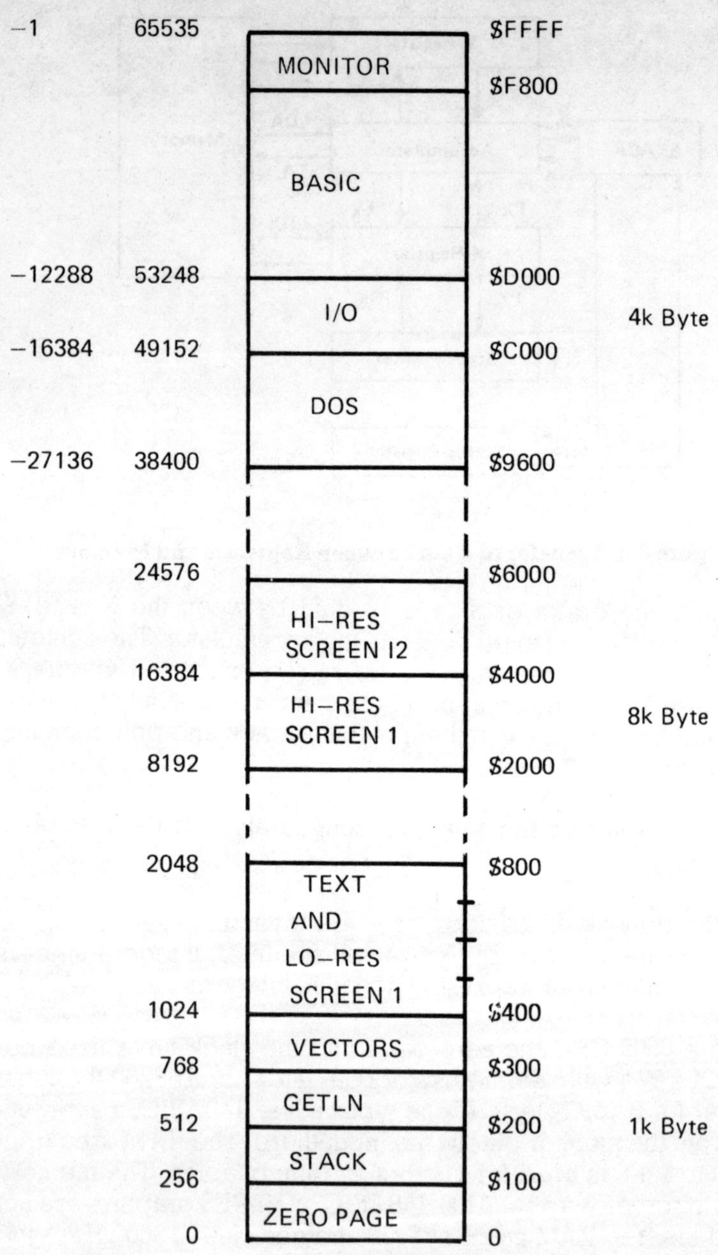

Figure 3-4: Organization of the Memory

At $D000 the ROM area starts. Here the APPLESOFT BASIC begins. The monitor is the last program at the top of the RAM. We will use this monitor to get familiar with machine code. In contrast to other computers the APPLE II makes it very easy to work with the monitor. It is recommended to read Chapter 3 of the APPLE II REFERENCE MANUAL prior to the programming examples in the next chapter.

3.2 A First Example

The best way to learn about computers and programming languages is to sit down and type in little programs and examples. Instead of a long paragraph on addressing modes and other technicalities we will learn with 'Hands on the APPLE'. As a first example we will add two numbers. In BASIC it is done very easy with the following lines:

```
10 HOME
20 A=5:B=3
30 PRINT A+B
```

The equivalent machine language program is:

```
JSR HOME
LDA #5
CLC
ADC #3
JSR PRTBYT
JMP MONITO
```

For writing this program we use the assembler mnemonics. Let's take a closer look at the commands.

Line 10 of our BASIC program erases the screen and places the cursor in the top left corner. The same is done by the subroutine HOME in the monitor. JSR is the mnemonic for Jump SubRoutine and is equivalent to the GOSUB statement in BASIC. The next command is LDA # 5. LDA is the mnemonic for LoaD Accumulator. The # sign specifies a specific addressing mode, the IMMEDIATE mode. Five is the number we want to store in the accumulator. The next command we look at is ADC # 3. ADC is the mnemonic for ADd with Carry. If the carry bit is set, it would be added to the result. Therefore we have to clear it with the command CLC (CLear Carry). The ADC command adds the two numbers 5 and 3 and places the result in the accumulator.

To print the result on the screen we use another routine from the monitor: PRTBYT. This routine prints the contents of the accumulator at the current cursor position. Our BASIC program ends here. In machine code we have to tell the program where to go. It jumps back into the monitor. JMP is the mnemonic for JuMP to an address.

Now we have to translate the mnemonic assembler program into a form which the CPU can recognize. The bytes in the RAM contain only bit patterns. These patterns are decoded and executed by the CPU. For this translation we use the lowest level of assembling a program. We use the 'Paper and Pencil' method. As an example, take a look at the Figure 3-5.

```
$800   20 58 FC   JSR HOME
$804   A9 05      LDA #05
$806   18         CLC
$807   69 03      ADC #03
$809   20 DA FD   JSR PRTBYT
$80C   4C 65 FF   JMP MONITO
```

Figure 3-5: Assembling with Paper and Pencil.

We take a sheet of paper and write down the mnemonics on the right side. Now the assembling begins. We take the command table from the appendix and search the code for JSR. At the branch commands we find the code 20. Next we need the starting address of the subroutine called HOME. Most of the subroutines which we can use for machine language are listed in Chapter 3 of the Reference Manual except this one (HOME) for which we are looking. The starting address for HOME is $FC58. Within a 6502 system an address is stored in the reverse order, first the low byte, then the high byte. Our first assembly line then reads:

```
20 58 FC      JSR HOME
```

This is a three byte instruction. The first byte is the OP-code; the following two bytes contain the address.

The next command is LDA # 5. We have to look for the code of LDA in the immediate addressing mode. We find A9. In this addressing mode the byte which has to be stored in the accumulator follows the OP-code. The next line then reads:

```
A9 05         LDA #5
```

This is a two byte instruction. The data follows the OP-code. The next instruction CLC is a one byte instruction. The code is 18 and the third line is:

```
18            CLC
```

The next instruction is ADC Once more the immediate addressing mode is used. For this OP-code we find 69. The fourth line of the assembling is:

```
69 03        ADC #3
```

For the next line we have to find the address of PRTBYT. It is $FDDA and we get:

```
20 DA FD     JSR PRTBYT
```

For the last line we need the OP-code for the JMP instruction. This is 4C. For returning into the editor we can use three different addresses. The entry at $FF59 is the same as pressing the reset key. The normal entry is $FF65. The APPLE beeps and the * prompt appears on the screen. To suppress the beep, enter the monitor at $FF69. In our example we use the normal entry at $FF65. The last line then reads:

```
4C 65 FF     JMP MONITO
```

This completes the translation of the mnemonics into the bit patterns. Maybe you may ask why we choose MONITO as a name instead of MONITOR. In an assembler these names are labels and most of the assembler programs allow labels only with six characters.

The next step we have to take is to store the program in the memory. Our small program is relocatable. We don't have any absolute addresses, except the monitor addresses. Figure 3-4 shows where to find free memory. We select $800 as starting address for the program. To enter the program we use the monitor.

From BASIC we get into the monitor by CALL -151. The prompt * of the monitor appears. The next input is:

```
800:20 58 FC A9 05 18 69 03 20 DA FD
4C 65 FF
```

A RETURN after the last FF stores the bytes in memory. To be sure that they are stored we type 800L. This disassembles the program. A disassembler is exactly the opposite of an assembler. It tries to translate machine code back into the mnemonics. The disassembled listing is shown in Figure 3-6.

```
0800-    20 58 FC    JSR    $FC58
0803-    A9 05       LDA    #$05
0805-    18          CLC
0806-    69 03       ADC    #$03
0808-    20 DA FD    JSR    $FDDA
080B-    4C 65 FF    JMP    $FF65
```

Figure 3-6: Disassembled program

Now the last step, to start and to execute the program, is reached. We type 800G; and if all is correct, the screen must go blank and a 08 must appear in the upper left corner, followed by a beep and the prompt of the monitor.

3.3 Using Branches

All programs contain loops which have to be executed until a certain condition is met. The condition can be whether the content of a memory location or a register is zero or not zero, or whether the result of a comparison is true or not true. A conditional branch tests the bits of the status register, and as result the branch is executed or bypassed. The instruction BEQ (Branch EQual) for example tests the zero flag. The zero flag is set to one if all eight bits are zero as result of an instruction.

Then the BEQ is performed. The BNE (Branch Not Equal) instruction is taken if the zero flag is reset to zero.

Let us give an example. We want to print ten characters "A" on the top of the screen. This is the program:

```
        JSR HOME
        LDX #10
M       LDA #$C1
        JSR COUT
        DEX
        BNE M
        JMP MONITO
```

The screen is cleared, the X-register is loaded with a decimal ten and the accumulator with the APPLE ASCII equivalent of the character "A". The subroutine COUT prints the contents of the accumulator as character at the current cursor position. The machine code looks like:

```
800   20 58 FC          JSR HOME
803   A2 0A             LDX #10
805   A9 C1        M    LDA #$C1
807   20 ED FD          JSR COUT
80A   CA                DEX
80B   D0 ??             BNE M
80D   4C 65 FF          JMP MONITO
```

We have to determine the contents of location 80C. The branch commands use the relative addressing mode. The second byte of the branch instruction is added to the content of the program counter.The program jumps to a location relative to the program counter and the value following the branch instruction. During the execution of a command the program counter of the 6502 always points to the beginning of the next instruction. In our example this is location 80D.

The instruction DEX decrements the index register X. As long as the content is not zero, the branch is taken. The program loops back to location 805. The contents of the program counter have to be decreased by eight or in other words a -8 has to be added to the contents of the program counter. The hexadecimal equivalent of -8 has to be stored in location 80C.

You can find this number in Table A-3 in the appendix. For -8 is found $F8. This number replaces the question marks in our program. Type it in as in the previous example and test it.

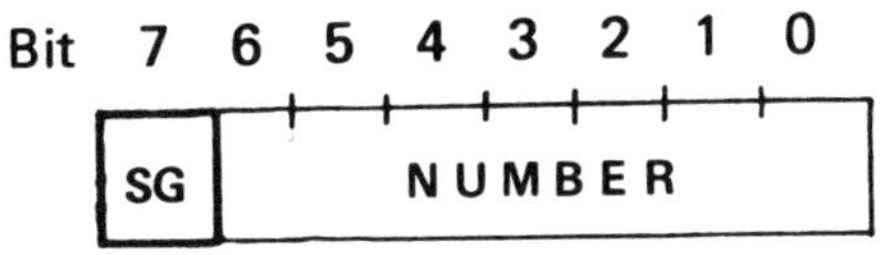

Figure 3-7: Signed Number

Here we take a closer look at the presentation of numbers. One byte can represent an unsigned or a signed number. The range for an unsigned number is 0 (all bits are zero) to 255 (all bits are ones). With a signed number the bit seven is used as sign bit. This is shown in Figure 3-7. For a positive number bit seven is zero, for a negative number bit seven is one. Positive numbers are:

0 = $0 = %0000 0000
1 = $1 = %0000 0001
2 = $2 = %0000 0010

127 = $7F = %0111 1111

For the presentation of negative numbers the two's complement is used. One gets the complement of a number the ones and the zeros are exchanged. To get the two's complement a one must be added. A step by step presentation of -1 is:

1 = %0000 0001

The complement is

= %1111 1110

The addition of one results in

-1 = %1111 1111

Negative numbers are:

-1 = $FF = %1111 1111
-2 = $FE = %1111 1110

-128 = $80 = %1000 0000

Thus relative branches can range only from -128 to + 127.

3.4 Comparisons

Comparisons are always made between the registers (accumulator, X- and Y-register) and the memory. There is no memory to memory or register to register comparison. Three bits of the status register are effected. Figure 3-8 shows how the bits are set by the comparison.

Comparison	N	Z	C
A, X, Y < M	1*	0	0
A, X, Y = M	0	1	1
A, X, Y > M	0*	0	1

Figure 3-8: Compare Instruction Results

If the contents of a register are smaller than the contents of a memory location, the zero and the carry bit are set. For these two bits the numbers are regarded as unsigned numbers (0 - 255). The negative bit is set by a comparison according to signed numbers.

For example:

The contents of the accumulator are 253 ($FD) and the contents of a memory location is 0. A comparison sets the C flag to one and the Z flag to zero because 253 is greater than zero. The N flag is set to one because -3 is less than zero. Next, the branch statements are listed which have to be used for the following conditions:

```
branch on  A <  M  then  BCC LABEL

           A <= M        BCC LABEL
                   and   BEQ LABEL

           A =  M        BEQ LABEL

           A >= M        BCS LABEL

           A >  M        BEQ NOT LABEL
                   and   BCS LABEL
```

We use the program in Figure 3-9 to print the contents of the status register in binary.

```
0800              2  HOME    EQU $FC58
0800              3  MONITO  EQU $FF65
0800              4  COUT    EQU $FDED
0800              5  ;
0800              6          ORG $800
0800              7  ;
0800 2058FC       8          JSR HOME
0803 A900         9          LDA #$00
0805 85FF        10          STA $FF
0807 A9FD        11          LDA #$FD
0809 C5FF        12          CMP $FF
080B 08          13          PHP
080C 68          14          PLA
080D 85FE        15          STA $FE
080F A008        16          LDY #$08
0811 06FE        17  L       ASL $FE
0813 9004        18          BCC L1
0815 A9B1        19          LDA #"1"
0817 D002        20          BNE L2
0819 A9B0        21  L1      LDA #"0"
081B 20EDFD      22  L2      JSR COUT
081E 88          23          DEY
081F D0F0        24          BNE L
0821 4C65FF      25          JMP MONITO
                 26          END
```

Figure 3-9: Binary Printout of the Status Register.

The listing in Figure 3-9 is the printout of an assembler. There are two pseudo OP-codes used in lines two to four and in line six. Pseudo OP-codes are directives for the assembler program, not for the machine code program. EQU equates a label name to an address. ORG sets the origin, the starting address.

The program starts in line eight. In this program a new addressing mode is used. It is the Absolute Zero-Page addressing mode. The zero page is the address range from 0 to 255 (0 to $FF). For this range one needs only one byte to specify an address. The instructions therefore are two bytes instructions. The first byte is the OP-code, the second byte a one byte address. The absolute addressing mode is used to address memory locations outside of the zero page. It uses three bytes, the OP-code and a two byte address.

In line 9 a zero is loaded into the accumulator and stored in location $FF in the zero page. Then the accumulator is loaded with $FD and compared with the contents of $FF in line 12. Lines 13 to 15 push the contents of the status register on the stack (PHP) and pull them into the accumulator (PLA). Then the contents of the accumulator are stored in memory location $FE. For the printout we use the Arithmetic Shift Left (ASL). The result of an ASL instruction is shown in Figure 3-10a.

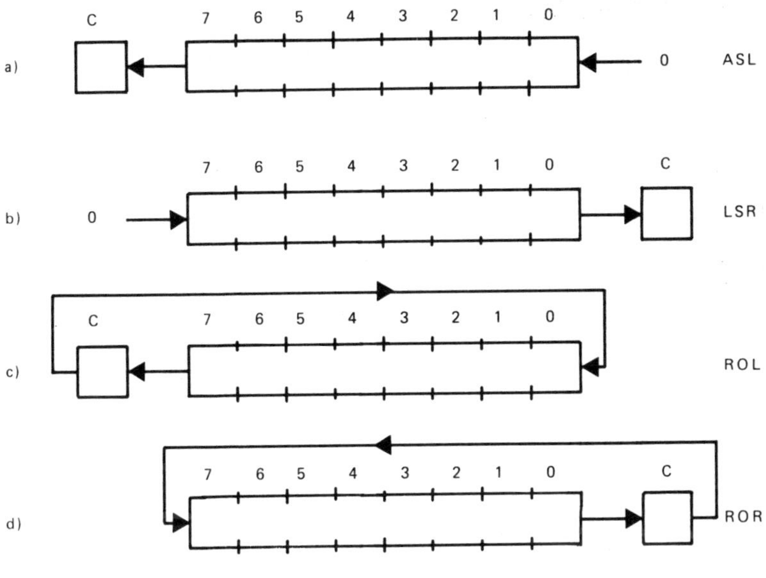

Figure 3-10: Shift Instructions

ASL $FE shifts the contents of $FE one place to the left. Bit seven is shifted into the carry bit. If it is zero, a "0" is loaded into the accumulator; otherwise a "1" is loaded and printed on the screen. This loop is repeated eight times. Figure 3-10 shows also the three other shift instructions: Logical Shift Right (LSR), ROtate Left (ROL) and ROtate Right (ROR).

The program in Figure 3-11 is an example for the input of data. The keyboard of the APPLE is read. If the ASCII character represents a hexadecimal number (0-9, A-F), it is converted to a number. The contents of two memory locations are multiplied by 16, and then the number is added. In such a way a 16-bit number is entered into memory. If the input represents no hexadecimal number, the program is left with the character in the accumulator.

The program starts in line 11. The screen is cleared, and the program jumps to the subroutine RDCHAR. Here the program waits for a keypress and leaves the subroutine with the character in the accumulator. Next a zero is stored in the two locations $FE and $FF. The first comparison takes place with the character "0". If the contents of the accumulator are less, it is no hexadecimal number.

This is also true if the contents of the accumulator are greater or equal than "G". If one looks at the Table A-4 he sees, that we have to filter out the characters from ":" to "@". If the contents of the accumulator are less than ":" then it is a number between 0 and 9. If it is less than "A", then it is no character from "A" to "F" and we leave the program. Otherwise we clear the higher four bits in the accumulator and add a nine. Let's look at the input of the hexadecimal number B. The APPLE ASCII character B is:

%11000010 = C1 = "B"

AND with %00001111 results in

%00000010 = 2

Now a nine is added to get the result 11.The AND instruction is used for masking single bits in the accumulator. See Table A-5 for the AND, OR and EOR functions.

```
0800        3  HOME    EQU $FC58
0800        4  MONITO  EQU $FF65
0800        5  COUT    EQU $FDED
0800        6  RDKEY   EQU $FD0C
0800        7  CR      EQU $FD8E
0800        8  PRTBYT  EQU $FDDA
```

```
0800                 ;
0800                        ORG $800
0800                 ;
0800 2058FC                 JSR HOME
0803 200CFD                 JSR RDKEY
0806 A200                   LDX #$00
0808 86FE                   STX $FE
080A 86FF                   STX $FF
080C C9B0            L      CMP #"0"
080E 9036                   BCC FIN
0810 C9C7                   CMP #"G"
0812 B032                   BCS FIN
0814 C9BA                   CMP #":"
0816 900B                   BCC CONV
0818 C9C1                   CMP #"A"
081A 902A                   BCC FIN
081C 290F                   AND #%00001111
081E 18                     CLC
081F 6909                   ADC #$09
0821 D002                   BNE CONV0
0823 290F            CONV   AND #%00001111
0825 A004            CONV0  LDY #$04
0827 06FE            CONV1  ASL $FE
0829 26FF                   ROL $FF
082B 88                     DEY
082C D0F9                   BNE CONV1
082E 18                     CLC
082F 65FE                   ADC $FE
0831 85FE                   STA $FE
0833 A5FF                   LDA $FF
0835 20DAFD                 JSR PRTBYT
0838 A5FE                   LDA $FE
083A 20DAFD                 JSR PRTBYT
083D 208EFD                 JSR CR
0840 200CFD                 JSR RDKEY
0843 18                     CLC
0844 90C6                   BCC L
0846 00              FIN    BRK
                            END
```

Figure 3-11: Input of a Two Byte Address.

Lines 29 to 33 perform the multiplication by 16. A shift left operation multiplies a number by two as it is shown in the following example:

00001100 = 12
00011000 = 24

Vice versa a shift right operation divides a number by two.

ASL $FE shifts the contents of $FE one place to the left and bit seven into the carry bit. ROL $FF shifts the carry bit into bit zero of $FF and the rest one place to the left. After the shifting, the contents of the accumulator are added to $FE, and the result is stored there. We use the PRTBYT routine to print the contents of the two locations on the screen. The subroutine CR issues one new line character, and the program waits for the next input in line 42. After this, the program jumps back to line 16. For this jumping the two instructions CLC and BCC L are used. The reason is that with these two commands our program remains relocatable. A JMP instruction would have introduced an absolute address.

If the character typed in doesn't represent a hexadecimal number the program is exited by the BRK command. This command is a software interrupt. The program displays the contents of all the registers and jumps into the monitor.

3.5 Indexed Addressing

In a previous example we wrote ten characters "A" into the memory of the screen. They are stored in the locations $400 to $409. If we want to transfer these ten characters to $401 - $40A.

we could write a program like this:

```
LDA $409
STA $40A
LDA $408
STA $409  etc. until
   .
   .

LDA $400
STA $401
```

This program is long and tedious. For a shorter program we use the indexed addressing mode. With this addressing mode the index register X or Y is used to modify the absolute address. The command LDA 400,X loads the accumulator with the contents of the memory location 400 + X. The contents of the X-register are added to the absolute address prior to loading. Instead of the X-register we can also use the Y-register. For moving the bytes we get the following program:

```
      LDX #9
M     LDA $400,X
      STA $401,X
      DEX
      BPL M
      BRK
```

We load the X-register with 9. The next command loads the contents of $400 + 9 = $409 into the accumulator and stores it in location $401 + 9 = $40A. Then the X-register is decremented. As long as the contents of X are positive (zero is a positive number), the program loops back to the label M.

The program in Figure 3-12 prints ten characters "A" on the screen. On pressing the "->" key the ten A's are shifted one byte towards higher memory. A space character overwrites the first A. On the screen the A's are shifted one place to the right.

```
0800                HOME    EQU $FC58
0800                MONITO  EQU $FF65
0800                COUT    EQU $FDED
0800                RDKEY   EQU $FD0C
0800                CR      EQU $FD8E
0800                PRTBYT  EQU $FDDA
0800                ;
0800                        ORG $800
0800                ;
0800  4C1B08                JMP MAIN
0803  A00A          MOVE    LDY #10
0805  8E3908                STX AUX
0808  BD0004        M1      LDA $400,X
080B  9D0104                STA $401,X
080E  CA                    DEX
080F  88                    DEY
0810  D0F6                  BNE M1
0812  A9A0                  LDA #$A0
0814  9D0004                STA $400,X
0817  AE3908                LDX AUX
081A  60                    RTS
081B                ;
081B  2058FC        MAIN    JSR HOME
081E  A20A                  LDX #10
0820  A9C1                  LDA #$C1
0822  20EDFD        M2      JSR COUT
0825  CA                    DEX
0826  D0FA                  BNE M2
0828                ;
0828  A209                  LDX #9
082A  200CFD        M3      JSR RDKEY
082D  C995                  CMP #$95
082F  D007                  BNE M5
0831  E8                    INX
0832  200308                JSR MOVE
0835  18                    CLC
0836  90F2                  BCC M3
0838  00            M5      BRK
0839  00            AUX     BYT 00
                            END
```

Figure 3-12: Moving Bytes

The program starts in line 11 with a jump to the main program part. In line 12 the subroutine MOVE starts. This subroutine moves up the ten characters. The end of the subroutine is the RTS (ReTurn from Subroutine) instruction. In line 36 this subroutine is called with the JSR (Jump SubRoutine) instruction. Figure 3-13 shows how the two instructions work. JSR places the address $834 on the stack and decrements the stackpointer by two. In a 6502 system the stack enlarges towards lower memory. The RTS instruction fetches the address from the stack and increments the stackpointer.

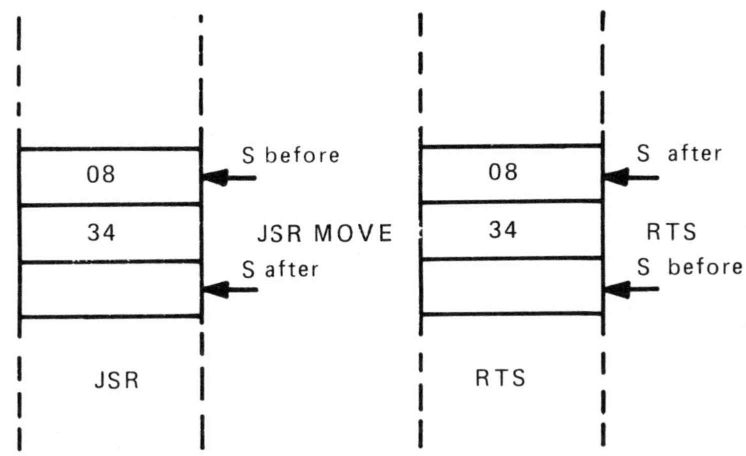

Figure 3-13: The JSR and the RTS Instruction

Subroutines may be nested. The maximum number of nested subroutines is 128. Within normal programs this never happens. But a subroutine can be called by itself. This is used in recursive techniques. Here one must be careful, that the number of nested subroutines doesn't exceed 128.

Some programs on interface cards use the JSR and the RTS instructions to determine in which slot the I/O interface is put in. Suppose the printer interface card is in slot 1. The program area which can be accessed from slot 1 is $C100 to C1FF; from slot 2 it is $C200 to $C2FF etc. The following sequence of statements gets the slot number:

```
        JSR  L
        TSX
        LDA  $100,X
        AND  #%00000001
L       RTS
```

If this program is executed in slot 1 the JSR L leaves a C1 on the stack at the current location of the stackpointer. This number is stored in the X-register via the TSX command. As the stack area starts at $100, the contents of $100 + X are fetched by the LDA $100,X instruction. This is C1 for slot 1. Masking with %00000001 leaves a 1 in the accumulator.

The program in Figure 3-12 shows the construction of the text screen of the APPLE computer. Continuous pressing of the "->" key shifts the ten A's in line one of the screen to the right. When the first A disappears in line one, it reappears not in line two but in line nine. After marching through this line, the characters appear in line 17. Leaving this line, nine characters disappear from the screen until the first A appears in line two. For an explanation see Figure 1 in the APPLE REFERENCE MANUAL.

Using the indexed addressing mode the maximum offset is 255. For moving more bytes we must use the indirect indexed or the indexed indirect addressing mode.

3.6 Indirect Indexed and Indexed Indirect Addressing

These two addressing modes are variations of the indirect addressing mode. The 6502 CPU has only one command with indirect addressing. This is the JMP (LOC) instruction. The destination for the jump is not the address LOC, it is the address stored in LOC and LOC + 1. Using parenthesis means that not the address but the contents stored at this address are significant.

An example for the indirect jump can be found in the ROM Monitor listing. Line 864 and line 865 reads:

```
FDED 6C 36 00   COUT    JMP (CSWL)
FDF0 C9 A0      COUT1   CMP #$A0
```

In line 864 the program jumps to an address stored in location $36 and $37 in the zero page. The normal contents of these two bytes are the address $FDF0 of the next instruction. COUT is the start of the character output routine. It is stored in ROM and cannot be changed. If the character is to be sent to another device prior to sending it to the screen write a routine and store the address in $36 and $37. At the end of the program jump to address $FDF0.

Notice! There is a well known error in the 6502 CPU. An indirect jump to an address which crosses a page boundary will crash the program.

Now let us look at the two modified indirect addressing modes.

A load instruction with INDIRECT INDEXED addressing is:

```
LDA (LOC),Y
```

LOC is a memory location in the zero page. For this addressing mode only the Y-register can be used. The contents of the Y-register are added to the address stored in LOC and LOC + 1. If there is a carry in adding the contents of the Y-register and LOC it is added to LOC + 1.

In most cases this addressing mode is used as an indirect addressing mode. The contents of the Y-register are zero. The sequence:

```
LDY #0
STA (LOC),Y
```

stores the contents of the accumulator in the memory location whose address is stored in LOC.

A load instruction with INDEXED INDIRECT addressing is:

```
LDA (LOC,X)
```

LOC is a location in the zero page and only the X-register can be used. To the contents of LOC are added the contents of the X-register. A resulting carry is discarded. The result is the lower byte of the effective address. The byte stored at LOC + 1 is the high byte of the effective address.

The program in Figure 3-14 takes text from the keyboard. Pressing the "->" key moves the contents of text screen one to text screen two. Pressing the "<-" switches back to text screen one.

```
0800           HOME   EQU $FC58
0800           MONITO EQU $FF65
0800           COUT   EQU $FDED
0800           RDKEY  EQU $FD0C
0800           CR     EQU $FD8E
0800           PRTBYT EQU $FDDA
0800           ;
0800           LOC1   EPZ $FC
0800           LOC2   EPZ $FE
0800           ;
0C00                  ORG $C00        ; PROGRAM STARTS AT $C00
0C00           ;                      ;
0C00 4C2B0C           JMP MAIN        ;
0C03 A000      MOVE   LDY #0          ;
0C05 84FC             STY LOC1        ;
0C07 84FE             STY LOC2        ; THE STARTING ADDRESS $400 IS
0C09 A904             LDA #04         ; STORED IN LOC1 AND LOC1+1
0C0B 85FD             STA LOC1+1      ; THE STARTING ADDRESS $800 IN
0C0D 0A               ASL             ; LOC2 AND LOC2+1
0C0E 85FF             STA LOC2+1      ;
0C10 B1FC      M1     LDA (LOC1),Y    ; LOAD CONTENT OF (LOC1)
0C12 293F             AND #%00111111  ; CHANGE CHARACTER TO INVERSE
0C14 91FE             STA (LOC2),Y    ; STORE IT IN (LOC2)
0C16 E6FC             INC LOC1        ; INCREMENT ADDRESS IN LOC1
0C18 D009             BNE M2          ; IF ZERO, INCREMENT LOC1+1
0C1A E6FD             INC LOC1+1      ;
0C1C A5FD             LDA LOC1+1      ; GET THE CONTENT OF LOC1+1
0C1E C908             CMP #$08        ; STOP MOVING IF IT IS 8
0C20 D001             BNE M2          ;
0C22 60               RTS             ;
0C23 E6FE      M2     INC LOC2        ; INCREMENT ADDRESS IN LOC2
0C25 D0E9             BNE M1          ; IF ZERO
0C27 E6FF             INC LOC2+1      ; INCREMENT LOC2+1
```

```
0C29 D0E5              BNE M1        ;
0C2B              ;                  ;
0C2B 2058FC      MAIN  JSR HOME      ; CLEAR SCREEN
0C2E 200CFD      MA0   JSR RDKEY     ; GET INPUT FROM KEYBOARD
0C31 C988              CMP #$88      ; IS IT THE <- KEY ?
0C33 D006              BNE MA1       ; IF YES
0C35 2C54C0            BIT $C054     ; SWITCH TO TEXTPAGE 1
0C38 18                CLC           ;
0C39 90F3              BCC MA0       ; GO BACK TO RDKEY
0C3B C995        MA1   CMP #$95      ; IS IT THE -> KEY ?
0C3D D009              BNE MA2       ; IF YES
0C3F 20030C            JSR MOVE      ; MOVE BYTES
0C42 2C55C0            BIT $C055     ; SWITCH TO TEXTPAGE 2
0C45 18                CLC           ;
0C46 90E6              BCC MA0       ; GO BACK TO RDKEY
0C48 C99B        MA2   CMP #$9B      ; IS IT THE ESC KEY ?
0C4A D003              BNE MA        ; IF YES
0C4C 4C65FF            JMP MONITO    ; JUMP TO THE MONITOR
0C4F 20EDFD      MA    JSR COUT      ; PRINT CHARACTER TO SCREEN
0C52 18                CLC           ;
0C53 90D9              BCC MA0       ; GO BACK TO RDKEY
0C55              ;
                     END
```

Figure 3-14: Moving 1K Bytes

The text in screen two is printed in inverse.

3.7 Using Subroutines

Now we will take a closer look at subroutines and on some useful routines of the Monitor. Working with subroutines is very convenient. they divide long programs into smaller parts and they can be tested separately. We have to make some comments on using subroutines.

Most subroutines change the contents of the registers. These contents must be saved if they are used after the return from the subroutine. You can use IOSAVE from the monitor. this routine starts at $FF4A and saves the A,X,Y,P and S registers in the zero page locations $45 to $49. To save only the registers a,x and y the following lines can be used:

```
PHA ; Push accu on the stack
TXA ; X-reg. into accu
PHA ; Save it on stack
TYA ; Y-reg. into accu
PHA ; Save it on stack
```

With the following lines the information is got back into the registers.

```
PLA ; Pull stack into accu
TAY ; Restore Y-reg.
PLA ;
TAX ; Restore X-reg.
PLA ; Restore accu
```

There are two possibilities to save the contents of the registers. it can be done in the main program before calling the subroutine or within the routine itself. This latter is sometimes easier. Save only those registers which are altered.

A second question is how to exchange data between the main program and the subroutine. There are three ways to do it.

1. Exchange via the registers. On exit of the keyboard input routine, for example, the character is in the accumulator.

2. Exchange via the stack. This technique is used for the exchange of data between PASCAL and machine code.

3. Both program parts, the main program and the subroutine, use a common area for the data.

An example is shown in Figure 3-15. The subroutine MSG prints text on the screen. This text is stored after the call of the routine and is terminated by $00.

```
0800            ;
0800            HOME   EQU $FC58
0800            MONITO EQU $FF65
0800            COUT   EQU $FDED
0800            TABV   EQU $FB5B
0800            ;
0800            AUX    EPZ $FE          Comment to Fig 3-15
0800            CH     EPZ $24
0800            CV     EPZ $25
0800            ;                       ;
0800                   ORG $800
0800            ;
0800 4C2208'           JMP MAIN         ; JUMP TO MAIN PROGRAM
0803            ;                       ; SUBROUTINE MESSAGE
```

```
0803 68         MSG    PLA              ; STORE RETURN ADDRESS -1
0804 85FE              STA AUX          ; = $830 IN AUX AND AUX+1
0806 68                PLA              ;
0807 85FF              STA AUX+1        ;
0809 A200              LDX #0           ; X-REG = 0
080B E6FE       MS1    INC AUX          ; INCREMENT AUX
080D D002              BNE MS2          ; IF ZERO
080F E6FF              INC AUX+1        ; INCREMENT AUX+1
0811 A1FE       MS2    LDA (AUX,X)      ; GET CONTENT OF (AUX,X)
0813 F006              BEQ MS3          ; IF ZERO, TEXT IS PRINTED
0815 20EDFD            JSR COUT         ; PRINT CHARACTER
0818 18                CLC              ; JUMP BACK TO GET NEXT
0819 90F0              BCC MS1          ; CHARACTER.
081B A5FF       MS3    LDA AUX+1        ; STORE CONTENT OF AUX+1
081D 48                PHA              ; AND AUX = $842 ON STACK
081E A5FE              LDA AUX          ; PROGRAM COMMENCES AT
0820 48                PHA              ; $843 AFTER RTS
0821 60                RTS              ;
0822            ;                       ;
0822 2058FC     MAIN   JSR HOME         ; CLEAR SCREEN
0825 A907              LDA #7           ; SET CURSOR HORIZONTAL
0827 8524              STA CH           ; POSITION TO 7
0829 A90A              LDA #10          ; SET CURSOR VERTICAL
082B 205BFB            JSR TABV         ; POSITION TO 10
082E 200308            JSR MSG          ; PRINT MESSAGE
0831 C1D0D0            ASC "APPLE II "  ; MESSAGE STARTS HERE
0834 CCC5A0                             ;
0837 C9C9A0                             ;
083A D0D2CF            ASC "PROGRAMS"   ;
083D C7D2C1                             ;
0840 CDD3                               ;
0842 00                HEX 00           ; END OF MESSAGE
0843 A900              LDA #0           ; SET CURSOR TO THE UPPER
0845 8524              STA CH           ; LEFT CORNER AND JUMP
0847 205BFB            JSR TABV         ; INTO THE MONITOR
084A 4C65FF            JMP MONITO
084D            ;
                       END
```

Figure 3-15: Output of Text

The program prints the text APPLE II PROGRAMS in the middle of the screen. The horizontal cursor position is stored in CV (=$24). For the vertical positioning of the cursor the subroutine TABV is used. It stores the contents of the accumulator in CV (=$25) and jumps to VTAB. The subroutine MSG takes the RETURN address from the stack and stores it in AUX and AUX+1. this is in our example the address $830. AUX is incremented by one, and the contents of (AUX,X) are loaded into the accumulator. This is an indirect addressing because the X-register is zero. If the contents of the accumulator are zero, all text is printed. Then the contents of AUX+1 and AUX are stored on the stack. The next RTS instruction takes this address (=$842) as the new RETURN address. The program commences at address $843. The cursor is positioned in the upper left corner of the screen and the program jumps into the Monitor.

In this program the pseudo OP-code ASC is used to store text within a program. It takes the characters between the quotation marks and stores the APPLE-ASCII equivalent in consecutive memory locations.

The program in Figure 3-16 shows the use of some subroutines of the low resolution graphics. It draws a rectangle on the screen and a ball bounces between the upper and lower limit of the rectangle. The program uses the routines HLIN, VLIN and PLOT for drawing and SCRN to detect the color of the next point. If this color is white the ball is reflected.

```
0800          GRAPH  EQU $C050
0800          TEXT   EQU $C051
0800          ALL    EQU $C052
0800          PAGE1  EQU $C054
0800          LORES  EQU $C056
0800          SETCOL EQU $F864
0800          PLOT   EQU $F800
0800          HLINE  EQU $F819
0800          VLINE  EQU $F828
0800          CLRSCR EQU $F832
0800          SCRN   EQU $F871
0800          KEYIN  EQU $FD1B
0800          KEY    EQU $C000
0800          KEYSTR EQU $C010
0800          ;
0800          BO     EPZ $FD      ; =1 MOVE DOWN, =0 UP
0800          HP     EPZ $FE      ; HORIZONTAL POSITION
0800          VP     EPZ $FF      ; VERTICAL POSITION
0800          ;                   ;
0800                 ORG $800     ; PROGRAM STARTS AT $800
0800 AD50C0          LDA GRAPH    ; SET GRAPHICS
0803 AD52C0          LDA ALL      ; WITHOUT TEXT
0806 AD54C0          LDA PAGE1    ; SELECT PAGE 1
0809 2032F8          JSR CLRSCR   ; CLEAR GRAPHICS SCREEN
080C A90F            LDA #$0F     ; SET COLOR TO WHITE
080E 2064F8          JSR SETCOL   ;
0811 A927            LDA #39      ; SET THE RIGHTMOST COORDI-
0813 852C            STA $2C      ; NATE TO 39
0815 A000            LDY #0       ; THE LEFTMOST TO 0
0817 A900            LDA #0       ; THE VERTICAL POSITION TO 0
0819 2019F8          JSR HLINE    ; DRAW A HORIZONTAL LINE
081C A92D            LDA #45      ; SET THE VERTICAL POS. TO 0
081E A000            LDY #0       ; THE LEFTMOST COORDINATE TO 0
0820 2019F8          JSR HLINE    ; DRAW A HORIZONTAL LINE
0823 A92D            LDA #45      ; SET THE BOTTOM VERTICAL COOR-
0825 852D            STA $2D      ; DINATE TO 45
0827 A900            LDA #0       ; THE TOP VERTICAL POS. TO 0
```

```
0829 A000            LDY #0          ; THE HORIZONTAL POS. TO 0
082B 2028F8          JSR VLINE       ; DRAW A VERTICAL LINE
082E A900            LDA #0          ; SET THE TOP TO 0
0830 A027            LDY #39         ; THE VERTICAL POS. TO 39
0832 2028F8          JSR VLINE       ; DRAW A VERTICAL LINE
0835 A914            LDA #20         ; SET THE HORIZONTAL AND THE
0837 85FE            STA HP          ; VERTICAL POSITION FOR THE
0839 85FF            STA VP          ; BALL TO 20
083B A901            LDA #1          ; SET THE DIRECTION DOWNWARDS
083D 85FD            STA BO          ;
083F A900      M     LDA #00         ; SET COLOR TO BLACK
0841 2064F8          JSR SETCOL      ;
0844 A5FF            LDA VP          ; PLOT A BLACK POINT AT HP, VP
0846 A4FE            LDY HP          ;
0848 2000F8          JSR PLOT        ; GET THE DIRECTION
084B A5FD            LDA BO          ; IF UP THEN DECREMENT
084D F004            BEQ M1          ; ELSE INCREMENT VP
084F E6FF            INC VP          ;
0851 D002            BNE M2          ;
0853 C6FF      M1    DEC VP          ; SET COLOR TO WHITE
0855 A90F      M2    LDA #$0F        ;
0857 2064F8          JSR SETCOL      ; PLOT A WHITE POINT AT HP, VP
085A A4FE            LDY HP          ;
085C A5FF            LDA VP          ;
085E 2000F8          JSR PLOT        ; WAIT A LONG TIME
0861 206B08          JSR WAIT        ; JUMP BACK TO PLOT THE
0864 18              CLC             ; NEXT POINT
0865 90D8            BCC M           ;
0867           ;
0867 201BFD          JSR KEYIN
086A 00              BRK
086B           ;
086B A240      WAIT  LDX #$40        ; THE X-REG. AND THE Y-REG.
086D A0FF      W     LDY #$FF        ; IS USED FOR DELAY
086F 88        W1    DEY             ;
0870 D0FD            BNE W1          ;
0872 CA              DEX             ;
0873 D0F8            BNE W           ;
0875 A6FF            LDX VP          ; GET THE NEXT POSITION
0877 A5FD            LDA BO          ; FOR PLOTTING
0879 F003            BEQ W3          ;
087B E8              INX             ;
087C D001            BNE W4          ;
087E CA        W3    DEX             ;
087F 8A        W4    TXA             ; DETECT THE COLOR OF THIS
0880 A4FE            LDY HP          ; POINT
0882 2071F8          JSR SCRN        ;
0885 C900            CMP #00         ; IF IT IS BLACK, GO ON
0887 F006            BEQ W2          ;
0889 A5FD            LDA BO          ; ELSE COMPLEMENT THE CON-
088B 4901            EOR #%00000001  ; TENT OF BO
088D 85FD            STA BO          ;
088F AD00C0    W2    LDA KEY         ; LOOK IF A KEY WAS PRESSED
0892 1007            BPL W5          ; IF NOT, RETURN TO MAIN PROG.
0894 2C10C0          BIT KEYSTR      ; ELSE RESET KEY-STROBE
0897 2051C0          JSR TEXT        ; SET TEXT MODE
089A 00              BRK             ; CLEAR SCREEN
089B 60        W5    RTS             ; AND BREAK INTO THE MONITOR
089C           ;
                     END
```

Figure 3-16: LOPLOT

3.8 Using the BASIC Command &

The BASIC command & performs a JSR to memory location \$3F5. In this location the machine code instruction 4C (JMP) is stored. The address of this JMP destination is \$FF58. This is an RTS instruction in the Monitor. This address can be changed to the starting address of a program in machine code. At the end of the program one jumps back to BASIC with RTS or with JMP \$3D0. If the RTS command is used BASIC tries to read the input buffer; and if it finds another BASIC command, this is executed.

Let's take a look at the input buffer. Starting at location \$200, every character typed in from the keyboard is stored. We use the following small program to move ten characters from \$200 to \$270.

```
02A0-   A2 0A      LDX   #$0A
02A2-   BD 00 02   LDA   $0200,X
02A5-   9D 70 02   STA   $0270,X
02A8-   CA         DEX
02A9-   10 F7      BPL   $02A2
02AB-   4C D0 03   JMP   $03D0
```

The program starts at \$2A0. The Monitor is used to store these few bytes. Then the address at \$3F6 is changed by

```
3F6:A0 02
```

and go back to BASIC. Here we type:

```
&L
```

We go into the Monitor and look at the bytes stored at location $270. Here we find:

```
AF 4C 8D 00 .....
```

AF is the token for the BASIC command &, and 4C is the ASCII code for the letter L. 8D is the CARRIAGE RETURN, and 00 marks the end of the input.

The program in Figure 3-17 uses the letters L, V and A after the & to branch in different parts of a program in machine code. This program calculates the length of a BASIC program (the length of the area used for variables and for arrays).

```
0800                       DCM "PR#1"
0800               ;
0800               HOME    EQU $FC58
0800               PRTBYT  EQU $FDDA
0800               COUT    EQU $FDED
0800               BELL    EQU $FF3A
0800               BASIC   EQU $3D0
0800               ;                           ; POINTER TO
0800               P       EPZ $69             ; BEGIN OF VARIABLES
0800               V       EPZ $6B             ; BEGIN OF ARRAYS
0800               A       EPZ $6D             ; END OF ARRAYS
0800               AUX     EPZ $FC             ; AUXILIARY LOCATIONS
0800               ;                           ;
4000                       ORG $4000           ; PROGRAM STARTS AT $4000
4000               ;                           ;
4000 2058FC                JSR HOME            ; CLEAR SCREEN
4003 209A40                JSR MSG             ; MESSAGE
4006 CCC5CE                ASC "LENGTH OF"     ;
4009 C7D4C8                                    ;
400C A0CFC6                                    ;
400F 00                    HEX 00              ;
4010 AD0102                LDA $201            ; GET 2ND CHARACTER
4013 C94C                  CMP #$4C            ; IS IT AN L ?
4015 D003                  BNE L1              ;
4017 4C2E40                JMP PL              ; THEN JUMP TO PL
401A C956          L1      CMP #$56            ; IS IT A V ?
401C D003                  BNE L2              ;
401E 4C4B40                JMP VL              ; THEN JUMP TP VL
4021 C941          L2      CMP #$41            ; IS IT AN A ?
4023 D003                  BNE L3              ;
4025 4C6A40                JMP AL              ; THEN JUMP TO AL
4028 203AFF        L3      JSR BELL            ; ELSE RING THE BELL
402B 4CD003                JMP BASIC           ; AND GO BACK TO BASIC
402E               ;                           ; PROGRAM-LENGTH
402E A569          PL      LDA P               ; GET LO BYTE
4030 38                    SEC                 ; SET CARRY
```

```
4031 E900                SBC #00          ; SUBTRACT 00 WITH CARRY
4033 85FE                STA AUX+2        ; STORE RESULT
4035 A56A                LDA P+1          ; GET HI BYTE
4037 E908                SBC #$08         ; SUBTRACT 08 WITH CARRY
4039 85FF                STA AUX+3        ; STORE RESULT
403B 209A40              JSR MSG          ; MESSAGE
403E A0D0D2              ASC " PROGRAM "  ;
4041 CFC7D2                               ;
4044 C1CDA0                               ;
4047 00                  HEX 00           ;
4048 4C8340              JMP FIN          ; JUMP TO FIN
404B              ;                       ; SPACE FOR VARIABLES
404B A56B         VL     LDA V            ; GET LO BYTE V
404D 38                  SEC              ; SET CARRY
404E E569                SBC P            ; SUBTRACT LO BYTE P
4050 85FE                STA AUX+2        ; STORE RESULT
4052 A56C                LDA V+1          ; GET HI BYTE V+1
4054 E56A                SBC P+1          ; SUBTRACT HI BYTE P+1
4056 85FF                STA AUX+3        ; STORE RESULT
4058 209A40              JSR MSG          ; MESSAGE
405B A0D6C1              ASC " VARIABLES " ;
405E D2C9C1                               ;
4061 C2CCC5                               ;
4064 D3A0                                 ;
4066 00                  HEX 00           ;
4067 4C8340              JMP FIN          ; JUMP TO FIN
406A              ;                       ; SPACE FOR ARRAYS
406A A56D         AL     LDA A            ; GET LO BYTE A
406C 38                  SEC              ; SET CARRY
406D E56B                SBC V            ; SUBTRACT LO BYTE V
406F 85FE                STA AUX+2        ; STORE RESULT
4071 A56E                LDA A+1          ; GET HI BYTE A+1
4073 E56C                SBC V+1          ; SUBTRACT HI BYTE V+1
4075 85FF                STA AUX+3        ; STORE RESULT
4077 209A40              JSR MSG          ; MESSAGE
407A A0C1D2              ASC " ARRAYS "   ;
407D D2C1D9                               ;
4080 D3A0                                 ;
4082 00                  HEX 00           ;
4083              ;                       ; PRINT RESULT
4083 A5FF         FIN    LDA AUX+3        ; GET HI BYTE
4085 20DAFD              JSR PRTBYT       ; PRINT IT
4088 A5FE                LDA AUX+2        ; GET LO BYTE
408A 20DAFD              JSR PRTBYT       ; PRINT IT
408D 209A40              JSR MSG          ; MESSAGE
4090 A0C2D9              ASC " BYTES"     ;
4093 D4C5D3                               ;
4096 00                  HEX 00           ;
4097 4CD003              JMP BASIC        ; GO BACK TO BASIC
409A              ;                       ; COMMENT FOR MSG SEE
409A 68           MSG    PLA              ; FIG 3-15
409B 85FC                STA AUX
409D 68                  PLA
409E 85FD                STA AUX+1
40A0 A200                LDX #0
40A2 E6FC         MS1    INC AUX
40A4 D002                BNE MS2
40A6 E6FD                INC AUX+1
40A8 A1FC         MS2    LDA (AUX,X)
40AA F006                BEQ MS3
40AC 20EDFD              JSR COUT
```

```
40AF 18              CLC
40B0 90F0            BCC MS1
40B2 A5FD      MS3   LDA AUX+1
40B4 48              PHA
40B5 A5FC            LDA AUX
40B7 48              PHA
40B8 60              RTS
40B9           ;
                     END
```

Figure 3-17: Calculating the Length of a basic Program and the Space Used for Variables and Arrays.

If the starting address $4000 is stored in $3F6 and $3F7, the input of &L calculates the length of a program, &V the space for variables, and &A the space for arrays.

A BASIC program starts at $801 and ends at the beginning of the area used to store the variables. The address in $69 and $6A points to this area. The pointer in $6B and $6C points to the end of the variables. This is the beginning of the area, where the arrays are stored.

Sometimes it is necessary to pass parameters from BASIC to a machine code program. For this purpose we can use two subroutines from the BASIC interpreter. The routine starting at $E6F8 reads one byte from the input buffer and stores it in $A1 and the X-register. The other routine reads the semicolon to divide the input of numbers.

The program in Figure 3-18, written by W. Bauer, is a demonstration with sound. To make sound only

&,225,255

has to be entered. The first number determines the frequency and the second number the duration of the sound.

The value passed to the subroutine may be an expression. Example:

&,F+10,D+5

For a wrong input the error messages

&,256,3 ILLEGAL QUANTITY ERROR

&,33 SYNTAX ERROR

&,A$,B$ TYPE MISMATCH ERROR

are issued.

```
0302-   AD 30 C0    LDA   $C030
0305-   88          DEY
0306-   D0 05       BNE   $030D
0308-   CE 01 03    DEC   $0301
030B-   F0 09       BEQ   $0316
030D-   CA          DEX
030E-   D0 F5       BNE   $0305
0310-   AE 00 03    LDX   $0300
0313-   4C 02 03    JMP   $0302
0316-   60          RTS
0320-   20 BE DE    JSR   $DEBE
0323-   20 F8 E6    JSR   $E6F8
0326-   8E 00 03    STX   $0300
0329-   20 BE DE    JSR   $DEBE
032C-   20 F8 E6    JSR   $E6F8
032F-   8E 01 03    STX   $0301
0332-   4C 02 03    JMP   $0302
```

Figure 3-18: Sound Demonstration

3.9 Pretty-Print

For the publication of BASIC programs it would be better to have the printout in a more readable form. The program in Figure 3-19 did the printout of the programs in the BASIC section. For a better understanding we look at a small BASIC program with two lines:

```
10 A = 10
20  PRINT A
```

The monitor is used to make a hexdump of 32 bytes starting at

$800:

```
*800.820

0800- 00 0A 08 0A 00 41 D0 31
0808- 30 00 11 08 14 00 BA 41
0810- 00 00 00 0A 45 4C 4C 4F
0818- 00 20 08 14 00 B2 20 00
0820- 28
*
```

The BASIC program starts at $801. The first two bytes are the starting address of the next line. This is $80A. Then the line number follows. The two bytes are stored in reverse order- first the lower byte (decimal 10), then the higher byte. The next byte is the ASCII code for the letter A. D0 is the token for the equal sign. 31 and 30 are the ASCII code for the numbers 1 and 0. 00 marks the end of the first line. Here the second line begins with the address of the third line. The line number is 20, and BA 41 stands for PRINT A. The 00 marks the end of the line, and 00 00, the end of the program.

The pretty-print program starts the printing at $803. It takes the line number and converts it into a decimal number. Then this number is printed right-justified. The highest bit of a token is always one. In a table the words for the tokens are stored in numerical order. They are separated by one space. $84 = 132 is, for example, the token for the word INPUT. The program subtracts 128 and searches the fourth space in the table. The subroutine OUT prints the characters until the next space is found. All bytes with the highest bit equal to zero represent ASCII characters.

The program uses a line counter to print 57 lines on a page. A new page starts always with a new line number. A column counter is used to count the printed characters. If the count exceeds 36, a new line is started at the next space or comma sign. Short statements are listed in one line.

A new line is also started with FOR and NEXT. The FOR indents the following lines two times. The indentation is reset by the next NEXT instruction. For more details see the comment in Figure 3-19.

```
0800            DDRB    EQU $C0C2
0800            DDRA    EQU DDRB+1
0800            TORA    EQU DDRB-1
0800            TORB    EQU DDRB-2
0800            ;
0800            S       EPZ $10
0800            A       EPZ S+3
0800            B       EPZ $1E
0800            PO      EPZ $F0
0800            CO      EPZ $F2
0800            TAB     EPZ $F4
0800            ;
0800            CCOUT   EQU $FDED
0800            HOME    EQU $FC58
0800            MONITO  EQU $FF59
0800            CR      EQU $FD8E
0800            PRTBYT  EQU $FDDA
0800            ;
4000                    ORG $4000
4000 A903       ANF     LDA #03          ; STORE ADDRESS OF FIRST
4002 8513               STA A            ; LINE NUMBER IN A AND A+1
4004 A908               LDA #08          ;
4006 8514               STA A+1          ;
4008 A907               LDA #7           ; SET TAB FOR NEW LINE
400A 85F4               STA TAB          ; WITHOUT LINE NUMBER
400C A901               LDA #1           ; SET TAB FOR NEW LINE
400E 85F5               STA TAB+1        ; WITH LINE NUMBER
4010 A900               LDA #00          ; SET LINE COUNT TO ZERO
4012 85F7               STA TAB+3        ;
4014 20D141             JSR MCR          ; MAKE FIVE CR'S
4017 A5F7       NEO     LDA TAB+3        ; GET LINE COUNT
4019 C939               CMP #57          ; IF SMALLER THAN 57 GO ON
401B 9012               BCC NEOO         ; ELSE SUBTRACT 58
401D 38                 SEC              ;
401E E93A               SBC #58          ; STORE RESULT IN TAB+3
4020 85F7               STA TAB+3        ; GET # OF LINES FOR FULL
4022 A90E               LDA #14          ; PAGE AND SUBTRACT TAB+3
4024 38                 SEC              ;
4025 E5F7               SBC TAB+3        ; TRANSFER A TO Y
4027 A8                 TAY              ; SET LINE COUNT TO ZERO
4028 A900               LDA #00          ;
402A 85F7               STA TAB+3        ; MAKE (Y) LINEFEEDS
402C 20D341             JSR MCR1         ; CHANGE LINE # TO DECIMAL
402F 20E340     NEOO    JSR BINBCD       ; PRINT LINE #
4032 201841             JSR DEZOUT       ; SET COLUMN COUNTER TO
4035 A900               LDA #0           ; ZERO
4037 85F2               STA CO           ;
4039 A001               LDY #$01         ; GET NEXT BYTE
403B B113               LDA (A),Y        ; IS IT "NEXT" THEN
403D C982               CMP #$82         ; DECREMENT TABS
403F D008               BNE NE3          ;
4041 C6F4               DEC TAB          ;
4043 C6F4               DEC TAB          ;
4045 C6F5               DEC TAB+1        ;
4047 C6F5               DEC TAB+1        ; SAVE ACCU ON STACK
4049 48         NE3     PHA              ; MAKE TABS
404A 20C641             JSR HTAB1        ; GET ACCU FROM STACK
404D 68                 PLA              ; IF IT IS NO TOKEN,
404E 3005               BMI NE           ; MAKE ONE SPACE
4050 A9A0               LDA #$A0         ;
4052 209141             JSR COUT         ; INCREMENT ADDRESS COUNTER
```

```
4055 205141   NE     JSR NEXT      ; GET NEXT BYTE
4058 B113            LDA (A),Y     ; IF IT IS LESS THAN 128
405A C980     NE4    CMP #$80      ;
405C B00C            BCS SU        ; COMPARE IT WITH ZERO
405E C900            CMP #$00      ; IF NOT EQUAL, GO ON
4060 D020            BNE N1        ; ELSE GET NEXT BYTE.
4062 C8              INY           ;
4063 B113            LDA (A),Y     ; IF ZERO, PRINTING IS
4065 C900            CMP #$00      ; FINISHED;
4067 D00A            BNE NN        ; IF NOT ZERO, END OF LINE
4069 00              BRK           ; JUMP TO BASIC
406A 205A41   SU     JSR SUCH      ; SEARCH WORD FOR TOKEN
406D 209741          JSR OUT       ; PRINT IT
4070 4C5540          JMP NE        ; GET NEXT BYTE
4073          ;                    ;
4073 20DA41   NN     JSR CRR       ; START A NEW LINE WITH
4076 205141          JSR NEXT      ; LINE #
4079 205141          JSR NEXT      ; JUMP OVER THE NEXT THREE
407C 205141          JSR NEXT      ; BYTES
407F 4C1740          JMP NE0       ;
4082 851E     N1     STA B         ; SAVE ACCU IN B
4084 209141   NE2    JSR COUT      ; PRINT CHARACTER
4087 A51E            LDA B         ; GET BYTE
4089 C93A            CMP #$3A      ; IS IT ":" ?
408B F010            BEQ N3        ; IF NOT, GET COLUMN COUNTER
408D A5F2            LDA CO        ;
408F C924            CMP #36       ; GREATER THAN 36 ?
4091 9049            BCC N5        ; IF NOT, GO ON
4093 A51E            LDA B         ;
4095 C920            CMP #$20      ; IS IT A SPACE CHARACTER
4097 F004            BEQ N3        ; MAKE LINE FEED
4099 C92C            CMP #$2C      ; IS IT A COMMA
409B D03F            BNE N5        ; MAKE LINE FEED
409D A5F2     N3     LDA CO        ; IF COLON AND COLUMN COUNTER
409F C914            CMP #20       ; GREATER THAN 20
40A1 9004            BCC N30       ; SET LINE FEED FLAG
40A3 A901            LDA #1        ;
40A5 85F6            STA TAB+2     ;
40A7 C8       N30    INY           ;
40A8 B113            LDA (A),Y     ; GET NEXT BYTE
40AA 851E            STA B         ; AND SAVE IT
40AC C981            CMP #$81      ; IS IT "FOR" ?
40AE D004            BNE N31       ;
40B0 A901            LDA #1        ; THEN SET LINE FEED FLAG
40B2 85F6            STA TAB+2     ;
40B4 A51E     N31    LDA B         ;
40B6 C982            CMP #$82      ; IS IT "NEXT" ?
40B8 D00C            BNE N4        ; IF NOT, GO ON
40BA A901            LDA #1        ; ELSE SET LINE FEED FLAG
40BC 85F6            STA TAB+2     ;
40BE C6F4            DEC TAB       ; DECREMENT TABS
40C0 C6F4            DEC TAB       ;
40C2 C6F5            DEC TAB+1     ;
40C4 C6F5            DEC TAB+1     ;
40C6 A5F6     N4     LDA TAB+2     ; GET LINE FEED FLAG
40C8 F012            BEQ N5        ;
40CA 20DA41          JSR CRR       ; IF SET, MAKE LINE FEED
40CD A51E            LDA B         ;
40CF 3005            BMI N41       ; IF NO TOKEN, MAKE ONE
40D1 A9A0            LDA #$A0      ; SPACE
40D3 209141          JSR COUT      ;
```

```
40D6 20BB41   N41    JSR HTAB       ; MAKE TABS
40D9 98              TYA            ; SET COLUMN COUNTER TO
40DA 85F2            STA CO         ; BEGIN OF NEW LINE
40DC A900     N5     LDA #0         ;
40DE 85F6            STA TAB+2      ; CLEAR LINE FEED FLAG
40E0 4C5540          JMP NE         ; GO ON PRINTING
40E3          ;                     ;
40E3          ;                     ;
40E3 A900     BINBCD LDA #00        ; BINARY TO DECIMAL CONV.
40E5 A8              TAY            ; SET Y-REG AND AUXILIARY
40E6 8510            STA S          ; LOCATIONS TO ZERO
40E8 8511            STA S+1        ;
40EA 8512            STA S+2        ;
40EC B113            LDA (A),Y      ; GET LO BYTE OF LINE #
40EE 851F            STA B+1        ; STORE IT
40F0 E613            INC A          ; INCREMENT ADDRESS COUNTER
40F2 D002            BNE B0         ;
40F4 E614            INC A+1        ;
40F6 B113     B0     LDA (A),Y      ; GET HI BYTE OF LINE #
40F8 851E            STA B          ; STORE IT
40FA A210            LDX #$10       ; SET X-REG TO 16
40FC 061F     B1     ASL B+1        ; SHIFT LEFT LO BYTE
40FE 261E            ROL B          ; ROTATE LEFT HI BYTE
4100 F8              SED            ; SET DECIMAL MODE
4101 A512            LDA S+2        ; ADD CARRY BIT AND DOUBLE
4103 6512            ADC S+2        ; THE CONTENTS OF THE AUX-
4105 8512            STA S+2        ; ILIARY LOCATIONS
4107 A511            LDA S+1        ;
4109 6511            ADC S+1        ;
410B 8511            STA S+1        ;
410D A510            LDA S          ;
410F 6510            ADC S          ;
4111 8510            STA S          ;
4113 D8              CLD            ; RESET DECIMAL MODE
4114 CA              DEX            ; REPEAT 16 TIMES
4115 D0E5            BNE B1         ;
4117 60              RTS            ;
4118          ;                     ;
4118 A200     DEZOUT LDX #00        ; SET X-REG TO ZERO
411A B510     D0     LDA S,X        ; GET HIGHEST NUMBER
411C D00D            BNE D1         ; IF ZERO
411E A9A0            LDA #$A0       ; PRINT TWO SPACES
4120 209141          JSR COUT       ;
4123 A9A0            LDA #$A0       ;
4125 209141          JSR COUT       ;
4128 E8              INX            ; INCREMENT X-REG AND
4129 D0EF            BNE D0         ; JUMP BACK
412B C90A     D1     CMP #10        ; IS NUMBER LESS THAN TEN ?
412D B010            BCS D2         ; IF NOT, GO PRINTING
412F A9A0            LDA #$A0       ; ELSE PRINT SPACE
4131 209141          JSR COUT       ;
4134 B510            LDA S,X        ; GET NUMBER ONCE MORE
4136 18              CLC            ;
4137 69B0            ADC #$B0       ; ADD $B0 TO GET ASCII CHAR
4139 209141          JSR COUT       ; PRINT IT
413C 18              CLC            ;
413D 9005            BCC D3         ; JUMP TO END
413F B510     D2     LDA S,X        ; GET NUMBER AND
4141 20DAFD          JSR PRTBYT     ; PRINT AS BYTE
4144 E8       D3     INX            ; INCREMENT X-REG
4145 E003            CPX #03        ; IF X-REG =3 ALL NUMBERS
```

```
4147 D0F6              BNE D2        ; ARE PRINTED.
4149 60                RTS           ;
414A             ;                   ;
414A E6F0        INCR  INC P0        ; INCREMENT TABLE COUNTER
414C D002              BNE INC       ;
414E E6F1              INC P0+1      ;
4150 60          INC   RTS           ;
4151             ;                   ;
4151 E613        NEXT  INC A         ; INCREMENT ADDRESS COUNTER
4153 D002              BNE N         ;
4155 E614              INC A+1       ;
4157 A000        N     LDY #$00      ; SET Y-REG TO ZERO
4159 60                RTS           ;
415A             ;                   ; SEARCH WORD FOR TOKEN
415A A000        SUCH  LDY #00       ; CLEAR THE REGISTERS
415C A200              LDX #00       ;
415E 38                SEC           ;
415F E980              SBC #$80      ; SUBTRACT 128
4161 8515              STA S+5       ; STORE THE RESULT
4163 C901              CMP #1        ; IS IT "FOR" ?
4165 D008              BNE S0        ; THEN INCREMENT THE TABS
4167 E6F4              INC TAB       ;
4169 E6F4              INC TAB       ;
416B E6F5              INC TAB+1     ;
416D E6F5              INC TAB+1     ;
416F A9DF        S0    LDA #TAB2     ; STORE THE STARTING ADDRESS
4171 85F0              STA P0        ; OF THE TABLE IN THE TOKEN
4173 A941              LDA /TAB2     ; COUNTER
4175 85F1              STA P0+1      ;
4177 A515              LDA S+5       ; GET TOKEN-128
4179 F015              BEQ SF        ; IF ZERO, NO SEARCH
417B B1F0        S1    LDA (P0),Y    ; GET BYTE FROM TABLE
417D C9A0              CMP #$A0      ; SEARCH FOR THE SPACE CHAR.
417F F005              BEQ S2        ; IF NO SPACE
4181 204A41            JSR INCR      ; INCREMENT TABLE COUNTER
4184 D0F5              BNE S1        ; GO ON SEARCHING
4186 E8          S2    INX           ; IF SPACE FOUND, INCREMENT
4187 E415              CPX S+5       ; X-REG. IF (XREG) = (S+5)
4189 F005              BEQ SF        ; THEN WORD STARTS AT P0 AND
418B 204A41            JSR INCR      ; P0+1
418E D0EB              BNE S1        ;
4190 60          SF    RTS           ;
4191             ;                   ;
4191 20EDFD      COUT  JSR CCOUT     ; PRINT CHARACTER AND
4194 E6F2              INC C0        ; INCREMENT COLUMN COUNTER
4196 60          02    RTS           ;
4197             ;                   ; PRINT WORD
4197 A5F2        OUT   LDA C0        ; GET COLUMN COUNTER
4199 C923              CMP #35       ; IF GREATER THAN 35
419B 900A              BCC OUTA      ;
419D A900              LDA #0        ; RESET COLUMN COUNTER
419F 85F2              STA C0        ;
41A1 20DA41            JSR CRR       ; MAKE CR
41A4 20BB41            JSR HTAB      ; AND TABS FOR NEW LINE
41A7 A000        OUTA  LDY #$0       ; ELSE GET CHARACTER
41A9 B1F0              LDA (P0),Y    ;
41AB 209141            JSR COUT      ; PRINT IT
41AE C8          OU1   INY           ; REPEAT UNTIL SPACE
41AF B1F0              LDA (P0),Y    ;
41B1 209141            JSR COUT      ;
41B4 C9A0              CMP #$A0      ;
```

```
41B6 D0F6                 BNE OU1         ;
41B8 A000          OU2    LDY #$00        ; CLEAR Y-REG
41BA 60                   RTS             ;
41BB               ;                      ;
41BB A4F4          HTAB   LDY TAB         ; PRINT TABS FOR A NEW LINE
41BD A9A0          HT     LDA #$A0        ; WITHOUT LINE #
41BF 209141               JSR COUT        ;
41C2 88                   DEY             ;
41C3 D0F8                 BNE HT          ;
41C5 60                   RTS             ;
41C6               ;                      ;
41C6 A4F5          HTAB1  LDY TAB+1       ; PRINT TABS FOR A NEW LINE
41C8 A9A0          HT1    LDA #$A0        ; WITH LINE #
41CA 209141               JSR COUT        ;
41CD 88                   DEY             ;
41CE D0F8                 BNE HT1         ;
41D0 60                   RTS             ;
41D1               ;                      ;
41D1 A005          MCR    LDY #5          ; MAKE FIVE LINE FEEDS
41D3 208EFD        MCR1   JSR CR          ;
41D6 88                   DEY             ;
41D7 D0FA                 BNE MCR1        ;
41D9 60                   RTS             ;
41DA               ;                      ;
41DA E6F7          CRR    INC TAB+3       ; INCREMENT LINE COUNTER
41DC 4C8EFD               JMP CR          ; MAKE LINE FEED
41DF               ;
41DF C5CEC4        TAB2   ASC "END
41E2 A0C6CF
41E5 D2A0CE
41E8 C5D8D4
41EB A0C4C1
41EE D4C1A0
41F1 C9CED0
41F4 D5D4A0
41F7 C4C5CC
41FA A0C4C9
41FD CDA0D2
4200 C5C1C4
4203 A0
4204 C7D2A0
4207 D4C5D8
420A D4A0D0
420D D2A3A0
4210 C9CEA3
4213 A0C3C1
4216 CCCCA0
4219 D0CCCF
421C D4A0C8
421F CCC9CE
4222 A0D6CC
4225 C9CEA0
4228 C8C7D2
422B B2A0C8
422E C7D2A0
4231 C8C3CF
4234 CCCFD2
4237 BDA0C8
423A D0CCCF
423D D4A0C4
4240 D2C1D7
4243 A0D8C4
4246 D2C1D7
4249 A0C8D4
424C C1C2A0
424F C8CFCD
4252 C5A0D2
4255 CFD4BD
4258 A0D3C3
425B C1CCC5
425E BDA0D3
4261 C8CCCF
4264 C1C4A0
4267 D4D2C1
426A C3C5A0
426D CECFD4
4270 D2C1C3
4273 C5A0
4275 CECFD2
4278 CDC1CC
427B A0C9CE
427E D6C5D2
4281 D3C5A0
4284 C6CCC1
4287 D3C8A0
428A C3CFCC
428D CFD2BD
4290 A0D0CF
4293 D0A0D6
4296 D4C1C2
4299 A0C8C9
429C CDC5CD
429F BAA0CC
42A2 CFCDC5
42A5 CDBAA0
42A8 CFCEC5
42AB D2D2A0
42AE D2C5D3
42B1 D5CDC5
42B4 A0D2C5
42B7 C3C1CC
42BA CCA0D3
42BD D4CFD2
42C0 C5A0
42C2 D3D0C5
42C5 C5C4BD
42C8 A0CCC5
42CB D4A0C7
42CE CFD4CF
42D1 A0D2D5
42D4 CEA0C9
42D7 C6A0D2
42DA C5D3D4
42DD CFD2C5
42E0 A0A6A0
42E3 C7CFD3
42E6 D5C2A0
42E9 D2C5D4
42EC D5D2CE
42EF A0D2C5
42F2 CDA0
```

```
42F4 D3D4CF
42F7 D0A0CF
42FA CEA0D7
42FD C1C9D4
4300 A0CCCF
4303 C1C4A0
4306 D3C1D6
4309 C5A0C4
430C C5C6A0
430F D0CFCB
4312 C5A0D0
4315 D2C9CE
4318 D4A0C3
431B CFCED4
431E A0CCC9
4321 D3D4A0
4324 C3CCC5
4327 C1D2A0
432A C7C5D4
432D A0CEC5
4330 D7A0D4
4333 C1C2A8
4336 A0D4CF
4339 A0
433A C6CEA0
433D D3D0C3
4340 A8A0D4
4343 C8C5CE
4346 A0C1D4
4349 A0CECF
434C D4A0D3
434F D4C5D0
4352 A0
4353 ABA0AD
4356 A0AAA0
4359 AFA0DE
435C A0C1CE
435F C4A0CF
4362 D2A0BE
4365 A0BDA0
4368 BCA0D3
436B C7CEA0
436E C9CED4
4371 A0C1C2
4374 D3A0D5
4377 D3D2A0
437A C6D2C5
437D A0D3C3
4380 D2CEA8
4383 A0D0C4
4386 CCA0D0
4389 CFD3A0
438C D3D1D2
438F A0D2CE
4392 C4A0CC
4395 CFC7A0
4398 C5D8D0
439B A0C3CF
439E D3A0D3
43A1 C9CEA0
43A4 D4C1CE
43A7 A0C1D4
43AA CEA0D0
43AD C5C5CB
43B0 A0CCC5
43B3 CEA0D3
43B6 D4D2A4
43B9 A0D6C1
43BC CCA0C1
43BF D3C3A0
43C2 C3C8D2
43C5 A4A0CC
43C8 C5C6D4
43CB A4A0D2
43CE C9C7C8
43D1 D4A4A0
43D4 CDC9C4
43D7 A4A0
```

```
SC "END FOR NEXT DATA INPUT DEL DIM READ "
SC "GR TEXT PR# IN# CALL PLOT HLIN VLIN HGR2 HGR "
SC "HCOLOR= HPLOT DRAW XDRAW HTAB HOME ROT= SCALE= SHLOAD TRACE NOTRACE "
SC "NORMAL INVERSE FLASH COLOR= POP VTAB HIMEM: LOMEM: ONERR RESUME RECALL STORE "
SC "SPEED= LET GOTO RUN IF RESTORE & GOSUB RETURN REM "
SC "STOP ON WAIT LOAD SAVE DEF POKE PRINT CONT LIST CLEAR GET NEW TAB( TO "
SC "FN SPC( THEN AT NOT STEP "
SC "+ - * / ^ AND OR > = < SGN INT ABS USR FRE SCRN( PDL POS "
SC "SQR RND LOG EXP COS SIN TAN ATN PEEK LEN STR$ VAL ASC "
SC "CHR$ LEFT$ RIGHT$ MID$ "
```

Figure 3-19: Pretty-Print

The binary to decimal conversion needs some explanation. This is given in Figure 3-20.

	DECIMAL RESULT	CARRY	BINARY NUMBER	SHIFT
0	00000000	0	01001000	
0	00000000	0	10010000	1
1	00000001	1	00100000	2
2	00000010	0	01000000	3
4	00000100	0	10000000	4
9	00001001	1	00000000	5
18	00011000	0	00000000	6
36	00110110	0	00000000	7
72	01110010	0	00000000	8

Figure 3-20: Binary Decimal Conversion

On every shift instruction the contents of the result are double, and an existing carry is added. This calculation is done in DECIMAL mode. Figure 3-20 shows the conversion of $48 into 72.

3.10 Input and Output with the 6522

In this chapter we will describe an interface card which can be used for many purposes. This card uses the 6522 VIA chip for the input and output of signals. On board are two 2114 RAM chips. The 1k memory is divided in four blocks with 256 bytes each. Figure 3-21 shows the schematic of the board and Figure 3-22 shows the assembled board. There is a prototyping area on the left side to mount other circuits, as AD- or DA converter etc.

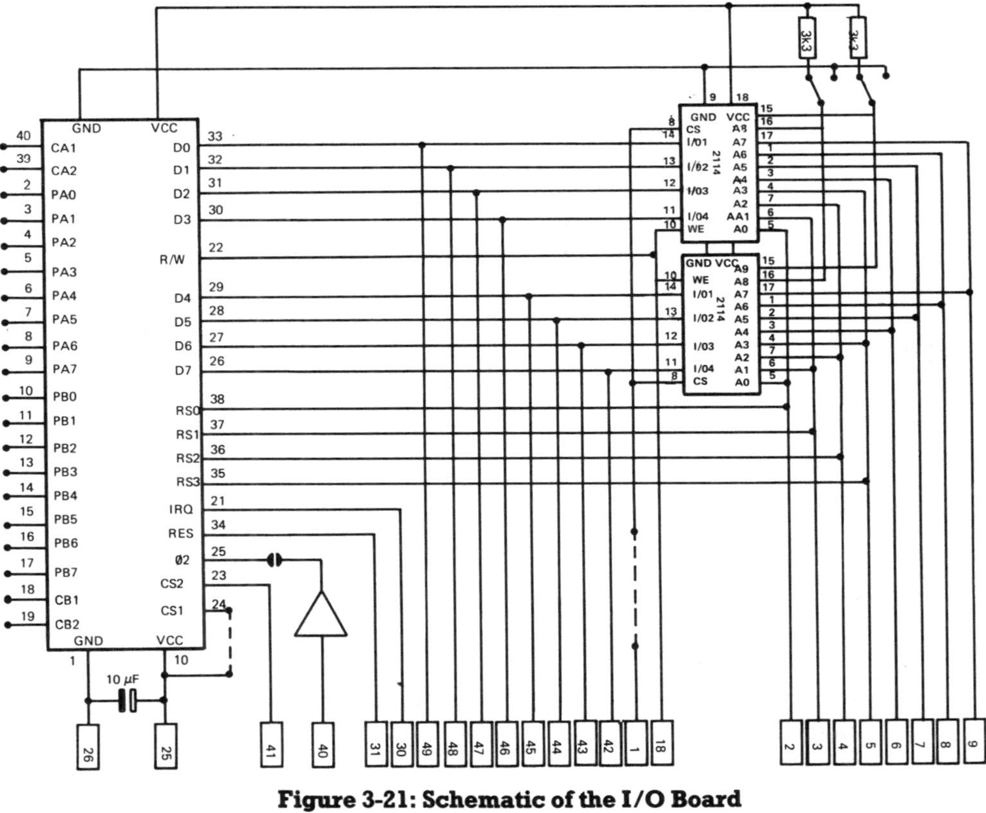

Figure 3-21: Schematic of the I/O Board

Figure 3-22: Photo of the Assembled Board

The RAM on the I/O board is accessed via the I/O SELECT signal. This line goes down for a write or read operation to addresses CN00 through CNFF. N is the slot number in which the board is plugged. If slot 4 is used, the address ranges from C400 to C4FF. With the two switches four different blocks of 256 bytes can be selected.

Programming the 6522

Register Number	RS Coding				Register Desig.	Description	
	RS3	RS2	RS1	RS0		Write	Read
0	0	0	0	0	ORB/IRB	Output Register "B"	Input Register "B"
1	0	0	0	1	ORA/IRA	Output Register "A"	Input Register "A"
2	0	0	1	0	DDRB	Data Direction Register "B"	
3	0	0	1	1	DDRA	Data Direction Register "A"	
4	0	1	0	0	T1C-L	T1 Low-Order Latches	T1 Low-Order Counter
5	0	1	0	1	T1C-H	T1 High-Order Counter	
6	0	1	1	0	T1L-L	T1 Low-Order Latches	
7	0	1	1	1	T1L-H	T1 High-Order Latches	
8	1	0	0	0	T2C-L	T2 Low-Order Latches	T2 Low-Order Counter
9	1	0	0	1	T2C-H	T2 High-Order Counter	
10	1	0	1	0	SR	Shift Register	
11	1	0	1	1	ACR	Auxiliary Control Register	
12	1	1	0	0	PCR	Peripheral Control Register	
13	1	1	0	1	IFR	Interrupt Flag Register	
14	1	1	1	0	IER	Interrupt Enable Register	
15	1	1	1	1	ORA/IRA	Same as Reg 1 Except No "Handshake"	

Figure 3-23: Internal Register of the 6522

Figure 3-23 shows the internal registers of the 6522. The 16 lines of Port A and Port B are bidirectional. The Data Direction registers DDRA and DDRB are used to program these lines as input or output. If a one is written into a bit of the Data Direction register, the corresponding line acts as output, and a zero marks the line as input. After turning on the computer and after RESET, all lines are marked as input lines. Figure 3-24 shows the program and Figure 3-25 the connections which have to be made to use the I/O card as a Centronics interface. Port A is used as an 8-bit output to the printer.

```
0800             PORTA  EQU $C081
0800             PORTB  EQU $C080
0800             DDRA   EQU $C083
0800             DDRB   EQU $C082
0800             ;
0800             CSWL   EPZ $36
0800             AUX    EQU $478
0800             ;
0800             RTS1   EQU $FF58
0800             ;
C400                    ORG $C400
C400             ;
C400 98          INIT   TYA             ; SAVE Y-REG
C401 48                 PHA             ;
C402 2058FF             JSR RTS1        ; GET THE SLOT #. JSR TO RTS
C405 BA                 TSX             ; STACK POINTER TO X-REG
C406 BD0001             LDA $100,X      ; GET CONTENT OF HI BYTE
C409 8537               STA CSWL+1      ; STORE IT IN CSWL
C40B 0A                 ASL             ; TIMES 16
C40C 0A                 ASL             ;
C40D 0A                 ASL             ;
C40E 0A                 ASL             ;
C40F A8                 TAY             ; TRANSFER TO Y
C410 8D7804             STA AUX         ; STORE IT IN AUX
C413 A9FF               LDA #$FF        ; SET PORTA AS OUTPUT
C415 9983C0             STA DDRA,Y      ;
C418 A903               LDA #$03        ; SET BIT 0 AND 1 OF PORTB
C41A 9982C0             STA DDRB,Y      ; AS OUTPUT
C41D A901               LDA #01         ; SET BIT 0 OF PORTB TO 1
C41F 9980C0             STA PORTB,Y     ;
C422 A929               LDA #PRINT      ; STORE LO BYTE OF ADDRESS
C424 8536               STA CSWL        ; PRINT IN CSWL
C426 68                 PLA             ; RESTORE Y-REG
C427 A8                 TAY             ;
C428 60                 RTS             ;
C429             ;                      ;
C429 C98D        PRINT  CMP #$8D        ; IS IT CR ?
C42B D002               BNE P0          ; IF YES, MAKE LINEFEED
C42D A98A               LDA #$8A        ; FIRST
C42F 8D7904      P0     STA AUX+1       ; SAVE ACCU IN AUX+1
C432 98                 TYA             ; SAVE Y-REG
C433 48                 PHA             ;
C434 AC7804             LDY AUX         ; GET SLOT # TIMES 16
C437 B980C0      P1     LDA PORTB,Y     ; WAIT, IF PRINTER IS
```

```
C43A 2940           AND #%01000000    ; BUSY
C43C D0F9           BNE P1            ;
C43E AD7904         LDA AUX+1         ; GET CHARACTER
C441 297F           AND #$7F          ; ZERO BIT 7
C443 9981C0         STA PORTA,Y       ; SEND IT TO PRINTER
C446 A900           LDA #$00          ;
C448 9980C0         STA PORTB,Y       ; MAKE STROBE
C44B A901           LDA #$01          ;
C44D 9980C0         STA PORTB,Y       ;
C450 B980C0    P2   LDA PORTB,Y       ; WAIT FOR ACKNOWLEDGE
C453 10FB           BPL P2            ;
C455 AD7904         LDA AUX+1         ; GET CHARACTER
C458 C98A           CMP #$8A          ; WAS IT LINEFEED ?
C45A D007           BNE P4            ;
C45C A98D           LDA #$8D          ; THEN SEND CARRIAGE RETURN
C45E 8D7904         STA AUX+1         ;
C461 D0D4           BNE P1            ;
C463 68        P4   PLA               ; RESTORE Y-REG
C464 A8             TAY               ;
C465 AD7904         LDA AUX+1         ; RESTORE ACCU
C468 4CF0FD         JMP $FDF0         ; JUMP TO COUT1 IN MONITOR
C46B           ;
                    END
```

Figure 3-24: Using the 6522 as a Centronics Interface

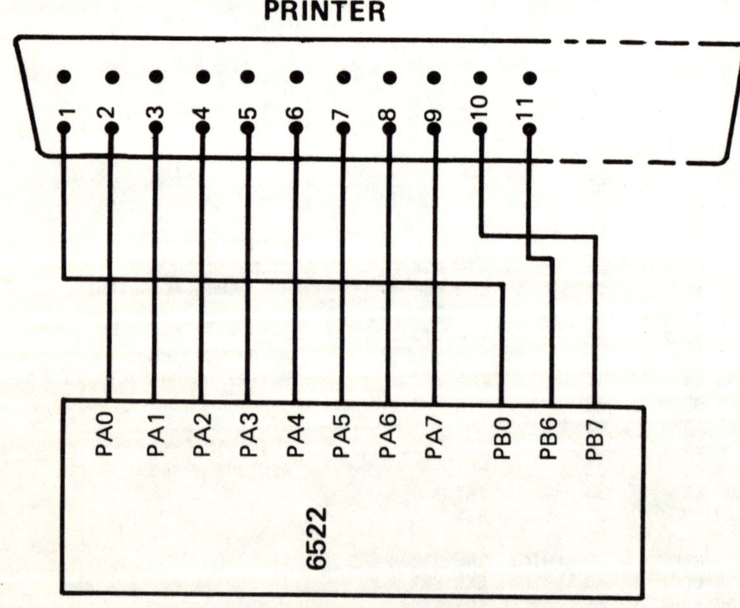

Figure 3-25: Connecting the Printer and the APPLE

The data is send to the printer via PORTA. PB7b senses the ACK line and PB6 the BUSY line. The STROBE output is PB0. First the program determines the slot number and stores the address of PRINT in CSWL. Every time when the COUT subroutine of the Monitor is called, the PRINT routine is executed in advance. The program is assembled for $C400, but it can be used for any slot. If the I/O card is put into slot # 1, the program is read from disk with

```
BLOAD CNTRX.MC,A$C100
```

Then the program is enabled with

```
PR#1
```

Programming the Timer

The 6522 has two timer T1 and T2. Timer 1 consists of two 8-bit latches and a 16-bit counter. The latches are used to store data which is loaded into the counter. With a write operation, data is stored in the low order latch. This data is transferred to the low order counter with a write operation to the high order latch. This write operation transfers also the data to the high order counter and starts it. The timer decrements the content at Φ2 clock rate. Bit 6 and 7 of the auxiliary register determine the operation mode of the counter. (See Figure 3-26)

T1 TIMER CONTROL (bits 7, 6)

7	6	OPERATION	PB7
0	0	TIMED INTERRUPT EACH TIME T1 IS LOADED	DISABLED
0	1	CONTINUOUS INTERRUPTS	
1	0	TIMED INTERRUPT EACH TIME T1 IS LOADED	ONE SHOT OUTPUT
1	1	CONTINUOUS INTERRUPTS	SQUARE WAVE OUTPUT

Figure 3-26: Operating Modes of Timer 1

Upon reaching zero, an interrupt flag will be set, and the IRQ line will go low if an interrupt is enabled. Depending on the modes, the timer will disable further interrupts or will automatically transfer the contents of the latches into the counter and will continue to decrement. In addition Timer 1 may be programmed to invert the signal at PB7 upon reaching zero.

Timer 2 operates as an interval timer or as a counter for negative pulses at PB6. Bit 5 of the auxiliary register determines the operating mode of Timer 2. With bit 5 equal to one, Timer 2 acts as a pulse counter. In this mode, the counter is first loaded with a number. Then this number is decremented with every negative pulse at PB6. Both timer are used to determine the run-time of BASIC-programs. The machine-language part is shown in Figure 3-27.

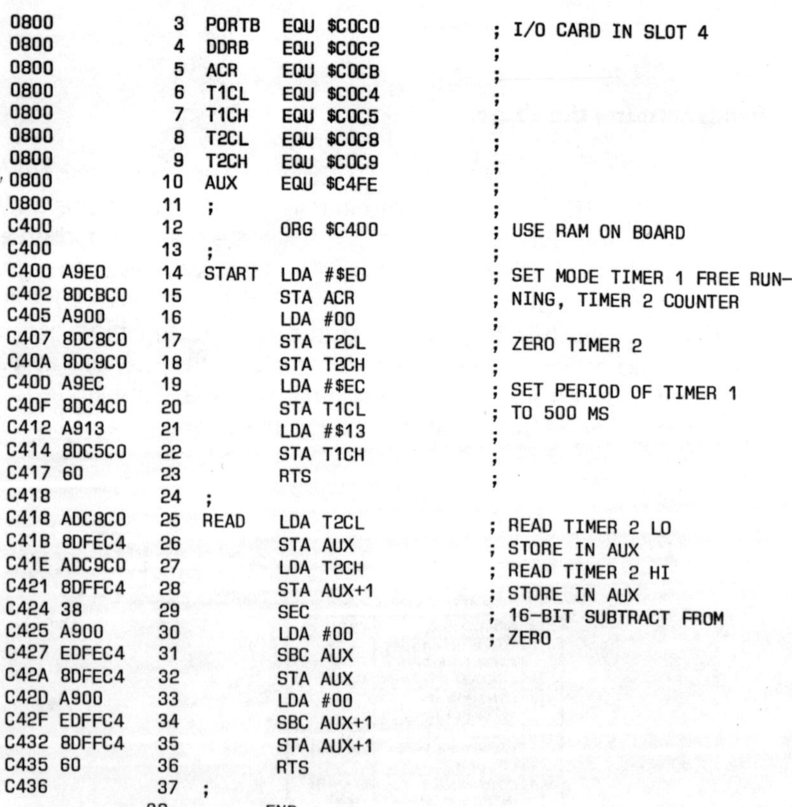

```
0800            PORTB  EQU $C0C0     ; I/O CARD IN SLOT 4
0800            DDRB   EQU $C0C2     ;
0800            ACR    EQU $C0CB     ;
0800            T1CL   EQU $C0C4     ;
0800            T1CH   EQU $C0C5     ;
0800            T2CL   EQU $C0C8     ;
0800            T2CH   EQU $C0C9     ;
0800            AUX    EQU $C4FE     ;
0800            ;                    ;
C400                   ORG $C400     ; USE RAM ON BOARD
C400            ;                    ;
C400 A9E0       START  LDA #$E0      ; SET MODE TIMER 1 FREE RUN-
C402 8DCBC0            STA ACR       ; NING, TIMER 2 COUNTER
C405 A900              LDA #00       ;
C407 8DC8C0            STA T2CL      ; ZERO TIMER 2
C40A 8DC9C0            STA T2CH      ;
C40D A9EC              LDA #$EC      ; SET PERIOD OF TIMER 1
C40F 8DC4C0            STA T1CL      ; TO 500 MS
C412 A913              LDA #$13      ;
C414 8DC5C0            STA T1CH      ;
C417 60                RTS           ;
C418            ;
C418 ADC8C0     READ   LDA T2CL      ; READ TIMER 2 LO
C41B 8DFEC4            STA AUX       ; STORE IN AUX
C41E ADC9C0            LDA T2CH      ; READ TIMER 2 HI
C421 8DFFC4            STA AUX+1     ; STORE IN AUX
C424 38                SEC           ; 16-BIT SUBTRACT FROM
C425 A900              LDA #00       ; ZERO
C427 EDFEC4            SBC AUX
C42A 8DFEC4            STA AUX
C42D A900              LDA #00
C42F EDFFC4            SBC AUX+1
C432 8DFFC4            STA AUX+1
C435 60                RTS
C436            ;
                       END
```

Figure 3-27: Machine Code Run-Time Test

Timer 1 produces a square wave of 1 ms. The time for half the period is stored in Timer 1. This value depends on the frequency of the quartz used for the 02 clock. The starting value for Timer 2 is zero. Pin PB7 is connected with pin PB6. In this manner Timer 2 decrements every 1 ms.

The BASIC Test program is shown in Figure 3-28. The subroutine under test is programmed, starting at line 1000. In the example it is a FOR...NEXT loop from 1 to 1000. CALL START starts the timer, CALL FIN is the call of READ. The subroutine starting at line 990 reads the contents of $C4FE, $C4FF and prints the result.

```
  10  REM  RUNTIME MEASUREMENT
  20  START =  - 15360:FIN =  - 15336
  30  LO =  - 15106
  40  D$ =  CHR$ (04)
  50  PRINT D$;"BLOAD RTIME.MC"
 100  CALL START
 110  GOSUB 1000
 120  CALL FIN: GOSUB 990:
     END
 990  PRINT "EXECUTION TIME=";
 992  H% =  PEEK (LO + 1):
      L% =  PEEK (LO)
 994  PRINT (H% * 256 + L%) / 100;" SECONDS"
 996  RETURN
 999  REM  PROGRAM UNDER TEST
1000  FOR I = 1 TO 1000:
      NEXT : RETURN
```

Figure 3-28: BASIC-Program Run-Time Test

3.11 Interrupts

An interrupt is the break of a program by a pulse. This pulse may be generated by an external device, which requests access to the computer, or by an internal timer. In multitasking systems, an interrupt of a timer is used to switch between different tasks.

The 6502 CPU has two interrupt entries. The NMI (Non Maskable Interrupt) and the IRQ (InterRupt Request). If the NMI line is pulled to ground, a jump to an address stored in location $FFFA is performed. This address is $3FB. At this address the interrupt service routine for the NMI starts. The jump vector for the IRQ is $FA40. Figure 3-29 shows the beginning of the interrupt service routine.

```
FA40-   85 45      STA   $45
FA42-   68         PLA
FA43-   48         PHA
FA44-   0A         ASL
FA45-   0A         ASL
FA46-   0A         ASL
FA47-   30 03      BMI   $FA4C
FA49-   6C FE 03   JMP   ($03FE)
```

Figure 3-29: The IRQ Service Routine.

If an interrupt occurs, the momentary address and the status of the processor are stored on the stack. First the accumulator is saved in $45. The status is pulled into the accumulator and pushed back on the stack.

Besides the two hardware interrupts, there is another interrupt, the software interrupt command BRK. A BRK instruction acts like an IRQ. In the status register the BRK flag instead of the IRQ flag is set. (See Figure 3-2). The program tests this bit and determines if a BRK or an IRQ has occurred. If it was an IRQ, the program jumps indirect to location $3FE. Here the starting address of the service routine must be programmed.

While the NMI cannot be turned off, the IRQ sets the interrupt bit in the status register and disables further interrupts. At the end of the service routine the interrupt flag has to be cleared with the CLI (CLear Interrupt bit) instruction. The RTI (ReTurn from Interrupt) instruction leads back to the address where the main program was left. One cannot use the RTS instruction because JSR saves only the program-counter, not the status register. During time-critical operation, such as writing to a disk or real time applications, an IRQ must often be disabled. This is done by the instruction SEI (SEt Interrupt bit).

The program in Figure 3-31 is a real time clock. It uses the Timer 1 and 2 in the same manner as in the previous example. Timer 1 generates a square wave of 0.1 s. Timer 2 divides the square wave by 10. At the time-out of Timer 2 an IRQ is generated. Every second the service routine updates the time and displays the result in the upper right corner of the screen.

Controlling interrupts with the 6522 involves three principal operations. The interrupt must be enabled in the Interrupt Enable Register (IER). The source of an interrupt can be determined in reading the Interrupt Flag Register (IFR). The last operation is to pass the interrupt to the CPU.

Figure 3-30 shows the control bits of the Interrupt Enable and the Interrupt Flag Register.

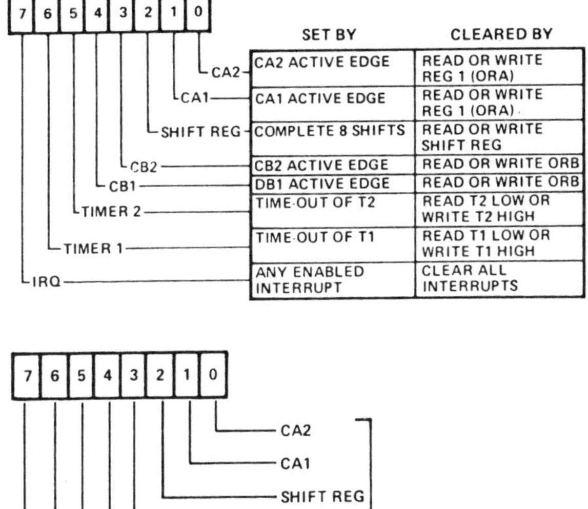

Figure 3-30: The IER and the IFR Register.

In lines 34 and 35 of Figure 3-31, $A0 is written to the IER. This causes the IRQ output of the 6522 to go low at the next time out of Timer 2. Then bit 7 and bit 5 of the IFR also go low, and an IRQ is signalled to the CPU.

```
0800           1         DCM "PR#1"
0800           2  ACR    EQU $C0CB      ; I/O CARD IN SLOT 4
0800           3  T1CL   EQU $C0C4      ;
0800           4  T2CL   EQU $C0C8      ;
0800           5  IFR    EQU $C0CD      ;
0800           6  IER    EQU $C0CE      ;
0800           7  HOME   EQU $FC58      ;
0800           8  PRTBYT EQU $FDDA      ;
0800           9  OUTCH  EQU $FDED      ;
0800          10  VTAB   EQU $FC22      ;
0800          11  MONITO EQU $FF59      ;
0800          12  ;                     ;
0800          13  CH     EPZ $24        ;
0800          14  CV     EPZ $25        ;
0800          15  ACC    EPZ $45        ;
0800          16  WNDTOP EPZ $22        ;
0800          17  ;                     ;
0800          18  HFZ    EQU $C4FC      ;
0800          19  ;                     ;
C400          20         ORG $C400
C400 A900     21  INIT   LDA #00        ; USE RAM ON BOARD
C402 8DFCC4   22         STA HFZ        ; STORE ZERO IN THE
C405 8DFDC4   23         STA HFZ+1      ; TIME LOCATIONS
C408 8DFEC4   24         STA HFZ+2      ;
C40B A902     25         LDA #2         ;
C40D 8522     26         STA WNDTOP     ; SET TOP OF WINDOW
C40F 2058FC   27         JSR HOME       ;
C412 A93E     28         LDA #IRQR      ; CLEAR SCREEN
C414 8DFE03   29         STA $3FE       ; GET LO BYTE OF SERVICE ROU-
C417 A9C4     30         LDA /IRQR      ; TINE. STORE IT IN $3FE
C419 8DFF03   31         STA $3FF       ; GET HI BYTE
C41C A9E0     32         LDA #$E0       ; STORE IT IN $3FF
C41E 8DCBC0   33         STA ACR        ; SET MODE: TIMER 1 FREE RUN-
C421 A9A0     34         LDA #$A0       ; NING, TIMER 2 COUNTER
C423 8DCEC0   35         STA IER        ; ENABLE INTERRUPT ON TIME
C426 A90A     36         LDA #10        ; OUT TIMER 2
C428 8DC8C0   37         STA T2CL       ; STORE 10 IN TIMER 2
C42B A900     38         LDA #00        ;
C42D 8DC9C0   39         STA T2CL+1     ;
C430 A93A     40         LDA #$3A       ;
C432 8DC4C0   41         STA T1CL       ; STORE 0.05 S IN TIMER 1
C435 A9B4     42         LDA #$B4       ; ( MUST BE ADJUSTED FOR
C437 8DC5C0   43         STA T1CL+1     ;   FOR ACCURACY )
C43A 58       44         CLI            ; START TIMER 1
C43B 4C59FF   45         JMP MONITO     ; ENABLE INTERRUPTS
C43E          46  ;                     ;
C43E          47  ;                     ;
C43E 8A       48  IRQR   TXA            ; START OF SERVICE ROUTINE
C43F 48       49         PHA            ; SAVE REGISTERS. ACCU WAS
C440 98       50         TYA            ; SAVED IN THE MONITOR
C441 48       51         PHA            ;
C442 A525     52         LDA CV         ; SAVE CURSOR POSITION IN
```

```
C444 8DFBC4          STA HFZ-1      ; MAIN PROGRAM
C447 A524            LDA CH         ;
C449 8DFAC4          STA HFZ-2      ;
C44C F8              SED            ; SET DECIMAL MODE
C44D A901            LDA #1         ; ADD 1 IN THE SECONDS
C44F 18              CLC            ; COUNTER
C450 6DFCC4          ADC HFZ        ;
C453 8DFCC4          STA HFZ        ;
C456 D8              CLD            ;
C457 C960            CMP #$60       ; SECONDS = 60 ?
C459 D024            BNE I1         ;
C45B A900            LDA #00        ; THEN ZERO TO SECONDS
C45D 8DFCC4          STA HFZ        ; COUNTER
C460 F8              SED            ;
C461 A901            LDA #1         ; ADD 1 TO MINUTES
C463 18              CLC            ; COUNTER.
C464 6DFDC4          ADC HFZ+1      ;
C467 8DFDC4          STA HFZ+1      ;
C46A D8              CLD            ;
C46B C960            CMP #$60       ; MINUTES = 60 ?
C46D D010            BNE I1         ;
C46F A900            LDA #00        ; THEN ZERO TO MINUTES
C471 8DFDC4          STA HFZ+1      ; COUNTER
C474 F8              SED            ;
C475 A901            LDA #1         ; ADD 1 TO HOURS COUNTER
C477 18              CLC            ;
C478 6DFEC4          ADC HFZ+2      ;
C47B 8DFEC4          STA HFZ+2      ;
C47E D8              CLD            ; CLEAR DECIMAL MODE
C47F A91E       I1   LDA #30        ; SET CURSOR POSITION
C481 8524            STA CH         ;
C483 A900            LDA #00        ;
C485 8525            STA CV         ;
C487 2022FC          JSR VTAB       ;
C48A ADFEC4          LDA HFZ+2      ; PRINT HOURS
C48D 20DAFD          JSR PRTBYT     ;
C490 A9BA            LDA #$BA       ; PRINT ":"
C492 20EDFD          JSR OUTCH      ;
C495 ADFDC4          LDA HFZ+1      ; PRINT MINUTES
C498 20DAFD          JSR PRTBYT     ;
C49B A9BA            LDA #$BA       ; PRINT ":"
C49D 20EDFD          JSR OUTCH      ;
C4A0 ADFCC4          LDA HFZ        ; PRINT SECONDS
C4A3 20DAFD          JSR PRTBYT     ;
C4A6 A90A       FIN  LDA #10        ; RESTORE TIMER 2
C4A8 8DC8C0          STA T2CL       ;
C4AB A900            LDA #00        ;
C4AD 8DC9C0          STA T2CL+1     ;
C4B0 A902            LDA #02        ;
C4B2 8522            STA WNDTOP     ; SET TOP OF WINDOW
C4B4 ADFAC4          LDA HFZ-2      ;
C4B7 8524            STA CH         ; RESTORE CURSOR
C4B9 ADFBC4          LDA HFZ-1      ; POSITION
C4BC 8525            STA CV         ;
C4BE 2022FC          JSR VTAB       ;
C4C1 58              CLI            ; ENABLE INTERRUPTS
C4C2 68              PLA            ; RESTORE REGISTERS
C4C3 A8              TAY            ;
C4C4 68              PLA            ;
C4C5 AA              TAX            ;
C4C6 A545            LDA ACC        ;
C4C8 40         FINI RTI            ; RETURN FROM INTERRUPT
                    END
```

Figure 3-31: A Real Time Clock

NOTES

4 Forth Section

The programming language FORTH was invented by CHARLES H. MOORE about ten years ago. Its first use was to control telescopes in the Kitt Peak Observatory. Today FORTH is widely used in control applications. One example is the control of movie cameras in the movie BATTLESHIP GALACTICA. Using the concept of virtual memory, FORTH also is used for data base management.

Figure 4-1 tries to compare the main differences between the three languages BASIC, PASCAL and FORTH.

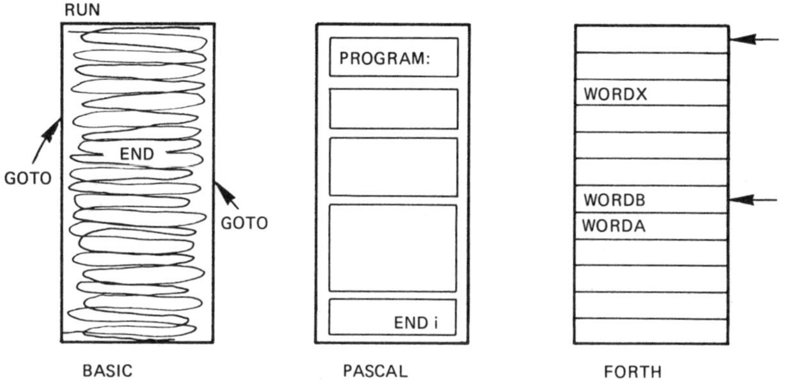

Figure 4-1: Differences between BASIC, PASCAL and FORTH.

BASIC is an unstructured queue of statements. The program is started with RUN at the beginning of the statements and ends with the END statement. One can enter a BASIC program from the side, using the GOTO statement.

PASCAL is a structured queue of statements. It begins with the PROGRAM statement and terminates at the last END statement. It is like a tube; there is no access to a program part inside the program. Testing a subroutine means writing a new program.

FORTH is quite different. The elements of a program in FORTH are stacked upon each other in slices, called WORDS. There is a free access to every slice, to every word. A FORTH program is started by calling a word. After the execution of the word, the FORTH interpreter waits for the input of a new word.

Changing only one statement in a PASCAL program means recompiling the whole program. This can be very tedious if it is a long program. Changing a word in FORTH means in most cases the compilation of only a few words.

If for example the word WORDX in Figure 4-1 has to be changed, only the words above WORDX have to be compiled. The rest remains unchanged.

In FORTH this queue of words is called the VOCABULARY. It is organized as a stack. In terms of a computer this is a LIFO (Last In, First Out) memory. The last item put on the stack is removed first.

There is another stack FORTH uses. This is called the PARAMETER stack. It is used for storing numbers and results of calculations and passes parameters from one word to the next.

Writing a FORTH program means to define new words by using other previously defined words. This makes FORTH a very dynamic language. Words can be rearranged to perform a new task. But all this freedom makes the programmer responsible for the correctness of a program. There are only a few error messages and warnings. Even if one programs the most foolish mistakes, FORTH almost always responds with OK.

In this FORTH section we will have only a short introduction. Mainly we will look at programs and FORTH specific programming techniques. For a more thorough introduction to FORTH "Starting Forth, " by L. BRODIE is recommended.

The FORTH version used for the following programs is an imlementation of FIG-FORTH Release 1.1. Special words for the APPLE II computer are described as they occur.

Sometimes it is said that FORTH programs are unreadable. They are unreadable like a PASCAL or a BASIC program, when the task and the programming idea are not known.

For documentation and understanding of FORTH words, it is necessary to show how the stack is effected by using a word. We will use the following abbreviations:

a	16-bit address
n	signed 16-bit number
u	unsigned 16-bit number
d	signed 32-bit number
b	8-bit byte
c	7-bit ASCII character
f	boolean number, flag

These abbreviations are used as follows:

WORD (STACK BEFOR - STACK AFTER)

Examples:

LOCK (an)

The word LOCK, a random selected word for this discussion, requests an address and a number on the stack before execution. The number n is on top of the stack; the address a is the second item on the stack. Both items are removed from the stack after execution.

FOUND (-f)

FOUND doesn't need any parameter before execution and leaves a boolean number f on the stack after execution.

COMP (aa'c -nf)

The word COMP needs two addresses and a character on top of the stack. After execution a number and a flag are left on the stack. In this representation the top of the stack (TOS) is always the rightmost character. To differ between several addresses or numbers, a apostrophe or a number can be added to the character like a' or n1 or n2.

4.1 Introduction into FORTH

4.11 The Stack and its Manipulation

One cell of the stack is a 16-bit cell. The stack may be changed in three ways. It can be enlarged, reduced or rearranged. All this can be done with the following words:

DUP (n - nn)
Duplicate the top of the stack.

DROP (n)
Throw away the top of the stack.

SWAP (nn' - n'n)
Reverse the top two elements.

OVER (n'n - n'nn')
Copy of the second element on top.

ROT (nn1n2 - n1n2n)
Rotate the top three elements counterclock wise.

Figure 4-2 shows how these words effect the stack.

				TOS	
	2	4	5	3	
2	4	5	3	3	DUP
2	4	3	3	5	ROT
2	4	3	5	3	SWAP
	2	4	3	5	DROP
2	4	3	5	3	OVER

Figure 4-2: Changing the Stack.

The rightmost element is always on top of the stack.

Two examples:

The stack contains the numbers 3 2 1 with the 1 on top of the stack. What words must be entered to obtain the sequence 3 2 2 1? The answer is :

```
     321
OVER 3213
SWAP 3221
```

On the stack we have the same sequence of numbers we started with above. Which words must be entered to get the sequence 2 3 3? This is the answer:

```
     321
DROP 32
SWAP 23
DUP  233
```

Exercise:

Start with 3 2 1 on the stack and get

```
A) 312
B) 213
C) 231
D) 123
E) 32121
```

For these exercises it is very useful to have a non destructive stack print. The print statement in FORTH is the . (dot). If one types

```
5.
```

the computer responds with

```
5 OK
```

Now the stack is empty. The definition for the print statement is:

. (n)
Prints the top of the stack on the screen.

Most of the utility packages contain the word .S (dot s, print stack). This word prints the contents of the stack with the top of the stack to the right. The input of

```
1 2 3 .S
```

prints

```
1 2 3 OK
```

The contents of the stack are not altered. On the other hand the input of

```
1 2 3 . . .
```

prints

```
3 2 1 OK
```

The last entered number is printed first and the contents of the stack are altered.

4.12 Words in FORTH

A word in FORTH may be any arbitrary string of characters excluding three special characters. These are the SPACE, BACKSPACE and RETURN characters. The SPACE character is the only delimiter between FORTH words. The BACKSPACE character is used for correcting typing errors, and the RETURN character is used to indicate that the input to the computer is completed.

Examples of Words:

FIRST 1TIMES .NAME @VALUE

THR EE is not recognized as one word, because of the additional space. It represents two words THR and EE.

The definition of a new word starts with the : sign, followed by a space and the name of the new word. Then all words used by this new word are listed. The definition ends with the ; sign.

: XXX
Start of a colon definition with name XXX.

;
End of a colon definition.

Example:

On the stack we have the three numbers 3 2 1, with the 1 on top of the stack. We want to define a word DROP3 which removes the 3 from the stack.

```
: DROP3 ( NN1N2-N1N2) ROT DROP ;
```

After the RETURN key, the new word is compiled into the vocabulary.

The contents of the vocabulary are listed on the screen with the word VLIST. We find the word DROP3 on top of the vocabulary stack. Once a word is compiled into the vocabulary, it can be used by all words defined later. With the word FORGET we can remove a word from the vocabulary.

FORGET XXX
Removes from the vocabulary the word XXX and all definitions made afterwards.

An example:

We use the word ." (print message) to print some messages on the screen and define

." XXX" ( )
Print message. Message ends with ".

```
: ONE ." ONE" ;
: TWO ." TWO" ;
: ONE ." THREE" ;
```

After the last definition we get the warning

ONE ISN'T UNIQUE

because ONE was already defined. This is not an error message; it is a warning. Nevertheless, the word is compiled into the dictionary.

If we now call ONE, we get the message THREE. FORGET ONE searches for the first occurrence of ONE from the top of the vocabulary and removes it. The call of ONE then prints the message ONE. Once more we FORGET ONE. If we now call TWO, we get the message

```
TWO ?
```

The word TWO is no longer in the vocabulary. It was removed by the second FORGET ONE.

There are two ways to enter new words into the dictionary. One we showed has a tremendous disadvantage. If an error is detected in one of the definitions, this definition and all definitions made later have to be retyped. The better way is to use the Editor. Here the definitions are entered into a textscreen. Figure 4-3 shows an example of a textscreen.

```
SCR # 024

 0 ( VKL                              ef)
 1 1 VARIABLE FNR
 2 : EIN ( nn') PAD RECLEN ERASE
 3   PAD ! PAD 2 + ! ;
 4 : (P) RECLEN 2 - + ;
 5 : ^P ( n) PAD (P) ! ;
 6 : P^ ( -n) PAD (P) @ ;
 7 : ?F# ( -f) 0 P# @ 1 =
 8   IF  1 ^P !MEM DROP 1 THEN ;
 9 : ^N ( an) (P) ! ;
10 : N^ ( a-n) (P) @ ;
11 : (@1EL) ( -a) 1 #INDEX ;
12 : COMP ( a-f) 0 SWAP @ PAD @
13   2DUP > IF 2DROP DROP 1 ELSE
14   = IF DROP 1 THEN THEN ;
15 -->
```

Figure 4-3: Textscreen

A screen has 16 lines with 32 characters. Some other Editors use screens with 16 lines and 64 characters. The lines are numbered from 0 to 15. There are some conventions in writing a screen. The first line should contain a comment which describes the task, date and initials of the programmer. A new definition should always start on a new line.

If one has written or changed a text screen, it must be saved on disk. The word FLUSH does this. The word LOAD compiles the words into the vocabulary, and LIST lists the contents of a screen on the TV screen. The definitions of these words are:

FLUSH (n)
Save screen n on disk.

LOAD (n)
Compile the definitions in screen n into the vocabulary.

LIST (n)
List screen n on the TV screen.

Another word, INDEX, is very useful. INDEX lists the contents of the first line of screens.

INDEX (nn')
List all first lines from screen n to screen n'.

There are numerous variations of the Editor in the various FORTH versions for the APPLE II. We don't describe an Editor in detail here. One should refer to the Reference Manuals.

4.13 Fundamental Operations in Arithmetic

As a stack oriented language FORTH uses the Reverse Polish Notation (RPN). This notation is also known as postfix notation. The operator for the calculation is entered after entering the numbers. If one types

3 6 +

the three is put on the stack and then the six. At this time the FORTH interpreter recognizes the word + . It takes the two top numbers, adds them together and places the result 9 on top of the stack. The . command prints a 9 on the screen.

Using the Reverse Polish Notation, there is no need to use brackets. Let us look at the following example:

(3 + 5)*(4-2)-7

A BASIC interpreter which has to decipher such an expression starts with the opening bracket, gets a number, then the operator, once more a number, and then the closing bracket. At this moment it can do the first calculation. The next step indicates a requirement for a multiplication. This can be done only after calculating the second, parenthetic expression.

Using RPN it is easier for the computer to calculate the following expression. In RPN we enter:

3 5 + 4 2 - * 7 -

Figure 4-4 shows the evaluation of the stack.

STACK					TOS	INPUT
					3	3
				3	5	5
					8	+
				8	4	4
			8	4	2	2
				8	2	–
					16	*
				16	7	7
					9	–

Figure 4-4: Calculating an Arithmetic Expression Using RPN.

To get familiar with RPN there are some exercises. Check your results with the . command.

Exercises:

```
3*4–7
(3*5+3)/6–4
5*5–4*4
(3+5)*2
20/(2*5)
```

The words for the fundamental operations of arithmetic are defined as follows:

+	(nn1 - n2)	n2=n+n1
-	(nn1 - n2)	n2=n-n1
*****	(nn1 - n2)	n2=n*n1
/	(nn1 - n2)	n2=n/n1

This arithmetic is done with 16-bit signed, fixed numbers. Two more words can be used to get the remainder or the quotient and the remainder of a division.

MOD (nn1 - n2)
n2 is the remainder of n/n1.

/MOD (nn1 - n2n3)
n2 is the remainder and n3 is the quotient of n/n1.

There is another interesting word */ (star slash). The definition is:

***/** (nn1n2 - n3)
n3=n*n1/n2 . The product n*n1 has a double precision intermediate.

We will see the use of double precision numbers and mixed operations in the examples.

To show that the arithmetic signs are words and not operators, we change the meaning of the + sign.

```
: + - ;
```

If we now enter 4 1 + ., a three instead of a five is displayed on the screen. It is better to FORGET this new + sign.

4.14 Comparisons

The comparison takes place with the two top numbers on the stack. They are replaced by the result of the comparison. The result is a one if the comparison was true, or the result is a zero if it was not true. This boolean flag is used by the control words to control the flow of the program. The following words can be used:

<	(nn' - f)	f = 1, if n less than n'.
>	(nn' - f)	f = 1, if n greater than n'.
=	(nn' - f)	f = 1, if n equal to n.
0<	(n - f)	f = 1, if n is less than zero.
0=	(n - f)	f = 1, if n is equal to zero.

Some examples:

```
2 3 < . 1  OK
3 2 < . 0  OK
3 2 = . 0  OK
-2 0< . 1  OK
```

If one wants to use the top two numbers on the stack after the comparison one has to duplicate them with

```
: 2DUP ( NN'-NN'NN') OVER OVER ;
```

4.15 Constants and Variables

Most of the data used for calculation is stored on the stack. Sometimes it is necessary to use a constant or a variable. The definitions are:

CONSTANT NAME (n)
Creates a constant NAME with the value n.

VARIABLE NAME (n)
Creates a variable NAME with the initial value n.

There is a difference in calling a constant or a variable. Calling a constant by name causes the value of the constant to be placed on the stack. Calling a variable by name causes the address of this variable to be placed on the stack. In order to get the value of the variable, the contents of this address have to be fetched. This is done by the word @ (fetch). To store the top of the stack in an address the word ! (store) is used.

@ (a-n)
Fetches the contents stored at address a.

! (na)
Stores n at address a.

Both instructions, fetch and store, use 16 bit numbers. In an 8-bit machine like the APPLE the low byte of the stack is stored at address a and the high byte at address a + 1. To fetch and to store a single byte one uses the words

C@ (a-b)
Fetch a single byte from address a.

C! (ba)
Store a single byte at address a.

Two more words are very often used with variables:

+! (na)
Adds n to the contents of address a.

? (a)
Fetches the contents of address a and prints them.

An example:

FORTH itself uses several constants and variables. For this example we will use the variable BASE. The contents of this variable determine the number base in which calculations are made. If the value of BASE is a decimal 10, all calculations are made in decimal. Changing this value to 16 causes the calculations to be made in hexadecimal. One may use however any other value for calculating in any other number base system.

Two words are defined to set a specific number base:

DECIMAL ()
Set decimal mode.

HEX ()
Set hexadecimal mode.

One can define:

```
: BIN 2 BASE ! ;
: TRI 3 BASE ! ;
: .BIN ( N) BIN . DECIMAL ;
: .TRI ( N) TRI . DECIMAL ;
```

The word BIN sets the number base to two and TRI to three. The trinary system uses the numbers 0, 1 and 2 to represent a number. The words .BIN and .TRI take a decimal value from the stack, convert it to a binary or trinary number, print this number and switch back to the decimal mode.

```
120 .BIN 1111000  OK
140 .TRI 12012  OK
```

Sometimes it is necessary to determine the current number base. If one enters BASE ?, the answer will always be 10 (why ?). In order to get the correct number base, one can define the word .BASE.

```
: .BASE BASE @ DUP DECIMAL .
  BASE ! ;
```

.BASE fetches the content of BASE, duplicates it, prints it in decimal and stores it again in BASE.

4.16 Input and Output

Two of the output words, . (print) and ." (print message), have already been discussed. There are some more words:

U. (n)
Print n as an unsigned number.

D. (d)
Print a double precision number.

.R (nn1)
Print number n right-justified in field. Fieldwidth is n1.

D.R (dn)
Print double precision number in field. Fieldwidth is n.

EMIT (c)
Prints ASCII character c.

CR ()
Prints a carriage-return.

SPACE ()
Print one space.

SPACES (n)
Print n spaces.

TYPE (an)
Print n bytes starting at address a.

KEY (-c)
Get character from keyboard.

?TERMINAL (-f)
f= 1, if any key was pressed.

EXPECT (an)
Expect n characters from the keyboard and store them starting at address a.

Examples for these words are found in the programs.

4.17 Control Structures

The words we have used until now didn't effect the flow of a program. Now we will take a closer look at these type words. Like in PASCAL there is no GOTO statement. This makes FORTH a structured, programming language. For the control of a program one uses a definite loop as

DO ... LOOP ,

conditional loops

BEGIN ... UNTIL or
BEGIN ... WHILE ...REPEAT and the

conditional branch

IF ... ELSE ... THEN .

These statements must be used within a colon definition. They cannot be executed directly by the interpreter.

The DO ... LOOP

This loop creates a finite number of program loops. The definition is

DO (nn')
Starts a loop from n' to n-1.

LOOP ()
Tests the upper limit of the loop and increments the index by one.

The program loop starts at n' and ends at n-1. As the comparison of the upper limit and the loop index is caused by the word LOOP, every loop is executed at least once.

FORTH uses a third stack, which hasn't been mentioned yet. This is the RETURN stack. This is the same stack that the CPU uses. During execution of a loop, FORTH places the loop index on top of this stack. The word I is used to get a copy of the top of the RETURN stack onto the PARAMETER stack.

An example:

Let us print the numbers from one to nine on the screen.

```
: .# 10 1 DO I . LOOP ;
  .# 1 2 3 4 5 6 7 8 9  OK
```

Just to show that a loop is executed at least once, we change the boundaries of the loop.

```
: .# 1 10 DO I . LOOP ;
  .# 10  OK
```

Loops can be nested. In the next example we print a row of numbers from 0 to 9.
Then in the next line we print numbers from 0 to 8 and so on until a single 0 is printed. The inner loop is defined as

```
: IL ( N) 0 DO I . LOOP ;
```

IL expects the upper limit + 1 on the stack. The outermost loop is defined as

```
: OL ( N) 0 DO CR 1 - DUP IL
  LOOP ;
```

OL expects the number of lines on the stack. If we enter 11 10 OL, OL takes the ten as upper limit for the outer loop. Next it issues a carriage return, and a one is subtracted from the remaining 11. The result is duplicated and IL takes one 10 as upper limit. The other 10 stays on the stack for the next call of IL. We should have added the word DROP after LOOP in OL. When the execution has finished, a 1 stays on the stack. The programmer has to take care that the stack remains after the execution of a task as it was before. Otherwise the stack grows and grows, and as it is limited, the system may crash.

The result of 11 10 OL is shown in Figure 4-5.

```
11 10 OL
0 1 2 3 4 5 6 7 8 9
0 1 2 3 4 5 6 7 8
0 1 2 3 4 5 6 7
0 1 2 3 4 5 6
0 1 2 3 4 5
0 1 2 3 4
0 1 2 3
0 1 2
0 1
0  OK
```

Figure 4-5: Triangle- Matrix.

Very often it is necessary to increment the loop index by another number instead of one or even decrement the loop index. Then the DO ... +LOOP must be used. The definition of DO is the same as above, but the +LOOP expects a number on the stack.

+LOOP (n)
Increments the index by n. If n is less zero, the loop index is decremented.

Some examples:

```
: +NR ( NN') DO I . 2 +LOOP ;  OK
10 0 +NR 0 2 4 6 8  OK

: -NR ( NN') DO I . -2 +LOOP ;  OK
0 10 -NR 10 8 6 4 2  OK
```

Another example of nested loops and the use of +LOOP is shown in Figure 4-6. A Rhombus is printed by the following words.

```
: STAR ( N) 0 DO 42 EMIT LOOP ;
: RI ( NN'N") DO CR 7 I -
  SPACES I 2 * 1 + STAR DUP
  +LOOP DROP ;
: RO 1 8 0 RI -1 -1 7 RI CR ;
```

The word STAR prints n times the character *. RI expects three parameters on the stack. N is the increment of the loop index. This is 1 in the upper part of the Rhombus and -1 in the lower part. N1 and n2 are the boundaries of the loop. RI first issues a carriage return; then it prints the spaces and the stars. As +LOOP removes the increment of the loop, it has to be duplicated. The word RO prints the upper and the lower parts of the Rhombus.

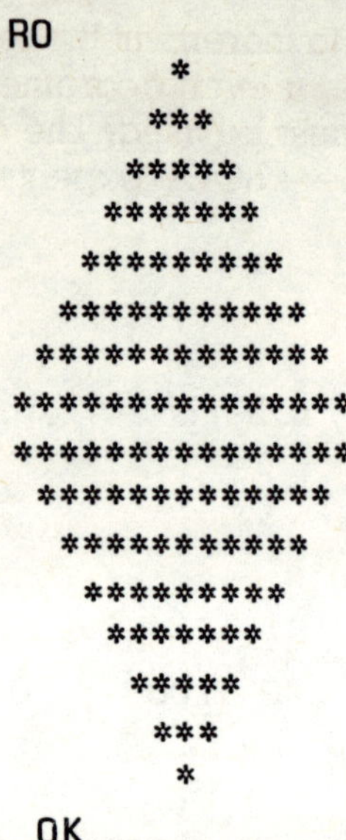

Figure 4-6: Rhombus.

We have mentioned the RETURN stack. FORTH uses this stack for loops and for the intermediate storage of addresses. With care a programmer can use this stack too. The word >R (to-R) puts the top number of the parameter stack on the return stack, and the word R> (R-from) returns it.

>**R**(n)
Put n to the return stack.

R> (-n)
Retrieves n from the return stack.

R (-n)
Copy the top of the return stack to the parameter stack. Same as I.

This words may be used only within a colon definition and outside of loops.

BEGIN ... UNTIL

This loop is a loop with an undetermined number of loops. The word UNTIL expects a flag on top of the stack. As long as this flag is zero, the words between BEGIN and UNTIL are repeated. A non-zero flag terminates the loop.

BEGIN ()
UNTIL (f)
The words between BEGIN and UNTIL are executed as long as the flag f is zero.

We use this loop to add together the numbers from 1 to 100. The words used are shown in Figure 4-7.

```
  0 VARIABLE X
: INCX ( -N) X @ 1 + DUP X ! ;
: SUM 0 DUP X ! BEGIN INCX +
  X @ 100 = UNTIL . ;
```

Figure 4-7: Adding Numbers with BEGIN ... UNTIL.

The variable X is used for counting. The word INCX increments the value of X. The +! is not used, as we have to add it to the previous sum. The loop is started with a zero on top of the stack. In SUM the value of X is incremented and added to the top of the stack. Then X is compared with 100. If it is less, the loop is repeated until it is equal 100. Then the loop is excited and the result is printed.

Another example for the BEGIN ... UNTIL loop is the word .E . This prints the character E on the screen as long as no key is pressed.

```
: .E BEGIN 69 EMIT ?TERMINAL
  UNTIL ;
```

BEGIN ... WHILE ... REPEAT

This loop is different from the BEGIN ... UNTIL loop. The word WHILE expects a flag on the stack. As long as this flag is non-zero, the words between WHILE and REPEAT are executed. An unconditional branch leads back to BEGIN. If WHILE finds a zero on the stack, the words between WHILE and REPEAT are skipped and the words following REPEAT are executed.

The definitions are:

BEGIN ()
WHILE (f)
REPEAT ()
The words between BEGIN, WHILE and REPEAT are executed as long as f is non-zero. If f is zero the program commences after REPEAT.

An example:

The same task as above, adding the numbers from 1 to 100, is demonstrated. The program is shown in Figure 4-8.

```
: TEST ( -F) 1 + DUP 101 < ;
: ADD DUP ROT + SWAP ;
: SUM 0 0 BEGIN TEST WHILE ADD
  REPEAT DROP . ;
```

Figure 4-8: Adding Numbers with BEGIN ... WHILE ... REPEAT.

First the word TEST is defined. A one is added to the top of the stack, and the result is duplicated and compared with 101. The next word ADD duplicates the top of the stack and rotates the first three elements. The third element is the amount of numbers that have been added until now.

The top two numbers are added, and the result is placed below the number of additions. The word SUM expects a zero as starting value on the stack. The word TEST is executed before WHILE. As long as the number of additions is less than 101, the word ADD is executed. If it is equal, the top of the stack is dropped, and the remaining number is printed.

IF ... THEN

IF ... ELSE ... THEN

This is a conditional branch. The definitions are:

IF (f)
THEN ()

IF expects a flag on the stack. If this flag is non-zero, the words between IF and THEN are executed.

IF (f)
ELSE ()
THEN ()

IF expects a flag on the stack. If this flag is non-zero, the words between IF and ELSE or the words between ELSE and THEN are executed.

An example:

The word COMP compares the top two numbers. If both numbers are equal the message EQUAL is printed. If they are not equal the message SMALLER or BIGGER is printed. The program is shown in Figure 4-9.

```
: 2DUP ( NN'-NN'NN') OVER OVER ;
: 2DROP ( NN') DROP DROP ;
: NOTEQUAL ( F) IF ." BIGGER "
  ELSE ." SMALLER " THEN ;
: COMP ( NN') 2DUP = IF
  ." EQUAL" 2DROP ELSE <
  NOTEQUAL THEN ;
```

Figure 4-9: Comparing two Numbers.

The word 2DUP duplicates the top two numbers and the word 2DROP drops them. The word NOTEQUAL expects a flag on the stack. If this flag is non-zero, the message BIGGER or SMALLER is printed.

The word COMP duplicates the top two numbers and compares them. If they are equal the message EQUAL is printed and the remaining two numbers are removed from the stack. If they are not equal, another comparison is performed. According to the result of this comparison the appropriate message is printed.

4.18 Access to the Disk

In a FORTH system the space on disk is an expansion of the memory in the computer. Data on disk is not stored as a file, it is stored in blocks. The size of a block may vary in different FORTH versions. Some have 256 bytes, others 1024. The constant B/BUF contains the number of bytes per block for the given FORTH version. The FORTH used for the examples in this book has 256 bytes per block. This is the same size as a sector on a disk. As we have 560 sectors on a formatted disk, we have 560 blocks of memory for storing data. The blocks are numbered from 0 to 559. The word BLOCK reads one block from the disk into the disk buffer. This is a special area in RAM reserved for these blocks.

BLOCK (n-a)

BLOCK places the starting address a of block n in RAM on the top of the stack. If this block is not present, it is read from disk into the disk buffer.

The relation between blocks on disk and RAM is shown in Figure 4-10.

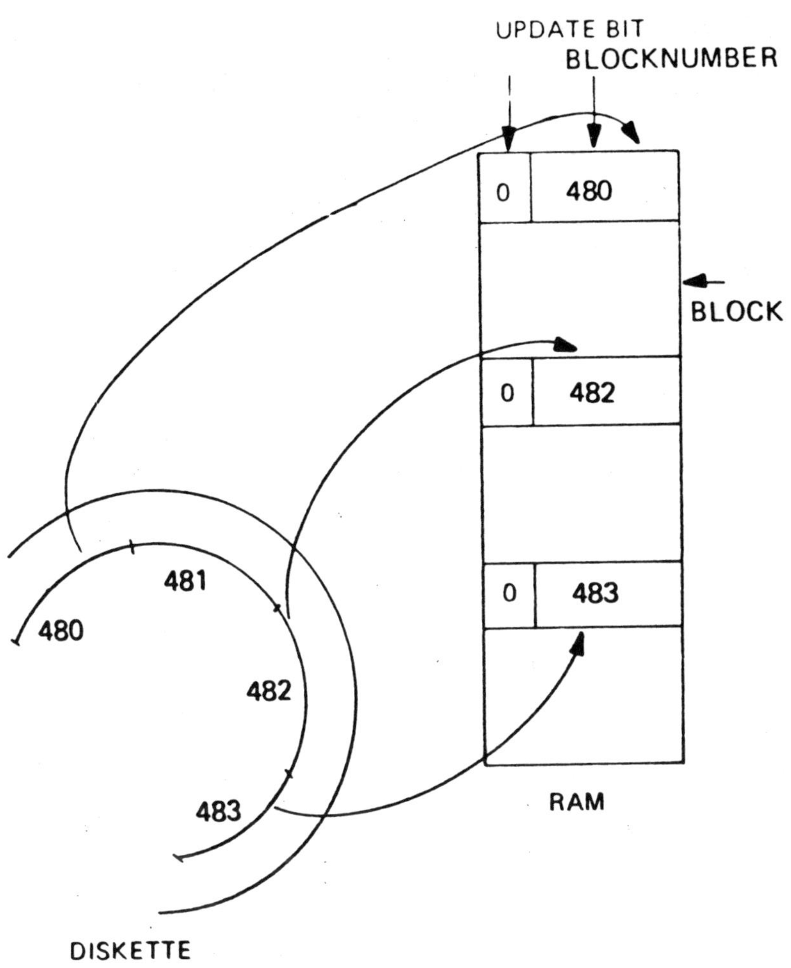

Figure 4-10: Blocks in RAM and on Diskette.

The header of a block is two bytes long. It contains the number of the block and the UPDATE-bit. If the contents of a block are changed and have to be rewritten on the disk with the word FLUSH, the block has to be marked as updated.

UPDATE ()
Mark the block most recently referenced as updated.

FLUSH ( )
Save all updated blocks on disk.

An updated block is also saved on disk, if the disk buffer is full and this block has to be overwritten. The word

EMPTY-BUFFERS ( )

clears the disk buffer. A zero is written into all headers. This is the reason why a block 0 cannot be used.

As the memory on disk is an open memory with a free access even to a single bit on the disk, a programmer has to pay attention. If a data or a program diskette has to be removed from a disk drive, the words FLUSH EMPTY-BUFFERS should first be entered. This saves all updated blocks on disk and leaves an empty disk buffer for the next disk.

As it was mentioned earlier, a text screen has 512 bytes (PWF 1.5). Two blocks are used to store the contents of a screen. The input of 30 LIST lists the contents of block 60 and 61.

An example:

On a BASIC disk the directory starts at track 17, sector 15. For FORTH this is block number 287 (17*16+15). 143 LIST lists the contents of the first two sectors of the BASIC directory. The directory starts in the second half of screen # 143.

Another direct access to the disk can be made with the word R/W.

R/W (anf)

With f=1, block n on the disk is stored at address a.
With f=0, 256 bytes starting at address a are written into block n on disk.

Examples for the transfer of data between disk and memory are found in the sample programs.

4.19 The Vocabulary Stack

Let us take a look at the construction of a FORTH word. The word HERE places the address of the first free memory location of the vocabulary stack onto the parameter stack. In Figure 4-11 first the content of HERE is printed, then a new definition

: ADD + ;

is made. Afterwards the definition HERE has moved up 12 bytes. The last two lines in Figure 4-11 show the hexdump of these 12 bytes.

```
23964 15 DUMP

ADDR: 5D9C
5D98   43   E A3   D 83 41 44 C4   C.#..ADD
5DA0   3E 5D B6   D 9C  C A3   D   >]6...#.
5DA8    4 44 55 4D 50  0 20   0   .DUMP. .
 OK
```

Figure 4-11: Hexdump of the Word Add

The construction of the word ADD is shown in Figure 4-13. The word begins with the NAME-FIELD. The first byte is the length byte. The lower four bits contain the length of the name. The maximum length of a name is therefore 16.

The next bytes contain the name in ASCII. The highest bit of the last character is set to one. This indicates to the Name Search routine of the interpreter the end of a name.

The next two bytes are the LINK-FIELD. The address stored here points to the name-field address of the previous definition.

	Hex address			Decimal address
HERE after the Definition →	5DA8			23976
	5DA6	A3	0D	23974
Parameterfield	5DA4	9C	0C	23972
Codefield	5DA2	B6	0D	23970
Linkfield	5DA0	3E	5D	23968
Namefield	5D9E	44	C4	23966
HERE →	5D9C	83	41	23964

Figure 4-12: Construction of the Word ADD.

The following two bytes are the CODE-FIELD. This address points to the beginning of the execution of the word. In the example this is the code-field address of the : definition. After the code-field the PARAMETER-FIELD starts. Here the code-field addresses of the words used in the definition are stored. In the example these are the code-field addresses of the word + and the word ;.

The definition of ADD ends here, and the pointer HERE points to the address of the next byte.

Now the word ADD is used in a new definition:

```
: #ADD DUP ROT ADD ;
```

Figure 4-13 shows the hexdump and Figure 4-14, the construction of the word # ADD.

```
23964 40 DUMP

ADDR: 5D9C
5D98   43  E A3  D 83 41 44 C4   C.#..ADD
5DA0   3E 5D B6  D 9C  C A3  D   >]6...#.
5DA8   83 23 41 C4 9C 5D B6  D   .#AD.]6.
5DB0   A4  A 23 11 A2 5D A3  D   $.#."]#.
5DB8    4 44 55 4D 50  0 20 20   .DUMP.
5DC0    0  0  0  0  0  0  0  0   ........
 OK
```

Figure 4-13: Hexdump of ADD and # ADD

The address in the link-field (17426) of the new word is the name-field address of ADD. The code-field addresses of DUP, ROT and ADD are stored in the parameter-field.

HERE after the Definition →	5DB8			23992
;	5DB6	A3	0D	23990
ADD	5DB4	A2	5D	23988
ROT	5DB2	23	11	23986
DUP	5DB0	A4	0A	23984
Codefield	5DAE	B6	0D	23982
Linkfield	5DAC	9C	5D	23980
Namefield	5DAA	41	C4	23978
HERE →	5DA8	83	23	23976

Figure 4-14: Construction of the Word # ADD.

When # ADD is executed, the words DUP and ROT are executed. Next the interpreter jumps to the code-field address of ADD. All words of this definition are worked out until the semicolon definition. Then the interpreter jumps back to the parameter-field of # ADD. The semicolon terminates the execution. If there are no more words, the interpreter prints OK and waits for the next input.

If the code-field address of a word is known, it can be executed with EXECUTE.

EXECUTE (a)
Execute word with code-field address a.

The vocabulary stack can also be used to store data. In the definition of HERE a system variable DP is used.

```
: HERE ( -A) DP @ ;
```

With

```
1000 HERE !
```

the number 1000 is stored at the top of the vocabulary. If another number is stored, two has to be added to DP. The word , (comma) stores a number and adds two to DP

, (n)
Stores n on top of the vocabulary stack and adds two to DP.

To store only a single byte the word C, is used.

C, (b)
Stores the byte b on the vocabulary stack and adds one to DP.

The word ALLOT makes a gap in the vocabulary.

ALLOT (n)
Leaves a gap of n bytes at the top of the dictionary.

Attention! The word ALLOT reserves n bytes in the vocabulary. To store n numbers 2*n bytes must be reserved.

4.1A Text and Strings

In the standard version of FORTH there are no strings or string functions implemented. Yet it is very easy to enter text or to printout text. For the input of text a special area in memory, PAD, can be used. The starting address of PAD is always 68 bytes beyond the top f the vocabulary stack.

PAD (-a)
The address of PAD is put on the stack.

The two words EXPECT and TYPE (see Chapter 4.16) are used to enter and to print characters.

Example:

The words

```
PAD 15 EXPECT
```

expect 15 characters to be entered into PAD. The RETURN after EXPECT does not start a new line. The input is terminated with another RETURN or automatically after the input of 15 characters.

A printout of these characters can be made with

```
PAD 15 TYPE
```

The text entered with EXPECT is printed, provided that the top of the vocabulary stack was not altered between EXPECT and TYPE. Only parts of the text can also be printed. With EXPECT we have entered the string

```
ABCDEFGHIJK
```

into PAD. The input of

```
PAD 2 + 3 TYPE
```

prints the characters

```
CDE
```

The use of the word WORD is another possibility to enter text into the computer.

WORD (c)
Read text from the input buffer until the delimiter c is encountered.

This is the FIG-FORTH definition of WORD. FORTH-79 uses a slightly different definition

WORD (c-an)
Read text from the input buffer until the delimiter c is encountered. Leave the starting address a of the text and the length n on the top of the stack.

The characters entered with WORD are stored at the top of the vocabulary stack. The first byte stored at HERE is the length byte. The word COUNT converts this byte into the starting address and the length of the text.

COUNT (a-a'n)
Converts the length byte at address a into the starting address a' and the length n.

As an example we write a word TEXT, which accepts text and moves it to PAD.

```
: TEXT ( C)
  PAD 72 32 FILL WORD HERE
  COUNT PAD SWAP CMOVE ;
```

The definitions of the two words FILL and CMOVE are:

FILL (nab)
Fill n bytes b into memory, starting at address a.

CMOVE (aa'n)
Moves n bytes from a to a'.

CMOVE moves the first byte from a to a', the second byte from a+1 to a'+1 etc.. The destination address a' must not be in the range of a<a'<a+n for a correct move of the bytes.

In TEXT, first PAD is filled with ASCII blanks, and WORD accepts characters until the delimiter c is found. HERE and COUNT place the starting address and the length of the text on the stack. PAD SWAP places the correct sequence of parameters for CMOVE on the stack.

An example:

```
13 TEXT THIS IS FORTH
```

There is only a RETURN after FORTH, not between TEXT and THIS. To be sure that the text has arrived in PAD, type 20 PAD TYPE. As delimiter, the ASCII character 13 (RETURN) was used.

The same sentence as above is entered. But now the delimiter 32 (SPACE) is used. After the RETURN, the computer asks:

```
IS ?
```

Only the word THIS was moved to PAD, as we used the delimiter 32. However the interpreter finds more text in the input buffer and tries to interpret it. IS is not a defined word, so the message IS ? is printed on the screen.

In some instances it is easier to enter a number as a string. This string is afterwards converted to a number.
For this FIG-FORTH uses the word NUMBER.

NUMBER (a-d)
Convert a string at a + 1 to a double precision number. At address a the length of the string is stored. The variable DPL contains the number of digits to the right of the decimal point. A minus sign may precede the string. The conversion ends if a space character if found. An error message is issued if a non-numeric character is found in the string.

An example for NUMBER is found in the program CASH REGISTER in Chapter 4.2.

For an output, a double precision number can be formatted.

The following words are used:

< (d)

Start converting a double precision number into a string.

#
Convert one digit.

 # S
Convert the remaining digits.

> (-an)
End of conversion. Leaves the starting address a and the length n ready for TYPE on the stack.

HOLD (c)
Insert character c into the string.

A word .$ is defined which prints the number 10000 as $100.00 .

```
: .$ ( D) <# # # 46 HOLD #S 36
   HOLD #> TYPE ;

   12345. .$ $123.45 OK
```

The conversion of this number to a string starts at the end of this number. The two digits 5 4 are converted. Next a decimal point is inserted, and the rest of the number is converted to a string. The $ sign is placed in front of the string. The conversion is terminated, and the string is printed on the screen.

Another example is the printout of an unsigned double precision number:

```
: UD. ( D) <# S# #> TYPE SPACE :
```

4.1B Defining Words

In FORTH a defining word is used to create new data structures. The compiler in FORTH is not closed as it is in other languages. New data structures can be entered in the compiler and used by the programmer. Figure 4-15 shows the construction of a defining word.

NAME	<BUILDS	COMPILE TIME BEHAVIOR	DOES>	RUN TIME BEHAVIOR

Figure 4-15: Construction of a Defining Word

After <BUILDS, all words are listed which are executed during compiling a word (compile time behavior). After DOES> all words are listed which executed during run time of a word (run time behavior)

An example:

The word CONSTANT is defined as

```
: CONSTANT <BUILDS , DOES> @ ;
```

During compiling the word CONSTANT, a number is stored in the vocabulary (,). In calling the word this number is fetched (@) from the vocabulary. As a second example, a one-dimensional array for 10 numbers is defined as

```
: ARRAY <BUILDS 20 ALLOT
        DOES> SWAP 2 * + ;
```

The word ARRAY is used to create words for the same class of data structures.

```
ARRAY VECTOR
```

creates the word VECTOR as a one-dimensional array for ten 16-bit numbers. The word VECTOR expects the index of the field in which a number is stored or is fetched from the top of the stack.

```
1000 0 VECTOR !
```

stores 1000 in the first field of VECTOR.

```
1 VECTOR @
```

fetches the contents of the second field. An example of a defining word is found in the program Language Translator.

In FORTH it is possible to change not only the compiler, but also the compile time behavior. During compilation the compiler can be turned off, the next word interpreted immediately, and then the compiler turned back on.

[turns off the compiler
] turns on the compiler

An example shows the following lines:

```
: STARS ( N) 0 DO [ HEX ] 2A
  EMIT [ DECIMAL ] LOOP ;
```

In stars the compiler is turned off, and the hexadecimal base is selected. After turning on the compiler, 2A is compiled as a hexadecimal number. Then the decimal number base is selected in the same manner.

Some words in FORTH are declared as IMMEDIATE. They are executed immediately upon calling in a definition. The following lines show an example:

```
: NOW ." NOW " ; IMMEDIATE  OK
: WRITE NOW ." HERE " ; NOW  OK
```

The word NOW, which prints the message NOW, is declared as IMMEDIATE, and it is used in WRITE. After the definition is entered and the RETURN key is pressed, the word NOW is executed immediately. The message NOW is printed between the ";" and the OK. The call of the word WRITE prints only the message HERE.

The word [COMPILE] compiles an immediate word into the vocabulary. The definition of WRITE is changed in

```
: WRITE ."  HERE" [COMPILE] NOW ;
```

The message NOW is not printed between ";" and OK as before. It is printed in calling the word WRITE.

```
WRITE  HERENOW  OK
```

One immediate word is ' (tick).

' XXX (-a)
Put the parameter-field address of XXX on the stack.

This word is used very often as compile-tick, as in the example below:

```
: ['] [COMPILE] ' ;
```

The compile-tick is used in the word PRINT. It fetches the parameter-field address of the next word on the stack. This address is converted to the codefield address and executed by EXECUTE.

```

: ['] [COMPILE] ' ;

: A ." I'LL BE SOON BACK" ;
: B ." DAILY HOURS FROM 8 AM TO
6 PM" ;
: C ." TODAY CLOSED" ;

: PRINT ['] 2 - EXECUTE ;

```

4.1C Some Naming Conventions

There are several words which are represented by only one character e.g. ! store, @ fetch . print . These words can be used to characterize the function of a word as

!MEM @VALUE .MES .

These words mean STORE MEMORY, FETCH VALUE and PRINT MESSAGE. This makes it easier to read FORTH programs. The character C is used to characterize 8-bit (single byte) words as in CMOVE, for example. Table A-6 in the appendix summarizes the Naming Conventions.

4.2 FORTH in Examples

In this chapter some examples in programming with FORTH are shown. The first program doesn't need any programming because it uses the FORTH vocabulary. Next there are some examples of the input of numbers and words, storing data on the disk, I/O programming, low resolution grafics, TURTLE grafics and a DBMS program.

4.21 Simple Programs

The concept of the vocabulary and defining new words can be used for a program which prints the meanings of abbreviations. For example:

```
: ABC ." AMERICAN BROADCASING CO
MPANY" ;
: BBC ." BRITISH BROADCASTING CO
MPANY" ;
: B.R.C.S. ." BRITISH RED CROSS
SOCIETY" ;
: ICPC ." INTERNATIONAL CRIMINAL
 POLICE" ;
: ETC ." AND SO ON" ;
```

In the same manner lists of chemical formulas, strange foreign words or a simple language translator can be programmed.

This is the example for an english to german translation:

```
: I ." ICH " ;
: AM ." BIN " ;
: GLAD ." FROH " ;

I AM GLAD ICH BIN FROH
```

Another language translator will be demonstrated later.

WEIGHTWATCHER:

This program calculates the amount of calories for a meal. The data is entered as follows:

```
BEER                    1  GLASS
BREAD                   1  SLICE
MUFFINS 2 PIECES etc..
```

The program is shown on screens 125 to 127.

```
SCR # 125

( AFB WEIGHTWATCHER            ef)
( UNIT GLAS: BEER, APPLEJUICE
        COCA-COLA, CHAMPAGNE
  UNIT SLICE: BREAD
  UNIT PIECE: CAKE, MUFFINS
  UNIT OZ: BEEF, HAM, CHIPS,
              NUTS, CHEESE
  UNIT TBSP [TABLESPOON] :
        BUTTER
  UNIT PKG: SEAFOOD
)
```

This screen contains only a comment about the units used for measurement. The unit GLAS for example, is used for beer, apple juice etc.. The unit OZ for beef, ham and so on.

```
SCR # 126

( AFB WEIGHTWATCHER CNTD      ef)
( MEASUREMENT UNITS)
: GLAS DROP + ;
: GLASSES * + ;
: SLICE DROP + ;
: SLICES * + ;
: PIECE DROP + ;
: PIECES * + ;
: OZ DROP + ;
: OZES * + ;
: TBSP DROP + ; : TBSPS * + ;
: PKG DROP + ; : PKGS * + ;
: CUP DROP + ; : CUPS * + ;
: START 0 ; : OF ;
```

The words for the units perform the following task. Every word expects a number on the stack. The second item on the stack is the amount of calories, and the third item is the sum of calories totalled. The word GLAS drops the quantity and adds the calories. The word GLASSES multiplies the quantity with the amount of calories and adds the result to the sum.

```
SCR # 127

( AFB WEIGHTWATCHER  cntd   ef)
( CALORIES )
: BEER 255 ; : COCA-COLA 88 ;
: BREAD 100 ;
: BUTTER 100 ; : BROWNIES 224 ;
: RICE 200 ; : GOUDA 108 ;
: MUFFINS 118 ;
: LASAGNE 241 ; : RAVIOLI 210 ;
: BURITO 47 ;    : CNCHIPS 166 ;
: PEANUTS 179 ; : PTCHIPS 156 ;


: AMOUNT DUP . ;
```

In screen 127 the amount of calories for the various items of food is programmed. The program is started with the word START. This places a zero on the stack. The input of

BEER 2 GLASSES

places the numbers 255 and 2 on the stack, multiplies them and adds the result to the previous sum. The word AMOUNT duplicates the top of the stack and prints it on the screen. Figure 4-16 is the example for a continental breakfast.

```
START  ?
 OK
 OK
START OK
BUTTER 2 TBSPS OK
BREAD 3 SLICES OK
COCA-COLA 2 GLASSES OK
GOUDA 3 OZES OK
AMOUNT 1000 OK
MUFFINS 2 PIECES OK
AMOUNT 1236 OK
.SCRN
```

Figure 4-16: Example of Weightwatcher

4.22 Input/Output for a Mailing List

Screen 41 contains words for the input and output of a mailing list. The memory area starting at PAD is used as text buffer.

```
SCR # 41
( APF MAILING I/O               EF)
: CL ( NA) PAD + SWAP BLANKS ;
: TIN ( A) 13 WORD HERE COUNT
   ROT PAD + SWAP CMOVE ;
: NA 20 0 CL 0 TIN ;
: ST 15 20 CL 20 TIN ;
: CY 20 35 CL 35 TIN ;
: CT 2 55 CL 55 TIN ;
: ZP 5 57 CL 57 TIN ;
: (OUT) ( NA) PAD + SWAP
    -TRAILING TYPE ;
: TOUT CR 20 0 (OUT) CR  15 20
   (OUT) CR 20 35 (OUT) SPACE
   2 55 (OUT) SPACE 5 57 (OUT) ;
```

CL (na) writes n space characters beginning at address PAD+a. TIN (a) accepts text at HERE. After a RETURN this text is moved to PAD+a. NA is the word to enter the name. It is used in the form

NA JEROME D. MILLER

There is no RETURN between NA and JEROME. In the same way the street (ST), the city (CY), the country (CT) and the zip-code (ZP) are entered. There is no need for a special sequence. The words can be entered arbitrarily. (OUT) (na) prints n bytes beginning at address PAD+a. TOUT prints the whole address.

4.23 Cash Register

This is an example for the input and the formatted output of numbers.

```
SCR # 40
( APF  CASHREG                    EF)
 5 VARIABLE H
 : CU ( NN') CH  CV  ;
 : >S ( D-AN) <# # # 46 HOLD #S
     36 HOLD #> ;
 : .$ 2DUP >S DUP 34 SWAP -
        1 SWAP CU TYPE ;
 : CL H @ 1+ 0 CU 20 0 DO 32
   EMIT LOOP ;
 : ?FIN H @ 16 = IF 5 H ! THEN ;
 : ERA 1 H +! ?FIN CL H @ 2 CU ;
 : $ ( -D) 13 WORD HERE NUMBER
      D+ .$ ERA  QUIT ;
 : CASH HOME 1 2 CU ." CASH"
   0. .$ 5 0 CU ." INPUT" QUIT ;

OK
```

The word CU (nn') uses two APPLE specific words:

CV (n)
Places the cursor in the vertical position n. (0< =n< =23)

CH (n)
Places the cursor at the horizontal position n. (0< =n< =39)

>S (d-an) converts a double precision number into a string with a preceding $ sign and a decimal point. .$ prints the converted string with the decimal point always in line 1, column 34. CL clears the place for the next entry on the screen. The variable H is used to count the entries. ?FIN checks if 10 entries have been made. Then the value H is reset to 5. ERA increments H, checks the number of entries, clears the screen for the next input and places the cursor there. The word $ is used for the input of numbers. $ (d-d') accepts text at HERE. After RETURN this text is converted into a number and added to the previous sum. Then the sum is reconverted and printed. The word QUIT terminates the execution of a word without printing OK.

The word CASH opens the cash register. HOME (APPLE specific) clears the screen. The word CASH is printed, and a double precision zero is placed on the stack. After printing INPUT the word CASH is terminated.

4.24 Two Mathematic Examples

Scr # 42 shows two examples in mathematics.

The word LCD calculates the largest common divisor of two numbers A and B. It uses the algorithm of EUCLID. The remainder of A and B is determined by A B MOD. If it is zero, B is the largest common divisor. If R is not zero, A is set to B, and B is set to the remainder R. Then the modulo division is repeated as long as R is non-zero. Figure 4-18 shows the evaluation on the stack.

```
42 LIST
SCR # 42
( APF MATH EXAMPLES              EF)
: LCD ( NN') BEGIN SWAP OVER MOD
   DUP 0= UNTIL DROP . ;

4 VARIABLE #ROW
: TEST ( N-F) MOD 0= ;
: .PRIM ( N-N) DUP 4 .R #ROW @
   DUP 0= IF CR DROP 4 ELSE 1 -
   THEN #ROW ! ;
: PTEST ( N) DUP 2 / 2 DO DUP
   I TEST IF 0 LEAVE THEN LOOP
   DUP IF .PRIM ELSE DROP THEN
   DROP ;
: PRIM ( NN') CR 4 #ROW !
   DO I PTEST LOOP CR ;
```

STACK					TOS	INPUT
					27	27
				27	21	21
				27	21	BEGIN
				21	27	SWAP
			21	27	21	OVER
				21	6	MOD
			21	6	6	DUP
			21	6	0	0=
				21	6	UNTIL
				6	21	SWAP
			6	21	6	OVER
				6	3	MOD
			6	3	3	DUP
			6	3	0	0=
				6	3	UNTIL
				3	6	SWAP
			3	6	3	OVER
				3	0	MOD
			3	0	0	DUP
			3	0	1	0=
				3	0	UNTIL
					3	DROP

 Figure 4-18: LCD, Evaluation on the Stack

The next words calculate the prime numbers between two boundaries. TEST (nn'-f) tests if the result of a modulo division is zero. It leaves a flag on the stack. .PRIM (n-n) prints a prime number right-justified in a field with the width 4. Four numbers are printed in one row. For counting the variable # ROW is used. Figure 4-19 shows the output with the prime numbers between 1 and 200.

```
     200 0 PRIM
  1   3   5   7  11
 13  17  19  23  29
 31  37  41  43  47
 53  59  61  67  71
 73  79  83  89  97
101 103 107 109 113
127 131 137 139 149
151 157 163 167 173
179 181 191 193 197
199
```

Figure 4-19: Prime Numbers

The word PTEST (n) tests if within a loop the number n is divisible by the loop index. This loop starts with two and ends with the half of the number under test. If a remainder of zero is found, the loop is terminated with LEAVE.

LEAVE ( )
Terminates a loop at the next LOOP.

If TEST finds a remainder equal to zero, a zero is placed on the stack, and the loop is excited. With a zero on the stack the word .PRIM is not executed and the top of the stack is dropped.

PRIM (nn') prints the prime numbers between n' and n.

4.25 Language Translator

The words in screen # 43 and # 44 form a language translator.

```
SCR # 43
( APF LANGUAGE TRANSLATOT    EF)
: LIS <BUILDS 8 ALLOT DOES>
  SWAP 2 * + ;

LIS 'LIST

: EN ." HELLO " ;
' EN 0 'LIST !
: DE ." GUTEN TAG " ;
' DE 1 'LIST !
: IT ." BON GIORNO " ;
' IT 2 'LIST !
: FR ." BON JOUR " ;
' FR 3 'LIST !

 -->
```

The defining word LIS creates a class of words which makes a gap for four numbers in the vocabulary stack during compile time. In run time these words expect a number on the stack. This number is used as an index to store or to fetch a number.
With LIS the word 'LIST (address list) is defined. The word EN prints the message HELLO. The parameter-field address of EN is stored in 'LIST. This is also done with the words DE, IT and FR.

```
SCR # 44
( APF LANG. TRANSLATOR CNTD  EF)
0 CONSTANT ENGLISH
1 CONSTANT GERMAN
2 CONSTANT ITALIEN
3 CONSTANT FRENCH

: GREETINGS ( N) 'LIST @ 2 -
  EXECUTE ;
```

The four constants ENGLISH ... FRENCH have the value 0 to 3. The word GREETINGS (n) fetches the nth parameter-field address from 'LIST, calculates the code-field address and executes the word. Figure 4-20 shows the printout of the language translator.

```
ITALIEN GREETINGS BON GIORNO  OK
FRENCH GREETINGS BON JOUR  OK
GERMAN GREETINGS GUTEN TAG  OK
ENGLISH GREETINGS HELLO  OK
```

Figure 4-20: Printout Language Translator

4.26 Storing Records on Disk

Screen # 45 is an example how to store records on disk. This screen needs screen # 41, the input and output for a mailing list, also to be loaded into memory.

```
SCR # 45
( APF VIRTUAL MEMORY             EF)
10 CONSTANT START
64 CONSTANT RCLN
: #INDEX ( N-A) RCLN B/BUF */MOD
   START + BLOCK + ;
: FIRST# ( -A) 0 #INDEX ;
: +NR 1 FIRST# +! UPDATE ;
: !DISK PAD FIRST# @ #INDEX RCLN
   CMOVE UPDATE +NR ;
: @DISK ( N) #INDEX PAD RCLN
   CMOVE TOUT ;
: INIT 1 FIRST# ! UPDATE ;
: .CONTENT CR FIRST# @ DUP 1 =
   1 XOR IF 1 DO I @DISK CR LOOP
   THEN ;
: FINI FLUSH EMPTY-BUFFERS ;
OK
```

The constant START determines the number of the block where the first record is stored. The constant RCLN is the length of one record. This number should always be a number 2 to the power of n, with n>0 and n<9. The length of the record used in the mailing list is 64. The word #INDEX (n-a) calculates the address a in the disk buffer for the record n. The evaluation #INDEX is shown in FIGURE 4-21. Record number 15 is stored on disk.

		15	
	15	64	RCLN
15	64	256	B/BUF
	192	3	*/MOD
192	3	10	START
	192	13	+
	192	a	BLOCK
		192+a	+

Figure 4-21: Calculating the Address for Record Number 15

The word */MOD has the same definition as */, but it leaves also the remainder on the stack. The result of the calculation in Figure 4-21 shows that the record 15 is stored in block 13, 192 bytes beyond the starting address of this block. In the first two bytes of block 10 the number called FIRST# is stored. This number points to the next free record on disk. The word INIT stores a one in FIRST# and initializes a new list of records.

The word !DISK calculates the address for the next record in the disk buffer. Then it moves the text from PAD into the buffer, UPDATEs the buffer and increments FIRST# by one. The word @DISK (n) fetches record number n from disk and displays the contents on the screen. The word .CONTENT prints all records on the screen.

4.27 Messages and Errors

In FORTH the error messages are stored on disk. It is proposed to use screen #4 and #5 for these messages, but very often other screens are used. The word

?ERROR (fn)

expects a flag and a number on the stack. N is the line number of the error message. If f is zero, the program continues in the normal way. If f is one, the error message n is printed, and the word QUIT is executed. The following lines are an example:

```
: TEST ( N) 6 ?ERROR ;  OK
0 TEST  OK
1 TEST  TEST ? DISK OUT OF RANGE
```

Screen # 46 is another example how to use messages. The word UMSG (n) fetches a user message from Block 6. We use these messages in a number guessing game. In screen # 3 the messages

```
SCR # 46
( APF MESSAGES AND ERRORS     EF)
: UMSG ( N) 32 * 6 BLOCK +
  32 -TRAILING TYPE ;
0 VARIABLE RND 78 @ RND !
: RANDOM ( -U) RND @ 31421 *
   6972 + DUP RND ! ;
: RND# ( U-U') RANDOM U* SWAP
   DROP ;
: MAKE# ( -N) 99 RND# ;
: GUESS ( N'N-N') 2DUP = IF
   3 UMSG DROP ELSE 2DUP < IF
   2 UMSG ELSE 1 UMSG THEN THEN
   DROP ;
OK
```

```
SCR # 3
  0 ( APF USER MESSAGES                    EF)
  1 TOO SMALL
  2 TOO BIG
  3 THAT'S RIGHT
```

Lines 4 to 8 form a RANDOM NUMBER GENERATOR. The random number produced with RND# (u-u') is in the range 0< =u'< =u. MAKEgenerates a random number between 0 and 99. GUESS expects the random number and the guessing number on the stack and leaves the random number there. The two numbers are compared, and the appropriate message is printed on the screen.

4.28 Low Resolution Graphics

For low resolution graphics the following words are implemented (POWER FORTH):

GR ( )
Set low resolution graphics.

COLOR (n)
Get color n.

LPLOT (lc)
A point is plotted in line l and column c.

HLINE (cc'l)
A horizontal line is plotted from column c to c' at line l.

VLINE (ll'c)
A vertical line is plotted from line l to l' at column c.

SCRN (lc-n)
Get the color of the point at line l and column c.

TEXT ( )
Switch back to text.

The screens # 47 and # 48 contain two examples.

```
SCR # 47
( APF LOW RES GRAFICS        EF)
: RNDP GR BEGIN 15 RND# COLOR
   36 RND# 39 RND# LPLOT
   ?TERMINAL UNTIL TEXT HOME  ;
16 VARIABLE X 10 VARIABLE Y
: (KAL)  11 1 DO I DUP 1 DO
15 RND# COLOR
Y @ OVER - X @ I - LPLOT
Y @ OVER - X @ I + LPLOT
Y @ OVER + X @ I + LPLOT
Y @ OVER + X @ I - LPLOT
X @ OVER - Y @ I - SWAP LPLOT
X @ OVER - Y @ I + SWAP LPLOT
X @ OVER + Y @ I + SWAP LPLOT
X @ OVER + Y @ I - SWAP LPLOT
LOOP DROP LOOP ; -->
```

```
SCR # 48
( APF LOW RES CNTD            EF)
: KAL GR BEGIN (KAL) ?TERMINAL
   UNTIL TEXT HOME ;
```

The word RNDP uses the Random Number Generator and produces a random patter on the screen. The generation is stopped with any key. The word KAL produces a patter in form of a kaleidoscope.

4.29 High Resolution Graphics

For high resolution graphics the following words are defined (POWER FORTH):

HGR ( )
Set high resolution graphics.

WHITE ( )
Set color to white.

BLACK ( )
Set color to black.

PLOT (xy)
Plot point at x ,y. x = 0 and y = 0 are the upper left corner.

LINE (xy)
Draw line to x,y.

An example is shown in screen # 49. This program produces the ray-shaped pattern shown in Figure 4-22.

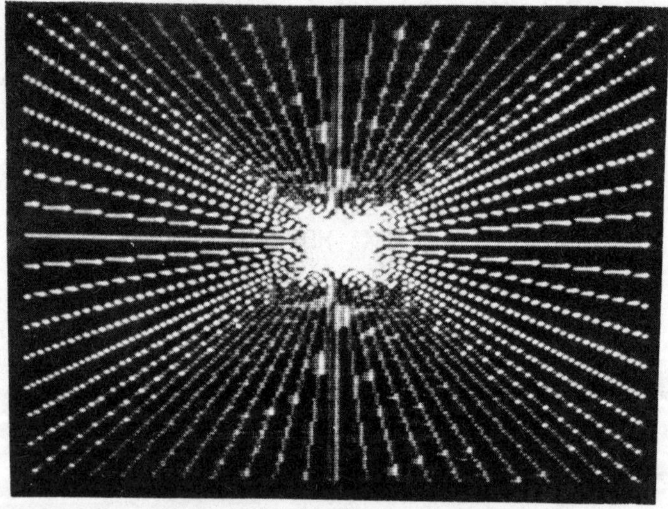

Figure 4-22: Ray-Shaped Pattern

The word PIC draws the picture. The word PIC2 first it draws the pattern with the color white and next with color black. The pattern appears and disappears.

```
SCR # 49
( APF HIGH RES GRAPHICS      EF)
200 VARIABLE X 10 VARIABLE Y
: CL HGR WHITE ;
: PL 100 80 PLOT ;
: ST 200 X ! 10 Y ! ;
: +X 10 X +! ; : -X -10 X +! ;
: +Y 10 Y +! ; : -Y -10 Y +! ;
: LI X @ Y @ LINE ;
: LL 20 0 DO PL LI -X LOOP ;
: DD 15 0 DO PL LI +Y LOOP ;
: RR 20 0 DO PL LI +X LOOP ;
: UU 15 0 DO PL LI -Y LOOP ;
: PIC CL PL ST LL DD RR UU ;
: (PI) LL DD RR UU ;
: PIC2 CL BEGIN WHITE (PI)
  BLACK (PI) ?TERMINAL UNTIL ;
```

With the words defined for high resolution grafics a simple TURTLE grafic is implemented. The trigonometric functions needed for this grafic are calculated from a SINE table. In screen # 75 and # 76 the SINE values for 0 degrees to 90 degrees are stored in steps of one degree. The scale factor is 10000. This means an accuracy of four digits. This is sufficient for the high resolution grafics.

```
SCR # 75
( TTG SIN-TAB                  EF)
: TABLE <BUILDS  DOES>
  SWAP 2 * + @ ;
   TABLE TSIN
0000 , 0175 , 0349 , 0523 ,
0698 , 0872 , 1045 , 1219 ,
1392 , 1564 , 1763 , 1908 ,
2079 , 2250 , 2419 , 2588 ,
2756 , 2924 , 3090 , 3256 ,
3420 , 3584 , 3746 , 3907 ,
4067 , 4226 , 4384 , 4540 ,
4695 , 4848 , 5000 , 5150 ,
5299 , 5446 , 5592 , 5736 ,
5878 , 6018 , 6157 , 6293 ,
6428 , 6561 , 6691 , 6820 ,
         -->
```

```
SCR # 76
( TTG SIN-TAB CNTD                    EF)
6947 , 7071 , 7193 , 7314 ,
7431 , 7547 , 7660 , 7771 ,
7880 , 7986 , 8090 , 8192 ,
8290 , 8387 , 8480 , 8572 ,
8660 , 8746 , 8829 , 8910 ,
8988 , 9063 , 9135 , 9205 ,
9272 , 9336 , 9397 , 9455 ,
9511 , 9563 , 9613 , 9659 ,
9703 , 9744 , 9781 , 9816 ,
9848 , 9877 , 9903 , 9925 ,
9945 , 9962 , 9976 , 9986 ,
9994 , 9998 , 10000 ,

( END SIN-TAB ) -->

```

```
SCR # 77
( TTG SIN COS                         EF)
: (SIN) ( N-N') DUP 90 >
  IF 180 SWAP - THEN TSIN  ;

: SIN ( N-N') 360 MOD DUP 0<
  IF 360 + THEN DUP 180 >
  IF 180 - (SIN) MINUS ELSE
  (SIN) THEN ;

: COS ( N-N') 360 MOD 90 + SIN ;





  -->

OK
```

The word SIN expects the number of degrees on the stack and leaves the SINE value modulo 10000 on the stack. The word COS does the same for the COSINE values.

In screens # 78 and # 79 the Turtle commands are defined. Two variables x and y are used. The starting values are x = 140 and y = 95. This is the middle of the screen. The word TURTLE initializes the turtle grafics and places the Turtle in the middle of the screen, looking to the right. The word TURN turns the direction of the Turtle. The word DRAW (n'n-n') draws a line of the length n in the direction n'. The direction n' stays on the stack. DRAWTO (n'n) turns the direction of the Turtle by n' degrees and draws a line of the length n. The unit of the length is one pixel. TPLOT plots a point at x,y, and GOTO (x,y) moves the Turtle to x,y without leaving a trail.

```
SCR # 78
( TTG COMMANDS                    EF)
  140 VARIABLE X  95 VARIABLE Y
: @XY X @ Y @ ;
: SI ( N'N-N") SWAP SIN 10000
  */ ;
: CO ( N'N-N") SWAP COS 10000
  */ ;
: TURTLE ( -N') 140 X ! 95 Y !
  HGR BLACK @XY PLOT 0 ;
: TURN ( N'-N") +  ;

: DRAW ( N'N-N') OVER SWAP
  DUP >R CO X +! DUP R>
  SI MINUS Y +! @XY LINE ;
: DRAWTO ( N'N) >R TURN R>
  DRAW ; -->
```

```
SCR # 79
( TTG COMMANDS CNTD               EF)
: TPLOT @XY PLOT ;
: GOTO ( XY) 95 SWAP - Y !
  140 SWAP + X ! TPLOT ;
```

The screens # 80 and # 81 contain some examples. With TI the Turtle is initialized to white. Figures 4-23 shows an example.

```
SCR # 80
( TTG                                    EF)
: SQUARE 4 0 DO 90 40 DRAWTO
  LOOP ;
: SQS 36 0 DO SQUARE 100 TURN
  40 DRAW LOOP ;
: SQ 0 DO 95 40 DRAWTO LOOP ;
: SQ1 36 0 DO SQUARE 10 TURN
  LOOP ;
```

```
SCR # 81
( TTG                                    EF)
: TI TURTLE WHITE TPLOT ;
: SQ2 60 0 DO 90 TURN 60 I -
  DRAW LOOP DROP ;
: SQ3 42 0 DO 92 TURN 60 I -
  DRAW LOOP DROP ;
: SQ4 30 -60 GOTO 8 0 DO
  45 TURN 60 DRAW LOOP DROP ;
: SQ5 30 -60 GOTO 60 0 DO
  47 TURN 60 I - DRAW LOOP
  DROP ;
```

Figure 4-23: Example

4.30 An Example for a DBMS System

The screens # 51 to # 56 contain an example for a Data Base Management System. A record of data is 128 bytes long. 64 bytes are used for four keywords with 16 characters and 64 bytes are used for text.

With the word INPUT the keywords and the text are entered into PAD and stored on disk. Screen # 53 is the same screen as screen # 45. Only the word TOUT was changed to (OUT). The word SEARCH searches for a given set of keywords. An example: The program is used to catalog programs and files on disk. The keywords have the following mening

KEYWORD 1 NAME OF THE PROGRAM
KEYWORD 2 CHARACTERISTIC 1
KEYWORD 3 CHARACTERISTIC 2
KEYWORD 4 CHARACTERISTIC 3

For Example:

FOURIER-ANALYSIS
BASIC
MATHEMATICAL
GRAFIC

TEXT: STORED ON DISK # 11

With

SEARCH
KEYWORD 1
KEYWORD 2 BASIC
KEYWORD 3 MATH
KEYWORD 4

all BASIC programs concerning mathematics are searched and

displayed on the screen. The word MATH is followed by one space. This is the delimiter used by (COMP$) (aa'c-f). This word compares two strings starting at address a and a' until the delimiter c is found in the string at address a. The flag f is one if the strings are equal.

```
SCR # 51
( DBMS  START                          EF)
: DESCR 0 VARIABLE -2 ALLOT ;
DESCR KEYW 4 , 16 ,
: 2@ ( A-D) DUP 2 + @ SWAP @ ;
KEYW 2@ DROP CONSTANT L
KEYW 2@ SWAP DROP CONSTANT F
KEYW 2@ * 64 + CONSTANT RCLN
: VEC <BUILDS 2 * ALLOT
     DOES> SWAP 2 * + ;
5 VEC #WO
: DUP2 ( N-NN) DUP DUP ;
: .MSG ( N) ." KEYWORD " . ;
: STORE ( NN') 1 - * PAD + SWAP
    EXPECT ;
: CLRP PAD RCLN 32 FILL ;
  -->
```

```
SCR # 52
( DBMS CNTD                            EF)
: (IN) HOME CR CLRP
   KEYW 2@ 1+ 1 DO I .MSG DUP2 I
   STORE CR LOOP DROP ;
: (OUT) F 1+ 1 DO CR I .MSG L
DUP I 1 - * PAD + SWAP TYPE LOOP
 CR ." TEXT:" PAD 64 + 64 TYPE ;
 : (COMP$) ( AA'C-F)
   BEGIN ROT DUP C@ >R OVER I =
    R> SWAP DUP IF 0 ELSE DROP
    >R ROT DUP C@ R> = DUP2 THEN
    WHILE 2DROP 1+ >R 1+ R> ROT
    REPEAT >R 2DROP 2DROP R> ;
: (MOV) PAD RCLN + RCLN ;
: <MOVE (MOV) PAD SWAP CMOVE ;
: MOVE> PAD (MOV) CMOVE ; -->
```

```
SCR # 53
( APF VIRTUAL MEMORY              EF)
10 CONSTANT START
: #INDEX ( N-A) RCLN B/BUF */MOD
   START + BLOCK + ;
: FIRST# ( -A) 0 #INDEX ;
: +NR 1 FIRST# +! UPDATE ;
: !DISK PAD FIRST# @ #INDEX RCLN
   CMOVE UPDATE +NR ;
: @DISK ( N) #INDEX PAD RCLN
   CMOVE (OUT) ;
: INIT 1 FIRST# ! UPDATE ;
: .CONTENT CR FIRST# @ DUP 1 =
   1 XOR IF 1 DO I @DISK CR LOOP
   THEN ;
: FINI FLUSH EMPTY-BUFFERS ;
       -->
OK
```

```
SCR # 54
( DBMS CNTD                       EF)
0 VARIABLE WO 1 VARIABLE #NR
0 VARIABLE #F 0 VARIABLE BO
: .ENTRY MOVE> #NR @ @DISK
   KEY DROP <MOVE ;
: LOOK KEYW 2@ 1+ 1 DO DUP I 1 -
  * PAD + @ 0 = IF 0 ELSE 1 THEN
  I #WO ! LOOP ;
: GOON 1 #NR ! ;
: #WO>#F F 1+ 1 DO I #WO @ IF
    I #F ! LEAVE THEN LOOP ;
: #F>WO #F @ 1 - L * WO ! ;
: WHAT CLRP (IN) LOOK #WO>#F
   #F>WO GOON ;
: COMP$ ( -F) PAD WO @ + #NR @
 #INDEX WO @ + 32 (COMP$) ; -->
OK
```

```
SCR # 55
( DBMS CNTD                              EF)
: NIL ." END OF LIST" ;
: NEXT ( N-NF) L WO +! 1+ DUP
   F 1+ = ;
: MUST ( N-NF) DUP #WO @ 0= ;
: ((SEARCH)) 1 BO +! #F @ BEGIN
   NEXT IF BO @ IF .ENTRY THEN
   0 ELSE MUST IF 1 ELSE COMP$
   THEN THEN 1 = WHILE REPEAT
   0 BO ! #F>WO ;
: (SAVE) FIRST# @ 8 MOD 0= IF
   FINI THEN ;
: (SEARCH) ( NN') DO I #NR !
   COMP$ DUP IF ((SEARCH))
   THEN LOOP ;
   -->

SCR # 56
( DBMS CNTD                              EF)
: FIN ( -F) FIRST# @ 1 - #NR
   @ = ;
: SEARCH WHAT FIRST# @ 1
   (SEARCH) FIN IF NIL THEN ;
: INTEX PAD 64 + 64 EXPECT ;

: INPUT (IN) ." TEXT:" 13 INTEX
  !DISK ;

: RUN HOME ." INPUT" CR
  ." SEARCH" CR ." .CONTENT" CR
  ." FINI" ;
```

Some other words used in the DBMS program: DESCR <NA-ME> creates an entry in the dictionary with <NAME>. The pointer HERE is reset to the code-field address. Starting at this address, the data is stored. Searching for a set of keywords, the program first Looks for what kind of keywords it has to search. This is marked in the vector # WO. The search starts with the first entry. If a match is found, the program searches with ((SE-ARCH)) for another match of keywords of the same entry. If all keywords are found, the word .ENTRY prints the contents on the screen. The contents of PAD are moved up with MOVE>, the entry is fetched from the disk and printed, and PAD is restored for further searching.

This program is used only as an example. For a real program some improvements must be made e.g. erasing an entry, stop printing if the screen is full etc.

Final remark:

FORTH is not easy to learn. But after a short time of experience, the time needed for writing application programs decreases considerably.

In this section only the most common words are mentioned. In Appendix F a FORTH WORD GLOSSARY is printed.

5 Appendix

Commands	symb. Code	Operation	UNM	ABS	ABS,X	ABS,Y	Z0	Z0,X	Z0,Y	(IND,X)	(IND),Y	REL	IND	ACCU	IMPL	N	Z	C	1	D	V
			Adressing modes													condition codes					
Transport	LDA	M → A	A9	AD	BD	B9	A5	B5		A1	B1					X	X	–	–	–	–
	LDX	M → X	A2	AE		BE	A6		B6							X	X	–	–	–	–
	LDY	M → Y	A0	AC	BC		A4	B4								X	X	–	–	–	–
	STA	A → M		8D	9D	99	85	95		81	91					–	–	–	–	–	–
	STX	X → M		8E			86		96							–	–	–	–	–	–
	STY	Y → M		8C			84	94								–	–	–	–	–	–
	TAX	A → X													AA	X	X	–	–	–	–
	TAY	A → Y													A8	X	X	–	–	–	–
	TXA	X → A													8A	X	X	–	–	–	–
	TYA	Y → A													98	X	X	–	–	–	–
	TXS	X → S													9A	–	–	–	–	–	–
	TSX	S → X													BA	X	X	–	–	–	–
	PLA	S+1 → S, Ms → A													68	X	X	–	–	–	–
	PHA	A → Ms, S–1 → S													48	–	–	–	–	–	–
	PLP	S+1 → S, Ms → P													28						
	PHP	P → Ms, S–1 → S													08	–	–	–	–	–	–
arithmetic-	ADC	A+M+C → A	69	6D	7D	79	65	75		61	71					X	X	X	–	–	X
	SBC	A–M–$\overline{C}$ → A	E9	ED	FD	F9	E5	F5		E1	F1					X	X	X	–	–	X
	INC	M+1 → M		EE	FE		E6	F6								X	X	–	–	–	–
	DEC	M–1 → M		CE	DE		C6	D6								X	X	–	–	–	–
	INX	X+1 → X													E8	X	X	–	–	–	–
	DEX	X–1 → X													CA	X	X	–	–	–	–
	INY	Y+1 → Y													C8	X	X	–	–	–	–
	DEY	Y–1 → Y													88	X	X	–	–	–	–
logic-	AND	A ∧ M → A	29	2D	3D	39	25	35		21	31					X	X	–	–	–	–
	ORA	A V M → A	09	0D	1D	19	05	15		01	11					X	X	–	–	–	–
	EOR	A ⊻ M → A	49	4D	5D	59	45	55		41	51					X	X	–	–	–	–
compare-	CMP	A–M	C9	CD	DD	D9	C5	D5		C1	D1					X	X	X	–	–	–
	CPX	X–M	E0	EC			E4									X	X	X	–	–	–
	CPY	Y–M	C0	CC			C4									X	X	X	–	–	–
	BIT	A ∧ M		2C			24									7	X	–	–	–	6
branch-	BCC	BRANCH ON C=0									90					–	–	–	–	–	–
	BCS	BRANCH ON C=1									B0					–	–	–	–	–	–
	BEQ	BRANCH ON Z=1									F0					–	–	–	–	–	–
	BNE	BRANCH ON Z=0									D0					–	–	–	–	–	–
	BMI	BRANCH ON N=1									30					–	–	–	–	–	–
	BPL	BRANCH ON N=0									10					–	–	–	–	–	–
	BVC	BRANCH ON V=0									50					–	–	–	–	–	–
	BVS	BRANCH ON V=1									70					–	–	–	–	–	–
	JMP		4C										6C			–	–	–	–	–	–
	JSR		20													–	–	–	–	–	–
SHIFT-	ASL			0E	1E		06	16						0A		X	X	X	–	–	–
	LSR			4E	5E		46	56						4A		0	X	X	–	–	–
	ROL			2E	3E		26	36						2A		X	X	X	–	–	–
	ROR			6E	7E		66	76						6A		X	X	X	–	–	–
Status-Register	CLC	C=0													18	–	–	0	–	–	–
	CLD	D=0													D8	–	–	–	–	0	–
	CLI	I=0													58	–	–	–	0	–	–
	CLV	V=0													B8	–	–	–	–	–	0
	SEC	C=1													38	–	–	1	–	–	–
	SED	D=1													F8	–	–	–	–	1	–
	SEI	I=1													78	–	–	–	1	–	–
Misc.	NOP	NO OPER													EA	–	–	–	–	–	–
	RTS	RETURN F. SUB													60	–	–	–	–	–	–
	RTI	RETURN F. INT													40						
	BRK	BREAK													00	–	–	–	1	–	–

Table A-1: The Commands of the 6502 CPU

LSD \ MSD	0	1	2	3	4	5	6	7	8	9	A	B	C	D	E	F
0	0	1	2	3	4	5	6	7	8	9	10	11	12	13	14	15
1	16	17	18	19	20	21	22	23	24	25	26	27	28	29	30	31
2	32	33	34	35	36	37	38	39	40	41	42	43	44	45	46	47
3	48	49	50	51	52	53	54	55	56	57	58	59	60	61	62	63
4	64	65	66	67	68	69	70	71	72	73	74	75	76	77	78	79
5	80	81	82	83	84	85	86	87	88	89	90	91	92	93	94	95
6	96	97	98	99	100	101	102	103	104	105	106	107	108	109	110	111
7	112	113	114	115	116	117	118	119	120	121	122	123	124	125	126	127

Table A-2: Forward Branch

LSD \ MSD	0	1	2	3	4	5	6	7	8	9	A	B	C	D	E	F
8	128	127	126	125	124	123	122	121	120	119	118	117	116	115	114	113
9	112	111	110	109	108	107	106	105	104	103	102	101	100	99	98	97
A	96	95	94	93	92	91	90	89	88	87	86	85	84	83	82	81
B	80	79	78	77	76	75	74	73	72	71	70	69	68	67	66	65
C	64	63	62	61	60	59	58	57	56	55	54	53	52	51	50	49
D	48	47	46	45	44	43	42	41	40	39	38	37	36	35	34	33
E	32	31	30	29	28	27	26	25	24	23	22	21	20	19	18	17
F	16	15	14	13	12	11	10	9	8	7	6	5	4	3	2	1

Table A-3: Backward Branch

LSD	MSD	0 000	1 001	2 010	3 011	4 100	5 101	6 110	7 111
0	0000	NUL	DLE	SP	0	@	P		p
1	0001	SOH	DC1	!	1	A	Q	a	q
2	0010	STX	DC2	"	2	B	R	b	r
3	0011	ETX	DC3	#	3	C	S	c	s
4	0100	EOT	DC4	$	4	D	T	d	t
5	0101	ENQ	NAK	%	5	E	U	e	u
6	0110	ACK	SYN	&	6	F	V	f	v
7	0111	BEL	ETB	'	7	G	W	g	w
8	1000	BS	CAN	(	8	H	X	h	x
9	1001	HT	EM	)	9	I	Y	i	y
A	1010	LF	SUB	*	:	J	Z	j	z
B	1011	VT	ESC	+	;	K	[	k	{
C	1100	FF	FS	,	<	L	\	l	|
D	1101	CR	GS	–	=	M	]	m	}
E	1110	SO	RS	•	>	N	↑	n	~
F	1111	SI	VS	/	?	O	←	o	DEL

Table A-4: ASCII Character Codes

Logical Functions

0	0	0
0	1	0
1	0	0
1	1	1

AND

0	0	0
0	1	1
1	0	1
1	1	1

OR

0	0	1
0	1	0
1	0	0
1	1	1

XOR

0	1
1	0

NOT

Table A-5: Logical Functions

Naming Conventions:

!NAME	Store into NAME	!DISK
#NAME	Quantity, Size	#POINTS
'NAME	Address of NAME	'S
(NAME)	Subroutine used in NAME	(FIND)
*NAME	Multiplication Scaling Factor	*SIZE
+NAME	Increment	+LOOP
	Switch on	
-NAME	Decrement	-TRAILING
	Switch off	
	Reverse Boolean	-DUP
/NAME	Division	
	Unsigned Counting per	/LOOP
1NAME	First Element in a Quantity	1SWITCH
2NAME	Second element in a Quantity	
:NAME	Start of a Definition	
;NAME	End of a Definition	
<NAME	Less than NAME	
	Direction	<MOVE
<NAME>	Service Routine for an Externel Device	
>NAME	To Destination NAME	>TAPE
	Direction	
?NAME	Question	
	Question with Error Code	?ERROR
@NAME	Fetch NAME	
CNAME	One Byte Long	C!
DNAME	Double Length	
UNAME	Unsigned Operation	
[NAME]	Compile Time Behavior	

Table A-6: Naming Conventions

FORTH-GLOSSARY

STACK MANIPULATION

DUP	(n-nn)	Duplicate the top of the stack.
DROP	(n)	Throw away the top element of the stack.
SWAP	(nn'-n'n)	Reverse the two top elements.
OVER	(nn'-nn'n)	Copy second element on top of the stack.
ROT	(nn1n2-n1n2n)	Rotate the top three elements counterclockwise.
>R	(n)	Move top element to the return stack.
R>	(-n)	Retrieve top element from the return stack.
R	(-n)	Copy top element of return stack to parameter stack

ARITHMETIC AND LOGICAL

+	(nn'-n1)	n1=n+n'
-	(nn'-n1)	n1=n-n'
*	(nn'-n1)	n1=n*n'
/	(nn'-n1)	n1=n/n'
*/	(n1n2n3-n)	n=n1*n2/n3 with double precision intermediate.
MOD	(nn'-n1)	n1 remainder of n/n'.
/MOD	(nn'-n1n2)	n1 remainder, n2 qoutient of n/n'.
*/MOD	(n1n2n3-nn')	n remainder, n' quotient of n1*n2/n3.
MINUS	(n- -n)	Change sign.
MAX	(nn'-n1)	n1=n if n>n' else n1=n'.
MIN	(nn'-n1)	n1=n if n<n' else n1=n'.
ABS	(n-n')	n' absolute of n.
D+	(dd'-d1)	d1=d+d' double precision addition.
DMINUS	(d-d')	Change sign.
DABS	(d-d')	d' absolute of d.
AND	(nn'-n1)	Logical AND bitwise.
OR	(nn'-n1)	Logical OR bitwise.
XOR	(nn'-n1)	Logical XOR bitwise.

CONTROL STRUCTURES

DO...LOOP		
DO	(nn')	Loops from n' to n-1, loop increment is one.
DO...+LOOP		
DO	(nn')	Loops from n' to n-1.
+LOOP	(n)	Loop increment is n (may be negative).
I	(n)	Put loop index on the stack, same as R.
LEAVE	( )	Terminate loop at next LOOP or +LOOP.
IF <words> THEN (ENDIF)		

IF	(f)	If f is not zero, <words> are executed.
IF <wordsl> ELSE <words2> THEN (ENDIF)		
IF	(f)	If f is not zero, <wordsl> are executed, else <words2>.
BEGIN <words> UNTIL (END)		
UNTIL (END)	(f)	<words> are repeated until f is non zero.
BEGIN <wordsl> WHILE <words2> REPEAT		
WHILE	(f)	If f is zero, program continues after REPEAT, else unconditional branch back from REPEAT to BEGIN.

MEMORY

@	(a-n)	Fetch content from address a and a+1.
C@	(a-b)	Fetch byte from address a.
!	(na)	Store n in address a and a+1.
C!	(ba)	Store byte b in address a.
?	(a)	Print content of address a and a+1.
+!	(na)	Add n to the content of address a and a+1.
CMOVE	(aa'n)	Move n bytes from a to a'. a+n<a'<a.
FILL	(anb)	Store n bytes b into memeory starting at address a.
ERASE	(an)	Store n ASCII 0 into memeory starting at address a.
BLANKS	(an)	Store n ASCII 32 into memory starting at address a.
,	(n)	Store n on top of dictionary. Add two to HERE.
C,	(b)	Store b on top of dictionary. Add one to HERE.
ALLOT	(n)	Leave gap of n bytes on top of dictionary.

COMPARSION

<	(nn'-f)	f=l, if n<n'.
>	(nn'-f)	f=l, if n>n'.
=	(nn'-f)	f=l, if n=n'.
0<	(n-f)	f=l, if n<0.
0=	(n-f)	f=l, if n=0.

NUMBER BASES

DECIMAL	( )	Set decimal base.
HEX	( )	Set hexadecimal base.
BASE	(-a)	Variable, contains number base.

INPUT-OUTPUT

.	(n)	Print n.
." xxx"	( )	Print message xxx. Message ends with " .
.R	(nn')	Print n, rightjustified in field. Fieldwidth is n'.
D.	(d)	Print double precision number d.
D.R	(dn)	Print d rightjustified in field. Fieldwidth is n.
U.	(n)	Print n as unsigned number u.
EMIT	(c)	Print ASCII character c.
TYPE	(an)	Print n bytes starting at address a.
KEY	(-c)	Get character from keyboard.
?TERMINAL	(-f)	f=1, if BREAK key was pressed.
EXPECT	(an)	Expects n bytes at address a.
WORD	(c)	Read characters from the input buffer until delimiter c is found.
COUNT	(a-a'n)	Change length byte at address a to a'=a+1 and length n. Ready for TYPE.

NUMBER FORMATTING

<#	( )	Start converting a number to a string.
#	( )	Convert one digit and add it to the string.
#S	( )	Convert remaining digits.
#>	(an)	End of conversion. Puts starting address a and length n on the stack. Ready for TYPE.
HOLD	(c)	Inserts the ASCII character into the string.
SIGN	(n)	Inserts sign of n into the string.
NUMBER	(a-d)	Convert a string at address a+1 to a double precision number. The length of the sring must be stored at address a.

DEFINING WORDS

: xxx	( )	Begin of a colon definition.
;	( )	End of a colon definition.
VARIABLE <name>	(n)	Create variable <name> with the initial value n.
<name>	(a)	The address a of the variable is put on the stack.
CONSTANT <name>	(n)	Create a constant <name> with the value n.
<name>	(n)	The value n of the constant is returned.
<BUILDS <words1> DOES> <words2>		Used to create a new defining word. <words1> are executed during compile time. <words2> are executed during run time.
CREATE <name>	( )	Creates an entry <name> into the vocabulary. The codefield address of <name> is the parameter field address.

Word	Stack	Description
VOCABULARIES		
CONTEXT	(a)	Returns address of CONTEXT vocabulary. This is searched first.
CURRENT	(a)	Returns address of CURRENT vocabulary. New definitions are put here.
FORTH	( )	Main FORTH vocabulary.
VOCABULARY <name>	( )	Opens new vocabulary. Sets CURRENT to <name>.
DEFINITIONS	( )	Sets CONTEXT to CURRENT.
VLIST	( )	Print all words.
FORGET <name>	( )	Forget all definitions back and including <name>.
' <name>	(a)	Get parameter field address of <name>.
DISK		
LIST	(n)	List content of text screen n.
LOAD	(n)	Compile text screen n into dictionary.
BLOCK	(n-a)	Read block n.
EMPTY-BUFFERS	( )	Erase all disk buffers.
UPDATE	( )	Mark last buffer accessed.
FLUSH	( )	Save all updated disk buffers.
INDEX	(nn')	List all first lines of text screens n to n'.
SOME VARIABLES		
DP	(-a)	Dictionary pointer. Contains the first free memory location on top of the vocabulary.
HERE	(-n)	Fetches DP.
PAD	(-a)	Scratch buffer PAD. 68 bytes above HERE.
TIB	(-a)	Terminal input buffer.
IN	(-n)	Offset to terminal input buffer.
S0	(-a)	Contains the initial address of the parameter stack.
SP@	(-a)	Fetch content of S0.
BLK	(-a)	Contains current block number.
SCR	(-a)	Contains current screen number.
B/BUF	(-n)	Constant, gives block size in bytes.

Table A-7: FORTH Word Set

Acknowledgement

The author wishes to thank W. BAUER for contributing the programs:

Keyword-File
Graphic 1
Maze

and WOLFGANG F. HAHN for contributing the program

Lunar Phase.

Also thanks to EDWARD WAGNER for the proofreading of this book.

☐ ALL PROGRAMS ON DISK US$19.95

☐ BARE BOARD, USED IN 3.10 US$19.95

☐ POWER-FORTH FOR APPLE US$39.00
(incl.Editor, HGR, LGR, Turtle-Grafic)

Use this sheet as order form.

This photo shows the populated board.

____

Name Please print

____

Address

____

City State/Country Code

Mail it to one of these addresses:

ELCOMP PUBLISHING, INC.
53 Redrock Lane
Pomona, CA 91766
USA
Phone: (714) 623-8314
Telex: 29 81 91

ELCOMP Computer (S) Pte. Ltd.
89 Short Street
Unit 03-07, Golden Wall Auto Centre
SINGAPORE 0718
Phone: 3382623, 3388228
Telex: 56516

Ing.W. Hofacker GmbH
Tegernseerstr. 18
D-8150 Holzkirchen
West-Germany
Phone: 08024 / 73 31
Telex: 52 69 73

PAYMENT: check, money order, VISA, MASTER CARD, Eurocheck, ACCESS, Interbank
Prepaid orders add $3.50 for shipping (USA)
$5.00 handling for C.O.D.
All orders outside USA: add 15 % shipping, California residents add 6.5 % sales tax.

Versatile Interface Adapter (VIA)

Synertek INCORPORATED

SY6522
SY6522A

MICROPROCESSOR PRODUCTS

Preliminary

APRIL 1979

- Two 8-Bit Bidirectional I/O Ports
- Two 16-Bit Programmable Timer/Counters
- Serial Data Port
- Single +5V Power Supply
- TTL Compatible
- CMOS Compatible Peripheral Control Lines
- Expanded "Handshake" Capability Allows Positive Control of Data Transfers Between Processor and Peripheral Devices
- Latched Output and Input Registers
- 1 MHz and 2 MHz Operation

The SY6522 Versatile Interface Adapter (VIA) is a very flexible I/O control device. In addition, this device contains a pair of very powerful 16-bit interval timers, a serial-to-parallel/parallel-to-serial shift register and input data latching on the peripheral ports. Expanded handshaking capability allows control of bi-directional data transfers between VIA's in multiple processor systems.

Control of peripheral devices is handled primarily through two 8-bit bi-directional ports. Each line can be programmed as either an input or an output. Several peripheral I/O lines can be controlled directly from the interval timers for generating programmable frequency square waves or for counting externally generated pulses. To facilitate control of the many powerful features of this chip, an interrupt flag register, an interrupt enable register and a pair of function control registers are provided.

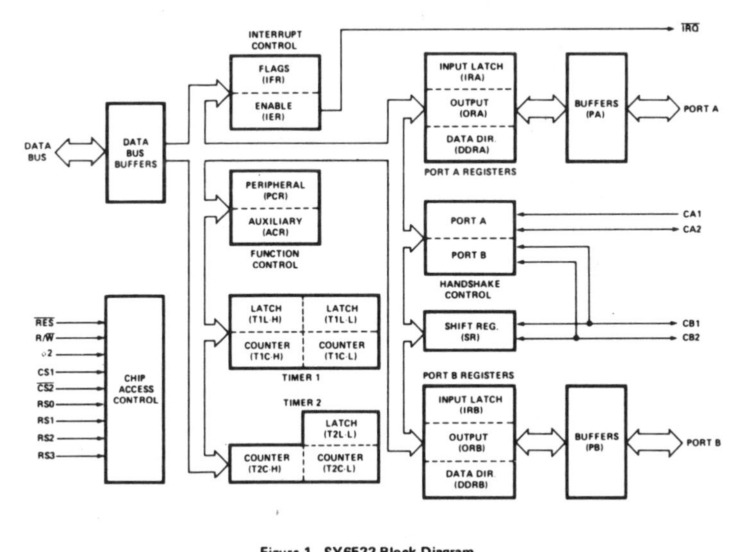

Figure 1. SY6522 Block Diagram

ABSOLUTE MAXIMUM RATINGS

Rating	Symbol	Value	Unit
Supply Voltage	V_{CC}	-0.3 to +7.0	V
Input Voltage	V_{IN}	-0.3 to +7.0	V
Operating Temperature Range	T_A	0 to +70	°C
Storage Temperature Range	T_{stg}	-55 to +150	°C

This device contains circuitry to protect the inputs against damage due to high static voltages. However, it is advised that normal precautions be taken to avoid application of any voltage higher than maximum rated voltages.

ELECTRICAL CHARACTERISTICS (V_{CC} = 5.0V ± 5%, T_A = 0–70°C unless otherwise noted)

Symbol	Characteristic	Min.	Max.	Unit
V_{IH}	Input High Voltage (all except φ2)	2.4	V_{CC}	V
V_{CH}	Clock High Voltage	2.4	V_{CC}	V
V_{IL}	Input Low Voltage	-0.3	0.4	V
I_{IN}	Input Leakage Current – V_{IN} = 0 to 5 Vdc R/$\overline{W}$, $\overline{RES}$, RS0, RS1, RS2, RS3, CS1, $\overline{CS2}$, CA1, Φ2	–	±2.5	μA
I_{TSI}	Off-state Input Current – V_{IN} = .4 to 2.4V V_{CC} = Max, D0 to D7	–	±10	μA
I_{IH}	Input High Current – V_{IH} = 2.4V PA0–PA7, CA2, PB0–PB7, CB1, CB2	-100	–	μA
I_{IL}	Input Low Current – V_{IL} = 0.4 Vdc PA0–PA7, CA2, PB0–PB7, CB1, CB2	–	-1.6	mA
V_{OH}	Output High Voltage V_{CC} = min, I_{load} = -100 μAdc PA0–PA7, CA2, PB0–PB7, CB1, CB2	2.4	–	V
V_{OL}	Output Low Voltage V_{CC} = min, I_{load} = 1.6 mAdc	–	0.4	V
I_{OH}	Output High Current (Sourcing) V_{OH} = 2.4V V_{OH} = 1.5V (PB0–PB7)	 -100 -1.0	 – –	 μA mA
I_{OL}	Output Low Current (Sinking) V_{OL} = 0.4 Vdc	1.6	–	mA
I_{OFF}	Output Leakage Current (Off state) $\overline{IRQ}$	–	10	μA
C_{IN}	Input Capacitance – T_A = 25°C, f = 1 MHz (R/$\overline{W}$, $\overline{RES}$, RS0, RS1, RS2, RS3, CS1, $\overline{CS2}$, D0-D7, PA0-PA7, CA1, CA2, PB0-PB7) (CB1, CB2) (Φ2 Input)	 – – –	 7.0 10 20	 pF pF pF
C_{OUT}	Output Capacitance – T_A = 25°C, f = 1 MHz	–	10	pF
P_D	Power Dissipation	–	700	mW

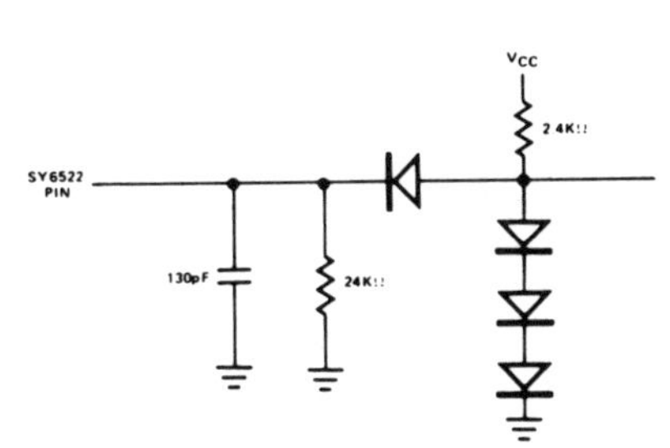

Figure 2. Test Load (for all Dynamic Parameters)

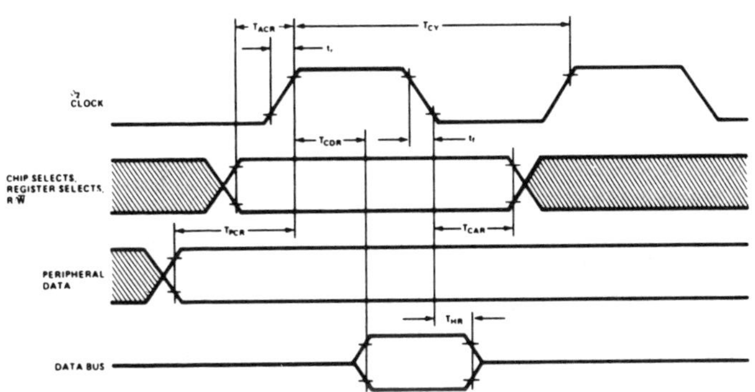

Figure 3. Read Timing Characteristics

READ TIMING CHARACTERISTICS (FIGURE 3)

Symbol	Parameter	SY6522		SY6522A		Unit
		Min.	Max.	Min.	Max.	
T_{CY}	Cycle Time	1	50	0.5	50	μs
T_{ACR}	Address Set-Up Time	180	–	90	–	ns
T_{CAR}	Address Hold Time	0	–	0	–	ns
T_{PCR}	Peripheral Data Set-Up Time	300	–	300	–	ns
T_{CDR}	Data Bus Delay Time	–	395	–	200	ns
T_{HR}	Data Bus Hold Time	10	–	10	–	ns

NOTE: tr, tf = 10 to 30ns.

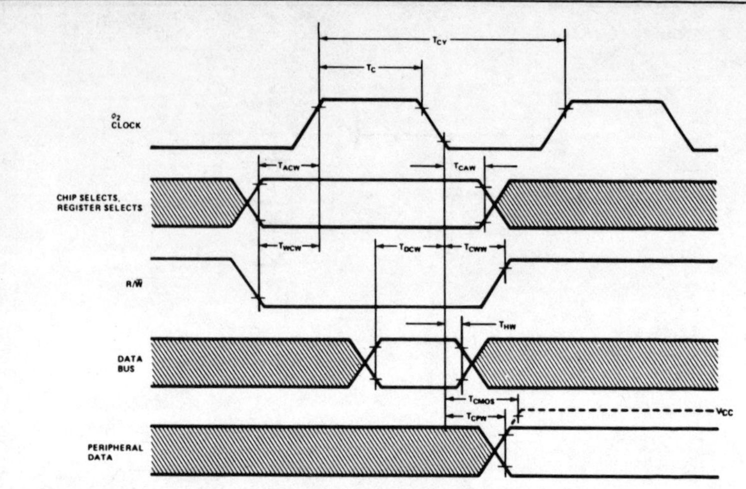

Figure 4. Write Timing Characteristics

WRITE TIMING CHARACTERISTICS (FIGURE 4)

Symbol	Parameter	SY6522		SY6522A		Unit
		Min.	Max.	Min.	Max.	
T_{CY}	Cycle Time	1	50	0.50	50	μs
T_C	φ2 Pulse Width	0.47	25	0.25	25	μs
T_{ACW}	Address Set-Up Time	180	–	90	–	ns
T_{CAW}	Address Hold Time	0	–	0	–	ns
T_{WCW}	R/W̄ Set-Up Time	180	–	90	–	ns
T_{CWW}	R/W̄ Hold Time	0	–	0	–	ns
T_{DCW}	Data Bus Set-Up Time	300	–	150	–	ns
T_{HW}	Data Bus Hold Time	10	–	10	–	ns
T_{CPW}	Peripheral Data Delay Time	–	1.0	–	1.0	μs
T_{CMOS}	Peripheral Data Delay Time to CMOS Levels	–	2.0	–	2.0	μs

NOTE: tr, tf = 10 to 30ns.

PERIPHERAL INTERFACE CHARACTERISTICS

Symbol	Characteristic	Min.	Max.	Unit	Figure
t_r, t_f	Rise and Fall Time for CA1, CB1, CA2, and CB2 Input Signals	–	1.0	μs	–
T_{CA2}	Delay Time, Clock Negative Transition to CA2 Negative Transition (read handshake or pulse mode)	–	1.0	μs	5a, 5b
T_{RS1}	Delay Time, Clock Negative Transition to CA2 Positive Transition (pulse mode)	–	1.0	μs	5a
T_{RS2}	Delay Time, CA1 Active Transition to CA2 Positive Transition (handshake mode)	–	2.0	μs	5b
T_{WHS}	Delay Time, Clock Positive Transition to CA2 or CB2 Negative Transition (write handshake)	–	1.0	μs	5c, 5d
T_{DS}	Delay Time, Peripheral Data Valid to CB2 Negative Transition	0	1.5	μs	5c, 5d
T_{RS3}	Delay Time, Clock Positive Transition to CA2 or CB2 Positive Transition (pulse mode)	–	1.0	μs	5c
T_{RS4}	Delay Time, CA1 or CB1 Active Transition to CA2 or CB2 Positive Transition (handshake mode)	–	2.0	μs	5d
T_{IL}	Set-up Time, Peripheral Data Valid to CA1 or CB1 Active Transition (input latching)	300	–	ns	5e
T_{SR1}	Shift-Out Delay Time – Time from ϕ_2 Falling Edge to CB2 Data Out	–	300	ns	5f
T_{SR2}	Shift-In Setup Time – Time from CB2 Data In to ϕ_2 Rising Edge	300	–	ns	5g
T_{IPW}	Pulse Width – PB6 Input Pulse	2	–	μs	5i
T_{ICW}	Pulse Width – CB1 Input Clock	2	–	μs	5h
I_{IPS}	Pulse Spacing – PB6 Input Pulse	2	–	μs	5i
I_{ICS}	Pulse Spacing – CB1 Input Pulse	2	–	μs	5h

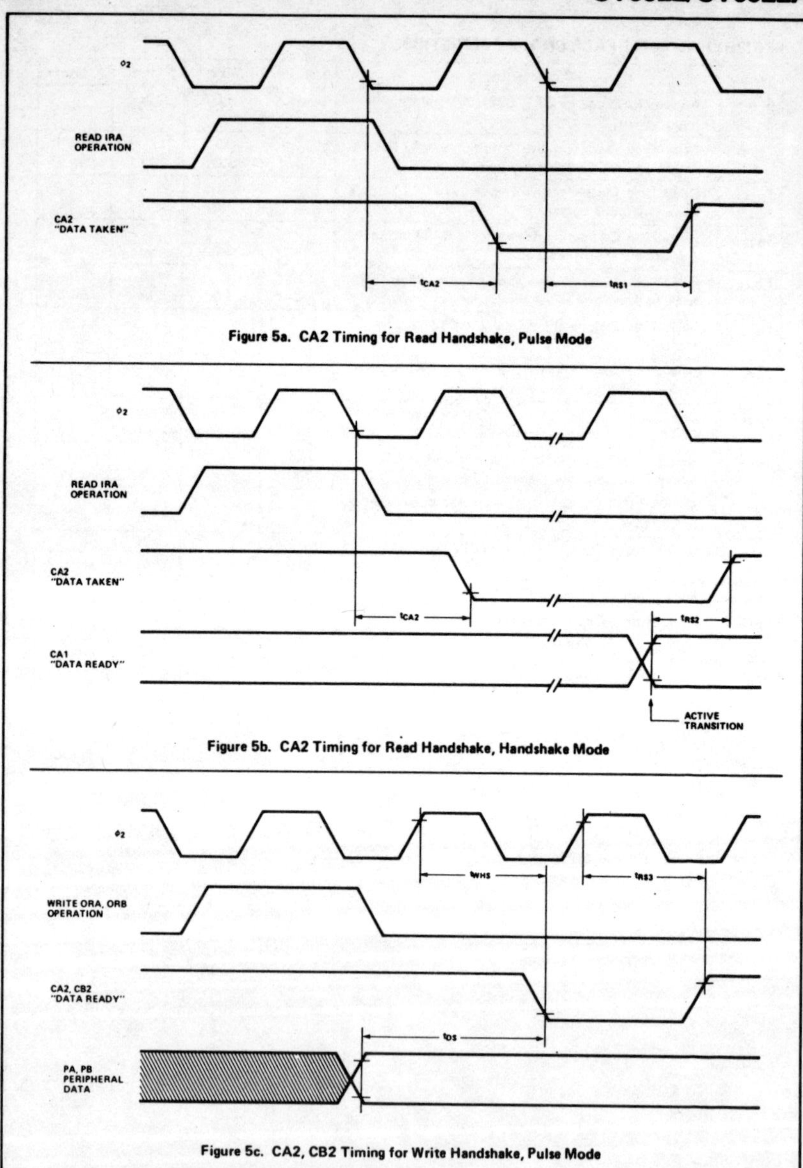

Figure 5a. CA2 Timing for Read Handshake, Pulse Mode

Figure 5b. CA2 Timing for Read Handshake, Handshake Mode

Figure 5c. CA2, CB2 Timing for Write Handshake, Pulse Mode

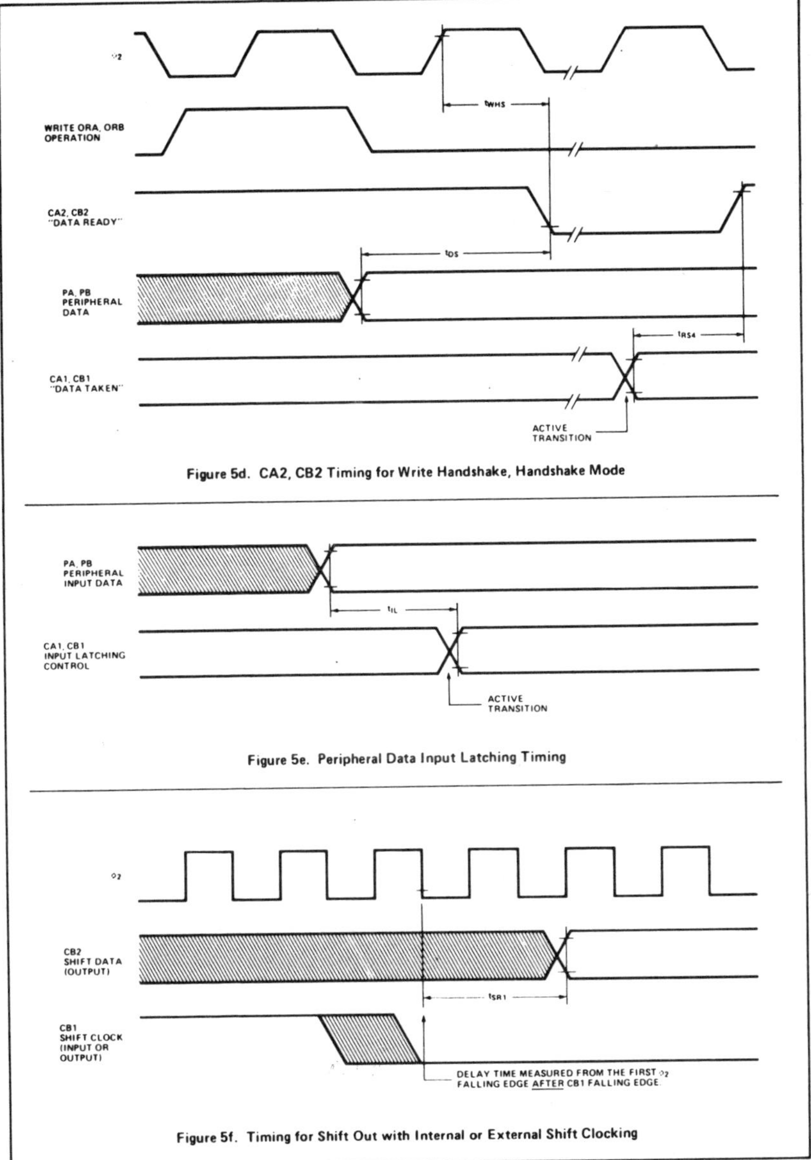

Figure 5d. CA2, CB2 Timing for Write Handshake, Handshake Mode

Figure 5e. Peripheral Data Input Latching Timing

Figure 5f. Timing for Shift Out with Internal or External Shift Clocking

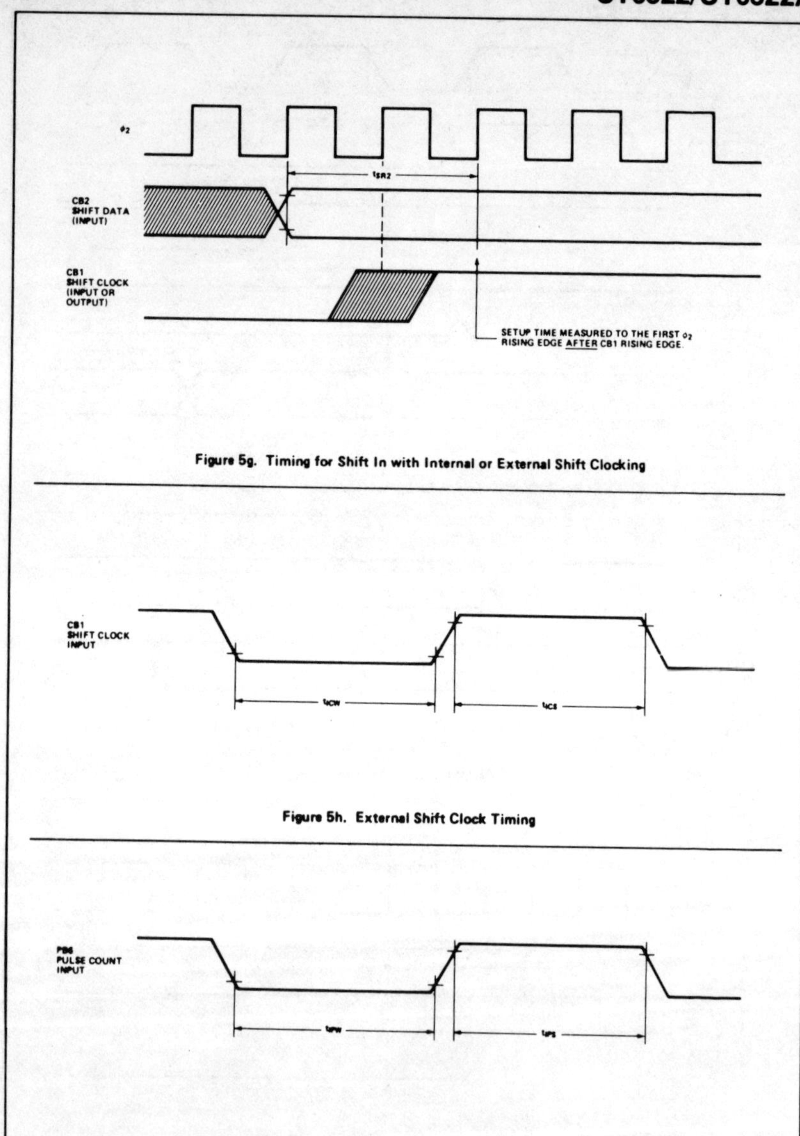

Figure 5g. Timing for Shift In with Internal or External Shift Clocking

Figure 5h. External Shift Clock Timing

Figure 5i. Pulse Count Input Timing

responding bit of the Output Register. A 1 in the Output Register causes the output to go high, and a "0" causes the output to go low. Data may be written into Output Register bits corresponding to pins which are programmed as inputs. In this case, however, the output signal is unaffected.

Reading a peripheral port causes the contents of the Input Register (IRA, IRB) to be transferred onto the Data Bus. With input latching disabled, IRA will always reflect the levels on the PA pins. With input latching enabled, IRA will reflect the levels on the PA pins at the time the latching occurred (via CA1).

The IRB register operates similar to the IRA register. However, for pins programmed as outputs there is a difference. When reading IRA, the level on the pin determines whether a 0 or a 1 is sensed. When reading IRB, however, the bit stored in the output register, ORB, is the bit sensed. Thus, for outputs which have large loading effects and which pull an output "1" down or which pull an output "0" up, reading IRA may result in reading a "0" when a "1" was actually programmed, and reading a "1" when a "0" was programmed. Reading IRB, on the other hand, will read the "1" or "0" level actually programmed, no matter what the loading on the pin.

Figures 9, 10, and 11 illustrate the formats of the port registers. In addition, the input latching modes are selected by the Auxiliary Control Register (Figure 16.)

Handshake Control of Data Transfers

The SY6522 allows positive control of data transfers between the system processor and peripheral devices

REG 0 – ORB/IRB

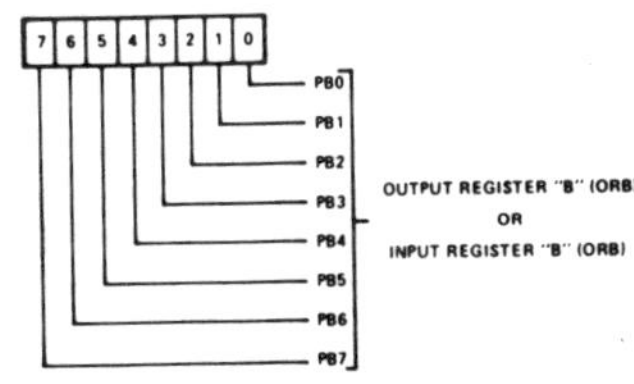

Pin Data Direction Selection	WRITE	READ
DDRB = "1" (OUTPUT)	MPU writes Output Level (ORB)	MPU reads output register bit in ORB. Pin level has no affect.
DDRB = "0" (INPUT) (Input latching disabled)	MPU writes into ORB, but no effect on pin level, until DDRB changed.	MPU reads input level on PB pin.
DDRB = "0" (INPUT) (Input latching enabled)		MPU reads IRB bit, which is the level of the PB pin at the time of the last CB1 active transition.

Figure 9. Output Register B (ORB), Input Register B (IRB)

REG 1 – ORA/IRA

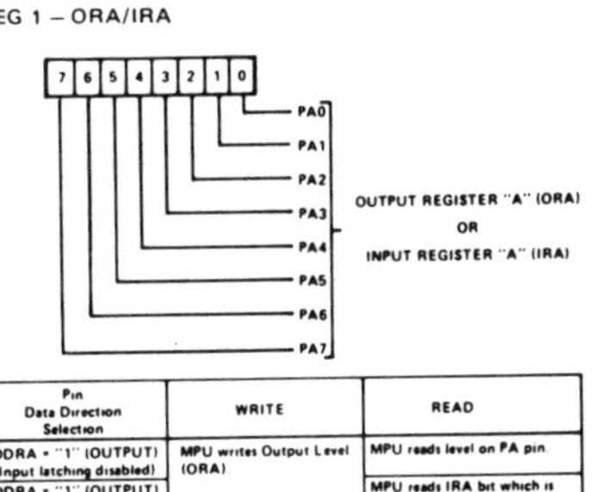

Pin Data Direction Selection	WRITE	READ
DDRA = "1" (OUTPUT) (Input latching disabled)	MPU writes Output Level (ORA)	MPU reads level on PA pin.
DDRA = "1" (OUTPUT) (Input latching enabled)		MPU reads IRA bit which is the level of the PA pin at the time of the last CA1 active transition.
DDRA = "0" (INPUT) (Input latching disabled)	MPU writes into ORA, but no effect on pin level, until DDRA changed.	MPU reads level on PA pin.
DDRA = "0" (INPUT) (Input latching enabled)		MPU reads IRA bit which is the level of the PA pin at the time of the last CA1 active transition.

Figure 10. Output Register A (ORA), Input Register A (IRA)

REG 2 (DDRB) AND REG 3 (DDRA)

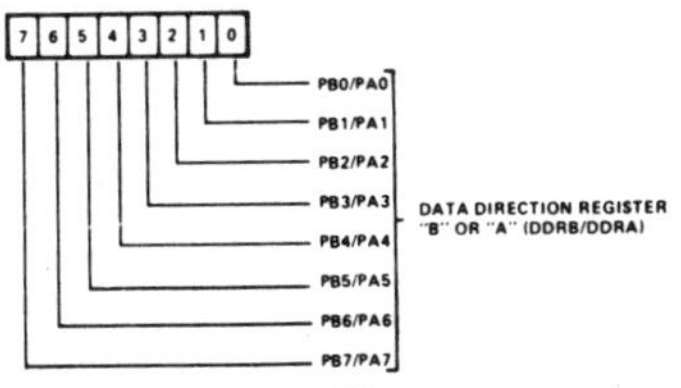

"0" ASSOCIATED PB/PA PIN IS AN INPUT (HIGH-IMPEDANCE)

"1" ASSOCIATED PB/PA PIN IS AN OUTPUT, WHOSE LEVEL IS DETERMINED BY ORB/ORA REGISTER BIT

Figure 11. Data Direction Registers (DDRB, DDRA)

through the operation of "handshake" lines. Port A lines (CA1, CA2) handshake data on both a read and a write operation while the Port B lines (CB1, CB2) handshake on a write operation only.

Read Handshake

Positive control of data transfers from peripheral devices into the system processor can be accomplished very effectively using Read Handshaking. In this case, the peripheral device must generate the equivalent of a "Data Ready" signal to the processor signifying that valid data is present on the peripheral port. This signal normally interrupts the processor, which then reads the data, causing generation of a "Data Taken" signal. The peripheral device responds by making new data available. This process continues until the data transfer is complete.

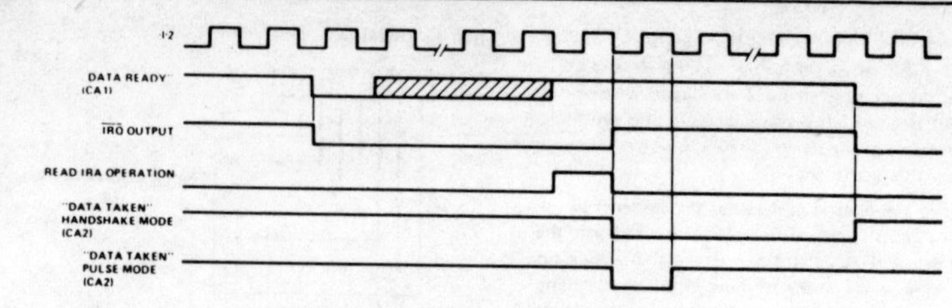

Figure 12. Read Handshake Timing (Port A, Only)

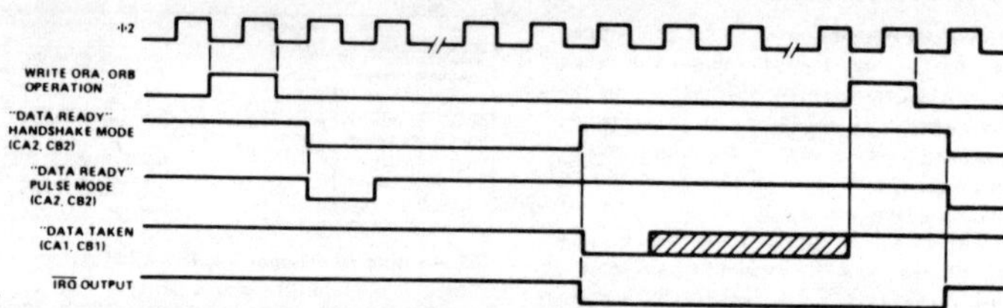

Figure 13. Write Handshake Timing

In the SY6522, automatic "Read" Handshaking is possible on the Peripheral A port only. The CA1 interrupt input pin accepts the "Data Ready" signal and CA2 generates the "Data Taken" signal. The "Data Ready" signal will set an internal flag which may interrupt the processor or which may be polled under program control. The "Data Taken" signal can either be a pulse or a level which is set low by the system processor and is cleared by the "Data Ready" signal. These options are shown in Figure 12 which illustrates the normal Read Handshaking sequence.

Write Handshake

The sequence of operations which allows handshaking data from the system processor to a peripheral device is very similar to that described for Read Handshaking. However, for Write Handshaking, the SY6522 generates the "Data Ready" signal and the peripheral device must respond with the "Data Taken" signal. This can be accomplished on both the PA port and the PB port on the SY6522. CA2 or CB2 act as a "Data Ready" output in either the handshake mode or pulse mode and CA1 or CB1 accept the "Data Taken" signal from the peripheral device, setting the interrupt flag and cleaning the "Data Ready" output. This sequence is shown in Figure 13.

Selection of operating modes for CA1, CA2, CB1, and CB2 is accomplished by the Peripheral Control Register (Figure 14).

Timer Operation

Interval Timer T1 consists of two 8-bit latches and a 16-bit counter. The latches are used to store data which is to be loaded into the counter. After loading, the counter decrements at $\phi 2$ clock rate. Upon reaching zero, an interrupt flag will be set, and $\overline{IRQ}$ will go low if the interrupt is enabled. The timer will then disable any further interrupts, or will automatically transfer the contents of the latches into the counter and will continue to decrement. In addition, the timer may be programmed to invert the output signal on a peripheral pin each time it "times-out". Each of these modes is discussed separately below.

The T1 counter is depicted in Figure 15 and the latches in Figure 16.

REG 12 – PERIPHERAL CONTROL REGISTER

7	6	5	4	3	2	1	0

Bits 7, 6, 5: CB2 CONTROL

7	6	5	OPERATION
0	0	0	INPUT NEGATIVE ACTIVE EDGE
0	0	1	INDEPENDENT INTERRUPT INPUT NEG EDGE
0	1	0	INPUT POSITIVE ACTIVE EDGE
0	1	1	INDEPENDENT INTERRUPT INPUT-POS EDGE
1	0	0	HANDSHAKE OUTPUT
1	0	1	PULSE OUTPUT
1	1	0	LOW OUTPUT
1	1	1	HIGH OUTPUT

Bit 4: CB1 INTERRUPT CONTROL

0 = NEGATIVE ACTIVE EDGE
1 = POSITIVE ACTIVE EDGE

Bits 3, 2, 1: CA2 CONTROL

3	2	1	OPERATION
0	0	0	INPUT-NEGATIVE ACTIVE EDGE
0	0	1	INDEPENDENT INTERRUPT INPUT-NEG EDGE
0	1	0	INPUT-POSITIVE ACTIVE EDGE
0	1	1	INDEPENDENT INTERRUPT INPUT-POS EDGE
1	0	0	HANDSHAKE OUTPUT
1	0	1	PULSE OUTPUT
1	1	0	LOW OUTPUT
1	1	1	HIGH OUTPUT

Bit 0: CA1 INTERRUPT CONTROL

0 = NEGATIVE ACTIVE EDGE
1 = POSITIVE ACTIVE EDGE

Figure 14. CA1, CA2, CB1, CB2 Control

Two bits are provided in the Auxiliary Control Register (bits 6 and 7) to allow selection of the T1 operating modes. The four possible modes are depicted in Figure 17.

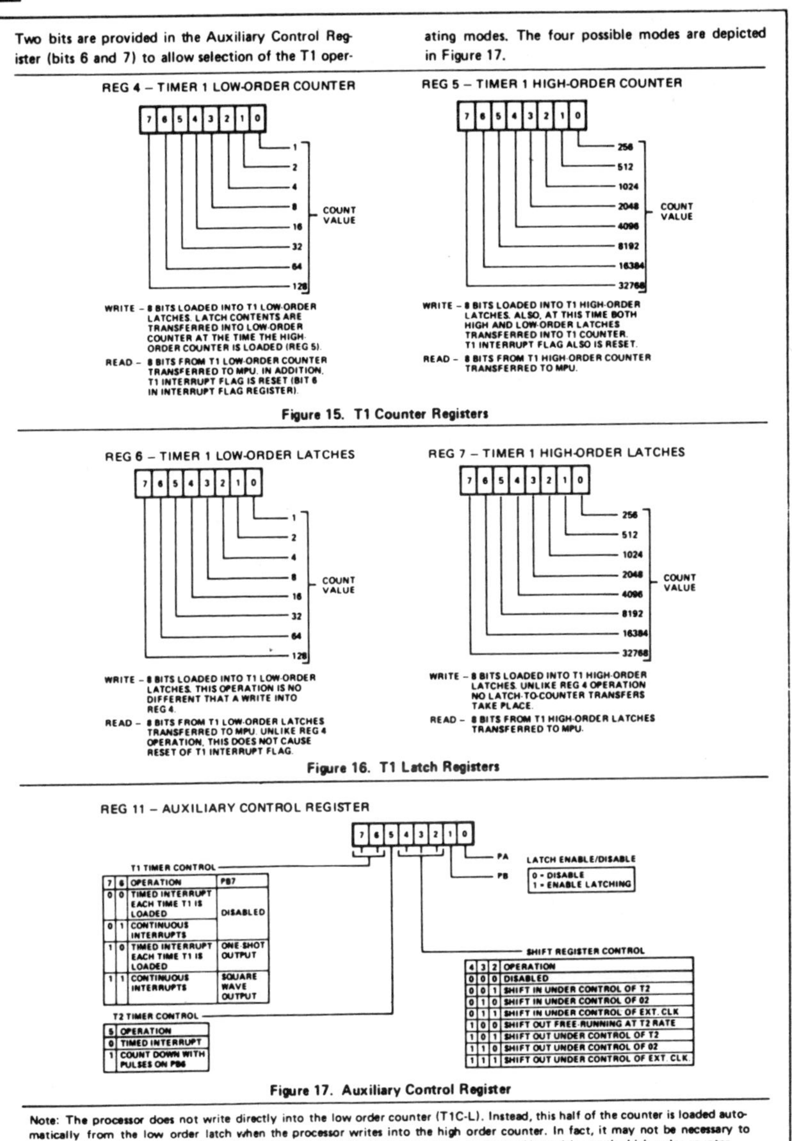

Figure 15. T1 Counter Registers

Figure 16. T1 Latch Registers

T1 TIMER CONTROL

7	6	OPERATION	PB7
0	0	TIMED INTERRUPT EACH TIME T1 IS LOADED	DISABLED
0	1	CONTINUOUS INTERRUPTS	
1	0	TIMED INTERRUPT EACH TIME T1 IS LOADED	ONE-SHOT OUTPUT
1	1	CONTINUOUS INTERRUPTS	SQUARE WAVE OUTPUT

T2 TIMER CONTROL

5	OPERATION
0	TIMED INTERRUPT
1	COUNT DOWN WITH PULSES ON PB6

SHIFT REGISTER CONTROL

4	3	2	OPERATION
0	0	0	DISABLED
0	0	1	SHIFT IN UNDER CONTROL OF T2
0	1	0	SHIFT IN UNDER CONTROL OF 02
0	1	1	SHIFT IN UNDER CONTROL OF EXT. CLK
1	0	0	SHIFT OUT FREE-RUNNING AT T2 RATE
1	0	1	SHIFT OUT UNDER CONTROL OF T2
1	1	0	SHIFT OUT UNDER CONTROL OF 02
1	1	1	SHIFT OUT UNDER CONTROL OF EXT. CLK.

Figure 17. Auxiliary Control Register

Note: The processor does not write directly into the low order counter (T1C-L). Instead, this half of the counter is loaded automatically from the low order latch when the processor writes into the high order counter. In fact, it may not be necessary to write to the low order counter in some applications since the timing operation is triggered by writing to the high order counter.

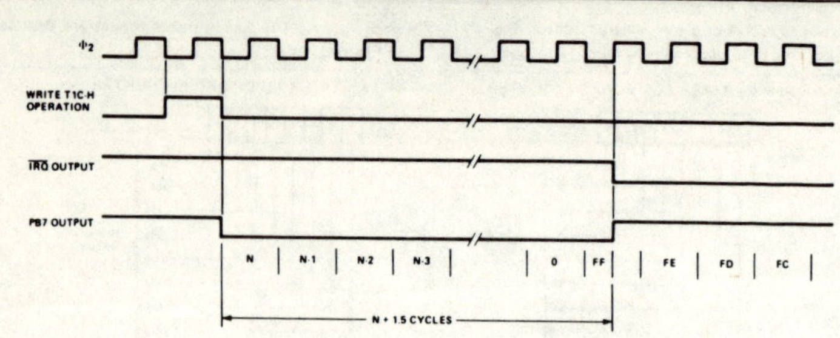

Figure 18. Timer 1 and Timer 2 One-Shot Mode Timing

Timer 1 One-Shot Mode

The interval timer one-shot mode allows generation of a single interrupt for each timer load operation. As with any interval timer, the delay between the "write T1C-H" operation and generation of the processor interrupt is a direct function of the data loaded into the timing counter. In addition to generating a single interrupt, Timer 1 can be programmed to produce a single negative pulse on the PB7 peripheral pin. With the output enabled (ACR7=1) a "write T1C-H" operation will cause PB7 to go low. PB7 will return high when Timer 1 times out. The result is a single programmable width pulse.

In the one-shot mode, writing into the high order latch has no effect on the operation of Timer 1. However, it will be necessary to assure that the low order latch contains the proper data before initiating the count-down with a "write T1C-H" operation. When the processor writes into the high order counter, the T1 interrupt flag will be cleared, the contents of the low order latch will be transferred into the low order counter, and the timer will begin to decrement at system clock rate. If the PB7 output is enabled, this signal will go low on the phase two following the write operation. When the counter reaches zero, the T1 interrupt flag will be set, the $\overline{IRQ}$ pin will go low (interrupt enabled), and the signal on PB7 will go high. At this time the counter will continue to decrement at system clock rate. This allows the system processor to read the contents of the counter to determine the time since interrupt. However, the T1 interrupt flag cannot be set again unless it has been cleared as described in this specification.

Timing for the SY6522 interval timer one-shot modes is shown in Figure 18.

Timer 1 Free-Run Mode

The most important advantage associated with the latches in T1 is the ability to produce a continuous series of evenly spaced interrupts and the ability to produce a square wave on PB7 whose frequency is not affected by variations in the processor interrupt response time. This is accomplished in the "free-running" mode.

In the free-running mode, the interrupt flag is set and the signal on PB7 is inverted each time the counter reaches zero. However, instead of continuing to decrement from zero after a time-out, the timer automatically transfers the contents of the latch into the counter (16 bits) and continues to decrement from there. The interrupt flag can be cleared by writing T1C-H, by reading T1C-L, or by writing directly into the flag as described later. However, it is not necessary to rewrite the timer to enable setting the interrupt flag on the next time-out.

All interval timers in the SY6522 are "re-triggerable". Rewriting the counter will always re-initialize the time-out period. In fact, the time-out can be prevented completely if the processor continues to rewrite the timer before it reaches zero. Timer 1 will operate in this manner if the processor writes into the high order counter (T1C-H). However, by loading the latches only, the processor can access the timer during each down-counting operation without affecting the time-out in process. Instead, the data loaded into the latches will determine the length of the next time-out period. This capability is particularly valuable in the free-running mode with the output enabled. In this mode, the signal on PB7 is inverted and the interrupt flag is set with each time-out. By responding to the interrupts with new data for the latches, the processor can determine the period of the next half cycle during each half cycle of the output signal on PB7. In this manner, very complex waveforms can be generated. Timing for the free-running mode is shown in Figure 19.

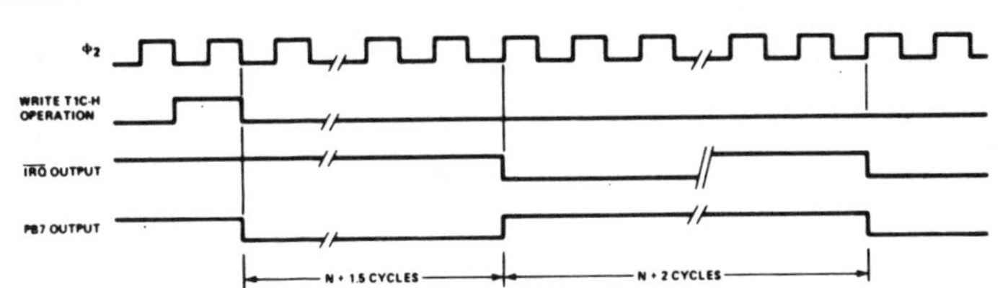

Note: A precaution to take in the use of PB7 as the timer output concerns the Data Direction Register contents for PB7. Both DDRB bit 7 and ACR bit 7 must be 1 for PB7 to function as the timer output. If one is 1 and the other is 0, then PB7 functions as a normal output pin, controlled by ORB bit 7.

Figure 19. Timer 1 Free-Run Mode Timing

Timer 2 Operation

Timer 2 operates as an interval timer (in the "one-slot" mode only), or as a counter for counting negative pulses on the PB6 peripheral pin. A single control bit is provided in the Auxiliary Control Register to select between these two modes. This timer is comprised of a "write-only" low-order latch (T2L-L), a "read-only" low-order counter and a read/write high order counter. The counter registers act as a 16-bit counter which decrements at Φ2 rate. Figure 20 illustrates the T2 Counter Registers.

Timer 2 One-Shot Mode

As an interval timer, T2 operates in the "one-shot" mode similar to Timer 1. In this mode, T2 provides a single interrupt for each "write T2C-H" operation. After timing out, the counter will continue to decrement. However, setting of the interrupt flag will be disabled after initial time-out so that it will not be set by the counter continuing to decrement through zero. The processor must rewrite T2C-H to enable setting of the interrupt flag. The interrupt flag is cleared by reading T2C-L or by writing T2C-H. Timing for this operation is shown in Figure 18.

REG 8 – TIMER 2 LOW-ORDER COUNTER

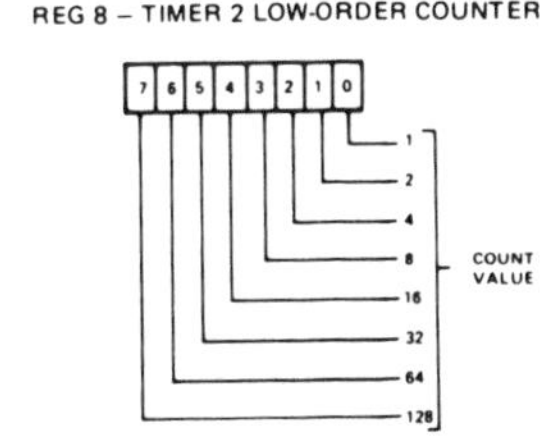

WRITE – 8 BITS LOADED INTO T2 LOW ORDER LATCHES
READ – 8 BITS FROM T2 LOW ORDER COUNTER TRANSFERRED TO MPU. T2 INTERRUPT FLAG IS RESET

REG 9 – TIMER 2 HIGH-ORDER COUNTER

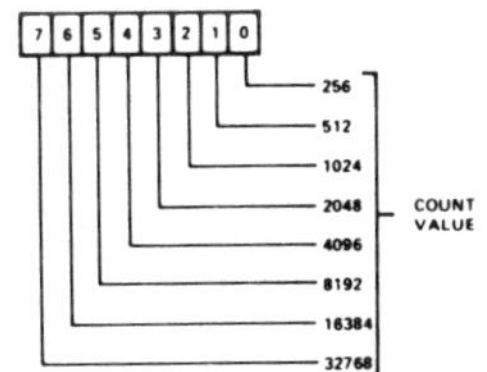

WRITE – 8 BITS LOADED INTO T2 HIGH ORDER COUNTER. ALSO, LOW ORDER LATCHES TRANSFERRED TO LOW ORDER COUNTER. IN ADDITION, T2 INTERRUPT FLAG IS RESET
READ – 8 BITS FROM T2 HIGH ORDER COUNTER TRANSFERRED TO MPU

Figure 20. T2 Counter Registers

Timer 2 Pulse Counting Mode

In the pulse counting mode, T2 serves primarily to count a predetermined number of negative-going pulses on PB6. This is accomplished by first loading a number into T2. Writing into T2C-H clears the interrupt flag and allows the counter to decrement each time a pulse is applied to PB6. The interrupt flag will be set when T2 reaches zero. At this time the counter will continue to decrement with each pulse on PB6. However, it is necessary to rewrite T2C-H to allow the interrupt flag to set on subsequent down-counting operations. Timing for this mode is shown in Figure 21. The pulse must be low on the leading edge of $\Phi 2$.

Shift Register Operation

The Shift Register (SR) performs serial data transfers into and out of the CB2 pin under control of an internal modulo-8 counter. Shift pulses can be applied to the CB1 pin from an external source or, with the proper mode selection, shift pulses generated internally will appear on the CB1 pin for controlling external devices.

The control bits which select the various shift register operating modes are located in the Auxiliary Control Register. Figure 22 illustrates the configuration of the SR data bits and the SR control bits of the ACR.

Figures 23 and 24 illustrate the operation of the various shift register modes.

Interrupt Operation

Controlling interrupts within the SY6522 involves three principal operations. These are flagging the interrupts, enabling interrupts and signaling to the processor that an active interrupt exists within the chip. Interrupt flags are set by interrupting conditions which exist within the chip or on inputs to the chip. These flags normally remain set until the interrupt has been serviced. To determine the source of an interrupt, the microprocessor must examine these flags in order from highest to lowest priority. This is accomplished by reading the flag register into the processor accumulator, shifting this register either right or left and then using conditional branch instructions to detect an active interrupt.

Associated with each interrupt flag is an interrupt enable bit. This can be set or cleared by the processor to enable interrupting the processor from the corresponding interrupt flag. If an interrupt flag is set to a logic 1 by an interrupting condition, and the corresponding interrupt enable bit is set to a 1, the Interrupt Request Output ($\overline{IRQ}$) will go low. $\overline{IRQ}$ is an "open-collector" output which can be "wire-or'ed" with other devices in the system to interrupt the processor.

In the SY6522, all the interrupt flags are contained in one register. In addition, bit 7 of this register will be read as a logic 1 when an interrupt exists within the chip. This allows very convenient polling of several devices within a system to locate the source of an interrupt.

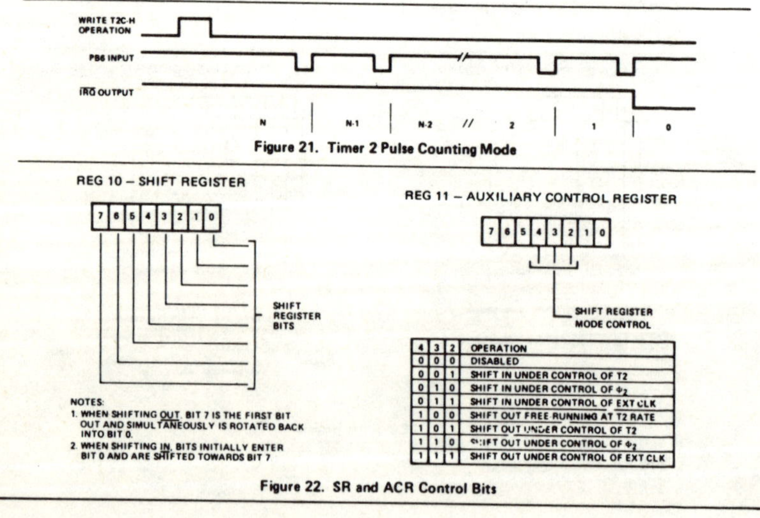

Figure 21. Timer 2 Pulse Counting Mode

4	3	2	OPERATION
0	0	0	DISABLED
0	0	1	SHIFT IN UNDER CONTROL OF T2
0	1	0	SHIFT IN UNDER CONTROL OF Φ_2
0	1	1	SHIFT IN UNDER CONTROL OF EXT CLK
1	0	0	SHIFT OUT FREE-RUNNING AT T2 RATE
1	0	1	SHIFT OUT UNDER CONTROL OF T2
1	1	0	SHIFT OUT UNDER CONTROL OF Φ_2
1	1	1	SHIFT OUT UNDER CONTROL OF EXT CLK

Figure 22. SR and ACR Control Bits

SR Disabled (000)

The 000 mode is used to disable the Shift Register. In this mode the microprocessor can write or read the SR, but the shifting operation is disabled and operation of CB1 and CB2 is controlled by the appropriate bits in the Peripheral Control Register (PCR). In this mode the SR Interrupt Flag is disabled (held to a logic 0).

Shift in Under Control of T2 (001)

In the 001 mode the shifting rate is controlled by the low order 8 bits of T2. Shift pulses are generated on the CB1 pin to control shifting in external devices. The time between transitions of this output clock is a function of the system clock period and the contents of the low order T2 latch (N).

The shifting operation is triggered by writing or reading the shift register. Data is shifted first into the low order bit of SR and is then shifted into the next higher order bit of the shift register on the negative-going edge of each clock pulse. The input data should change before the positive-going edge of the CB1 clock pulse. This data is shifted into the shift register during the ϕ_2 clock cycle following the positive-going edge of the CB1 clock pulse. After 8 CB1 clock pulses, the shift register interrupt flag will be set and $\overline{IRQ}$ will go low.

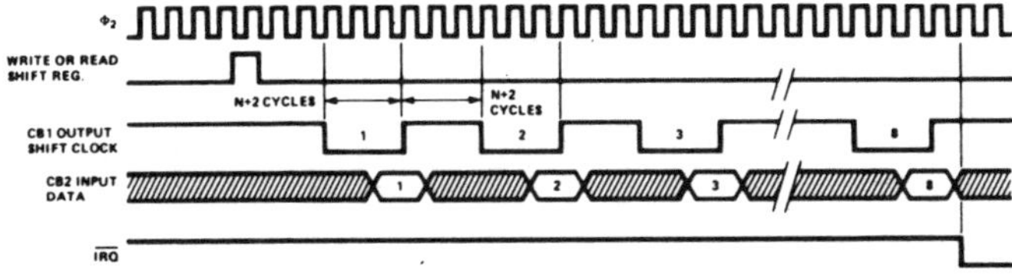

Shift in Under Control of ϕ_2 (010)

In mode 010 the shift rate is a direct function of the system clock frequency. CB1 becomes an output which generates shift pulses for controlling external devices. Timer 2 operates as an independent interval timer and has no effect on SR. The shifting operation is triggered by reading or writing the Shift Register. Data is shifted first into bit 0 and is then shifted into the next higher order bit of the shift register on the trailing edge of each ϕ_2 clock pulse. After 8 clock pulses, the shift register interrupt flag will be set, and the output clock pulses on CB1 will stop.

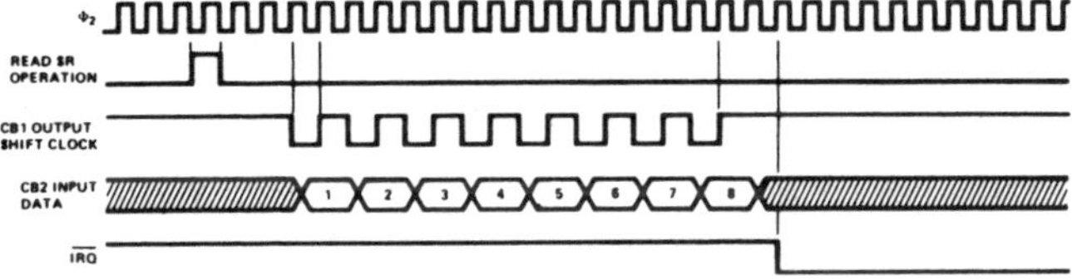

Shift in Under Control of External CB1 Clock (011)

In mode 011 CB1 becomes an input. This allows an external device to load the shift register at its own pace. The shift register counter will interrupt the processor each time 8 bits have been shifted in. However, the shift register counter does not stop the shifting operation; it acts simply as a pulse counter. Reading or writing the Shift Register resets the Interrupt flag and initializes the SR counter to count another 8 pulses.

Note that the data is shifted during the first system clock cycle following the positive-going edge of the CB1 shift pulse. For this reason, data must be held stable during the first full cycle following CB1 going high.

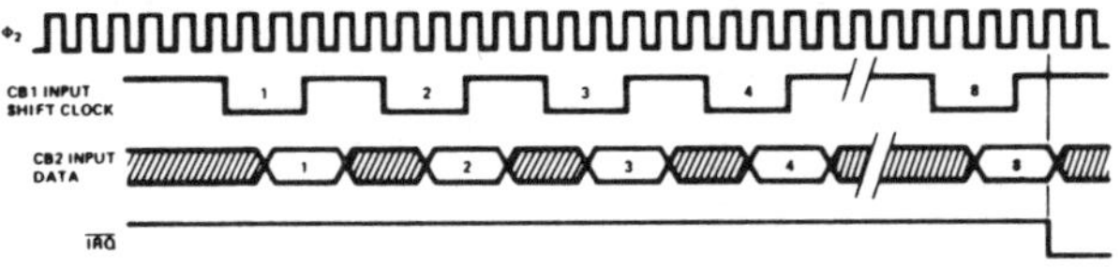

Figure 23. Shift Register Input Modes

Shift Out Free-Running at T2 Rate (100)

Mode 100 is very similar to mode 101 in which the shifting rate is set by T2. However, in mode 100 the SR Counter does not stop the shifting operation. Since the Shift Register bit 7 (SR7) is recirculated back into bit 0, the 8 bits loaded into the shift register will be clocked onto CB2 repetitively. In this mode the shift register counter is disabled.

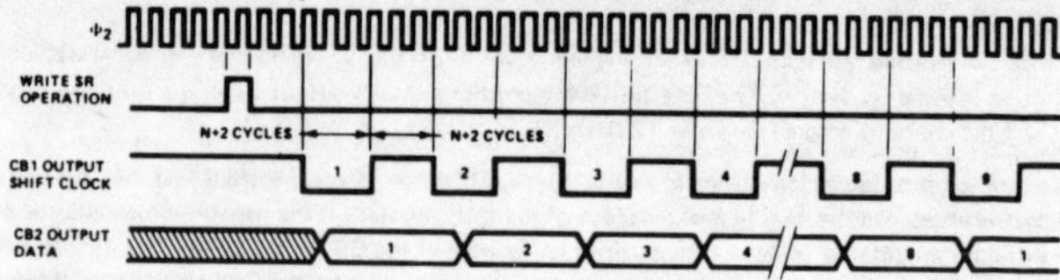

Shift Out Under Control of T2 (101)

In mode 101 the shift rate is controlled by T2 (as in the previous mode). However, with each read or write of the shift register the SR Counter is reset and 8 bits are shifted onto CB2. At the same time, 8 shift pulses are generated on CB1 to control shifting in external devices. After the 8 shift pulses, the shifting is disabled, the SR Interrupt Flag is set and CB2 remains at the last data level.

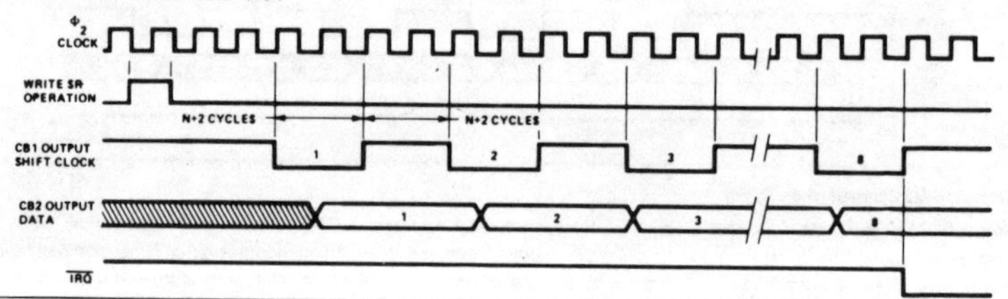

Shift Out Under Control of ϕ_2 (110)

In mode 110, the shift rate is controlled by the ϕ_2 system clock.

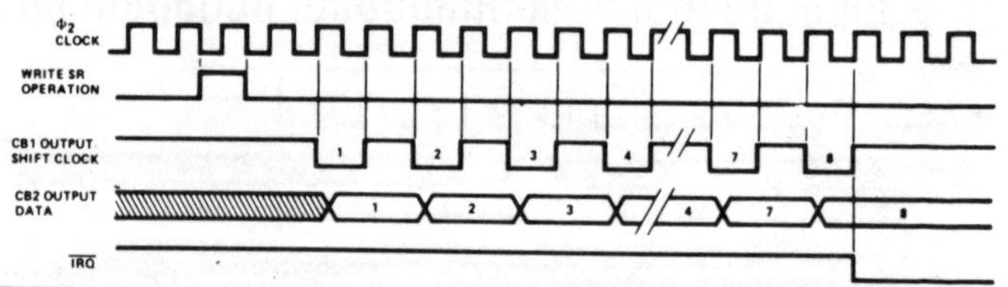

Shift Out Under Control of External CB1 Clock (111)

In mode 111 shifting is controlled by pulses applied to the CB1 pin by an external device. The SR counter sets the SR Interrupt flag each time it counts 8 pulses but it does not disable the shifting function. Each time the microprocessor writes or reads the shift register, the SR Interrupt flag is reset and the SR counter is initialized to begin counting the next 8 shift pulses on pin CB1. After 8 shift pulses, the interrupt flag is set. The microprocessor can then load the shift register with the next byte of data.

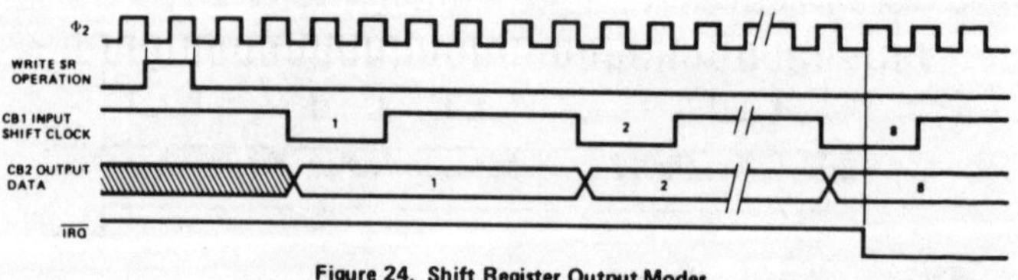

Figure 24. Shift Register Output Modes

The Interrupt Flag Register (IFR) and Interrupt Enable Register (IER) are depicted in Figures 25 and 26, respectively.

The IFR may be read directly by the processor. In addition, individual flag bits may be cleared by writing a "1" into the appropriate bit of the IFR. When the proper chip select and register signals are applied to the chip, the contents of this register are placed on the data bus. Bit 7 indicates the status of the IRQ output. This bit corresponds to the logic function: IRQ = IFR6 x IER6 + IFR5 x IER5 + IFR4 x IER4 + IFR3 x IER3 + IFR2 x IER2 + IFR1 x IER1 + IFR0 x IER0. Note: X = logic AND, + = Logic OR.

The IFR bit 7 is not a flag. Therefore, this bit is not directly cleared by writing a logic 1 into it. It can only be cleared by clearing all the flags in the register or by disabling all the active interrupts as discussed in the next section.

REG 13 – INTERRUPT FLAG REGISTER

Bit		SET BY	CLEARED BY
0	CA2	CA2 ACTIVE EDGE	READ OR WRITE REG 1 (ORA)
1	CA1	CA1 ACTIVE EDGE	READ OR WRITE REG 1 (ORA)
2	SHIFT REG	COMPLETE 8 SHIFTS	READ OR WRITE SHIFT REG
3	CB2	CB2 ACTIVE EDGE	READ OR WRITE ORB
4	CB1	DB1 ACTIVE EDGE	READ OR WRITE ORB
5	TIMER 2	TIME-OUT OF T2	READ T2 LOW OR WRITE T2 HIGH
6	TIMER 1	TIME-OUT OF T1	READ T1 LOW OR WRITE T1 HIGH
7	IRQ	ANY ENABLED INTERRUPT	CLEAR ALL INTERRUPTS

Figure 25. Interrupt Flag Register (IFR)

For each interrupt flag in IFR, there is a corresponding bit in the Interrupt Enable Register. The system processor can set or clear selected bits in this register to facilitate controlling individual interrupts without affecting others. This is accomplished by writing to address 1110 (IER address). If bit 7 of the data placed on the system data bus during this write operation is a 0, each 1 in bits 6 through 0 clears the corresponding bit in the Interrupt Enable Register. For each zero in bits 6 through 0, the corresponding bit is unaffected.

Setting selected bits in the Interrupt Enable Register is accomplished by writing to the same address with bit 7 in the data word set to a logic 1. In this case, each 1 in bits 6 through 0 will set the corresponding bit. For each zero, the corresponding bit will be unaffected. This individual control of the setting and clearing operations allows very convenient control of the interrupts during system operation.

In addition to setting and clearing IER bits, the processor can read the contents of this register by placing the proper address on the register select and chip select inputs with the R/W line high. Bit 7 will be read as a logic 0.

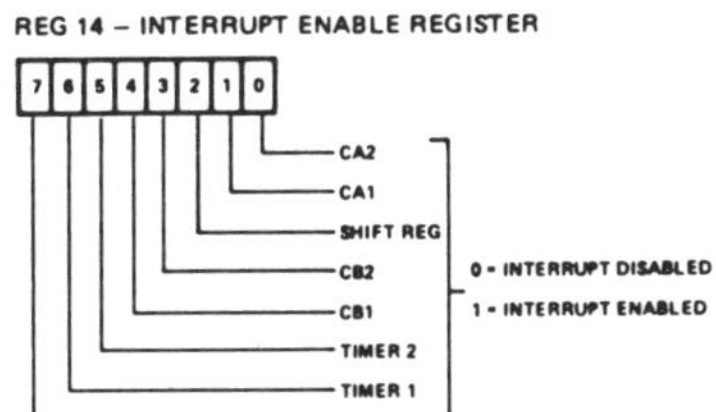

NOTES:
1. IF BIT 7 IS A "0", THEN EACH "1" IN BITS 0 - 6 DISABLES THE CORRESPONDING INTERRUPT.
2. IF BIT 7 IS A "1", THEN EACH "1" IN BITS 0 - 6 ENABLES THE CORRESPONDING INTERRUPT.
3. IF A READ OF THIS REGISTER IS DONE, BIT 7 WILL BE "0" AND ALL OTHER BITS WILL REFLECT THEIR ENABLE/DISABLE STATE.

Figure 26. Interrupt Enable Register (IER)

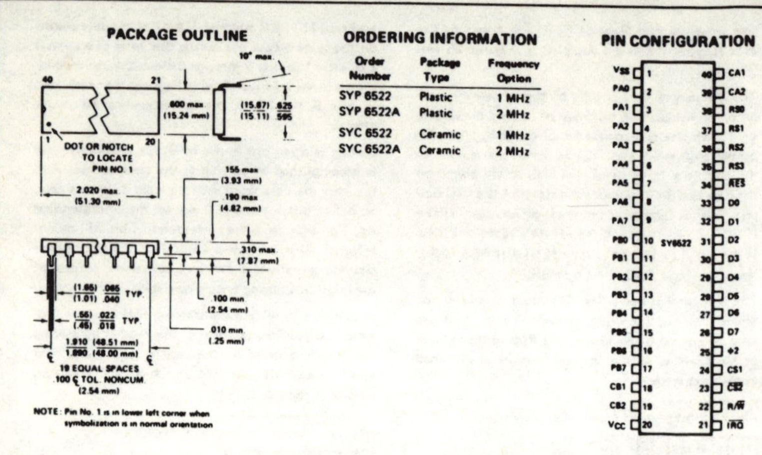

ORDERING INFORMATION

Order Number	Package Type	Frequency Option
SYP 6522	Plastic	1 MHz
SYP 6522A	Plastic	2 MHz
SYC 6522	Ceramic	1 MHz
SYC 6522A	Ceramic	2 MHz